SELECTED ESSAYS OF
Hugh MacDiarmid

A Select List of Books by HUGH MACDIARMID

POETRY

Sangschaw, 1925
Penny Wheep, 1926
A Drunk Man Looks at the Thistle, 1926
To Circumjack Cencrastus, 1930
First Hymn to Lenin and other poems, 1931
Scots Unbound and other poems, 1932
Stony Limits and other poems, 1934
Second Hymn to Lenin and other poems, 1935
A Kist of Whistles, 1947
In Memoriam James Joyce, 1955
Three Hymns to Lenin, 1957
The Battle Continues, 1957
The Kind of Poetry I Want, 1961
Collected Poems, 1962, revised edition, 1967
A Lap of Honour, 1967

PROSE

Annals of the Five Senses, 1923 (also verse)
Contemporary Scottish Studies, 1926
Albyn: or Scotland and the Future, 1927
At the Sign of the Thistle, 1934 (essays)
Scottish Scene, 1934 (with Lewis Grassic Gibbon)
Scottish Eccentrics, 1936
The Islands of Scotland, 1939
Lucky Poet, 1943
Cunninghame Graham: A Centenary Study, 1952
Francis George Scott, 1955
Burns Today and Tomorrow, 1959

David Hume: Scotland's Greatest Son, 1961
The Man of (almost) Independent Mind, 1962
The Ugly Birds Without Wings, 1962
The Company I've Kept, 1966 (autobiographical)

EDITED

Northern Numbers, 1920, 1921, 1922
The Golden Treasury of Scottish Poetry, 1940, reissued 1946, etc.
William Soutar, Collected Poems, 1948
Robert Burns, 1949
Selections from the Poems of William Dunbar, 1952
Robert Burns, Love Poems, 1962

HUGH MACDIARMID *By Rosalie M. J. Loveday*

SELECTED ESSAYS

OF

Hugh MacDiarmid

Edited with an Introduction by
DUNCAN GLEN

UNIVERSITY OF CALIFORNIA PRESS

Berkeley and Los Angeles · 1970

UNIVERSITY OF CALIFORNIA PRESS
Berkeley and Los Angeles, California

Standard Book Number 520–01618–1
Library of Congress Catalog Card Number: 76–99506

FOR MY FRIENDS
ALEXANDER SCOTT
Senior Lecturer in Scottish Literature
at Glasgow University
AND HIS WIFE CATHY

CONTENTS

INTRODUCTION BY DUNCAN GLEN   13

PART ONE

1   The Politics and Poetry of Hugh MacDiarmid (1952)   19
2   A Russo-Scottish Parallelism (1923)   38
3   Art and the Unknown (1926)   44
4   Paul Valéry (1927)   49
5   My Native Place (1931)   53
6   The Caledonian Antisyzygy and the Gaelic Idea (1931–2)   56
7   Charles Doughty and the Need for Heroic Poetry (1936)   75
8   John Singer (1942)   86
9   William Soutar (1944)   92

PART TWO

10   The Scottish Renaissance: The Next Step (1950)   105
11   The Quality of Scots Internationalism (1950)   111
12   The Significance of Cunninghame Graham (1952)   121
13   Robert Fergusson: Direct Poetry and the Scottish Genius (1952)   129
14   Economic Independence for the Individual (1952)   150
15   Norman Douglas (1953)   157
16   Encouraging the Creative Arts (1953)   162
17   Towards a Celtic Front (1953)   171
18   Robert Burns: His Influence (1959)   177
19   To a Young Poet (1959)   183
20   Lewis Grassic Gibbon (1960)   188
21   John Davidson: Influences and Influence (1961)   197

Contents

22 Contemporary Scottish Literature and the National Question (1965)   205

23 The Scottish Renaissance Movement After Forty Years (1966)   216

24 The Upsurge of Scottish Nationalism (1967)   228

25 Poetry and Science (1967)   233

REFERENCE NOTES   249

ACKNOWLEDGMENTS

The essays in this collection appeared in the following books, newspapers, magazines and B.B.C. programmes and we gratefully acknowledge permission to reproduce them: 'The Politics and Poetry of Hugh MacDiarmid' (*National Weekly*, and reprinted as pamphlet of the same title); 'A Russo-Scottish Parallelism' (*The Glasgow Herald*); 'Art and the Unknown' (*The New Age*); 'Paul Valéry' (*The New Age*); 'My Native Place' (*Scots Observer*); 'The Caledonian Antisyzygy and the Gaelic Idea' (*The Modern Scot*); 'Charles Doughty and the Need for Heroic Poetry' (*The Modern Scot*, and reprinted as the pamphlet of the same title); 'John Singer' ('Introduction', *The Fury of the Living. Poems by John Singer*, Maclellan, 1942); 'William Soutar' ('Introduction', *William Soutar: Collected Poems*, Dakers, 1948); 'The Scottish Renaissance — the Next Step' (*Jabberwock*); 'The Quality of Scots Internationalism' (*Scottish Art and Letters*); 'The Significance of Cunninghame Graham' (*National Weekly*); 'Robert Fergusson: Direct Poetry and the Scottish Genius' (*Robert Fergusson, 1750–1774*, ed. Sydney Goodsir Smith, Nelson, 1952); 'Economic Independence for the Individual' (*Scottish Journal*); 'Norman Douglas' (B.B.C. talk); 'Encouraging the Creative Arts' (*Scottish Journal*); 'Towards a Celtic Front' (*Scottish Journal*); 'Robert Burns: His Influence' (*Scottish Field*); 'To a Young Poet' (*Saltire Review*); 'Lewis Grassic Gibbon' (B.B.C. programme); 'John Davidson: Influences and Influence' (*John Davidson: a Selection of His Poems*, ed. Maurice Lindsay, Hutchinson, 1961); 'Contemporary Scottish Literature and the National Question' (Lecture delivered at Humboldt University, German Democratic Republic); 'The Scottish Renaissance Movement After Forty Years' (*The Library Review*); 'The Upsurge of Scottish Nationalism' (*The Glasgow Herald*); 'Poetry and Science' (Part of lecture delivered at Lund University, Sweden, and the University of Massachusetts, Amherst).

The frontispiece is reproduced by kind permission of the artist, Rosalie M. J. Loveday.

INTRODUCTION

During the last ten years there has been a growing awareness that 'Hugh MacDiarmid' (Christopher Murray Grieve) is a poet whose work puts him beside the very great poets of this century. His poetry is now increasingly reaching the wider, and more critical, audience that it demands and would have reached decades ago but for the so-thought difficulties of his Scots, and other reasons of a non-literary character. His prose writings, however, remain largely uncollected and exceedingly difficult to find. In his autobiography, *Lucky Poet*,[1] MacDiarmid wrote: 'I am the author of about twenty books and enough uncollected essays to make twice as many again.' By now the total must be more like four times as many again.

By the standards of a world which finds the occupation 'Poet' a joke, Hugh MacDiarmid is a journalist. He was a full-time journalist before the 1914–18 war and again after his demobilization in 1919 until the early 'thirties. Most of this time was spent in Angus as chief reporter of the weekly paper *The Montrose Review* but he had a spell in London as acting editor of the short-lived radio magazine *Vox*. He was also a publicity officer for a year in Liverpool. Most of this journalism is outside our interests here but this training as a journalist must, however, have encouraged MacDiarmid in his ability to produce vast quantities of provocative and lively prose at great speed. It perhaps also gave him the inclination to be more concerned with getting his copy out than with being obsessed by refinements of style or with editorial cutting and organization. Of course, this attitude also, to some extent, reflects MacDiarmid's own restless personality and his prose is an impressive expression of his hard, searching, never-still intelligence.

Also, of course, MacDiarmid has devoted himself — again restlessly — to many causes, and his prose has been one of his weapons, whether on behalf of his critical and poetical stances, his Scottish nationalism, his Douglasism, his communism, or the revaluation of neighbours' houses in the Shetlands. Almost always,

13

as a prose writer he has been an educator, a publicist, a propagandist. His success can, perhaps, be judged by the vituperative correspondence he aroused—and arouses—in newspapers, and by the ridicule, poverty and hardship he endured in the Shetlands during the 'thirties and in Glasgow and elsewhere in the 'forties and 'fifties. His achievement can also be seen in the changed attitude to Scottish literature now prevailing not only in Scotland but also throughout the world. Of course, always, there was behind his prose the strength of his great poetry.

To discuss the diversity and range of MacDiarmid's contributions of prose to newspapers, magazines and books other than his own would fill another book, but the major groupings can be shown. There are his contributions to magazines he himself edited (*The Scottish Chapbook, The Scottish Nation* and *The Northern Review* in the 'twenties; *The Voice of Scotland* in 1939 and again when it was revived in the 'fifties). His *Scottish Chapbook* causeries are where he first expounded his belief in the importance of the Scots language to a twentieth-century Scottish poet; in *The Voice of Scotland* he had an organ for his Scottish republicanism. Most of the early articles in the *Voice* were absorbed into *Lucky Poet*. In the 'twenties MacDiarmid contributed a series of articles to *The Dunfermline Press*, generally on literary topics. More important is his literary criticism in *The New Age* which was the magazine which gave MacDiarmid, or Grieve, his first contacts with the larger literary world and which influenced him towards Major Douglas's Social Credit movement.

In Scotland MacDiarmid was commissioned to do a most ambitious series, 'Contemporary Scottish Studies', in which, it was announced, he would 'discuss in all the work of no fewer than three hundred men and women of Scotland' involved in cultural activities. These articles in the official organ of the Scottish Educational Association, *The Scottish Educational Journal*, did much to create MacDiarmid's *kulturkampf;* some of them are collected in the 1926 volume *Contemporary Scottish Studies*.[2] To this time also belongs much anonymous and pseudonymous writing by him, including a series syndicated to dozens of local Scottish papers each week.

In the 'thirties MacDiarmid had become even more unpopular with respectable Scottish institutions, including the press, and it was mostly to little magazines that he contributed, including *The Modern Scot* and *The Free Man* in Scotland, and Douglasite journals in London. T. S. Eliot printed the important essay 'English Ascendency in British Literature' — which was reprinted in *At the Sign of the Thistle*[3] — and two reviews in *Criterion*. In the 'forties and 'fifties MacDiarmid was mainly associated with lively but short-lived Scottish journals, including *Scottish Journal*, *The National Weekly* and the annual *Scottish Art and Letters*, but towards the end of the 'fifties international publication came with his acceptance and recognition after some twenty years in the desert.

Outside the periodical field MacDiarmid has always been a generous contributor of introductions and prefaces to other writers' books and of articles to books edited by others, although until recently the former would exceed the latter.

Of the twenty or so books referred to in *Lucky Poet* seven are prose works; I have not printed anything from these books or from *Lucky Poet*, which should be reissued by its publishers, as should the collection of essays, *At the Sign of the Thistle*, which shows admirably the strength of MacDiarmid as a writer of English prose. Also too long out of print is *Scottish Scene*, written in collaboration with Lewis Grassic Gibbon — the collaborators 'drew up a synopsis and went their separate ways, each to write his separate sections'. A number of Grieve's essays have been reprinted as pamphlets but they are very rare and I have not excluded them from my considerations. I have also considered MacDiarmid's work for the B.B.C. and have included two talks which were broadcast. Some of MacDiarmid's work for the B.B.C. was absorbed into *Lucky Poet* and these talks I have not considered for the reason given above.

The essays are arranged in chronological order with the exception of the first one which was first published under the pseudonym of 'Arthur Leslie' but it is MacDiarmid on MacDiarmid — a uniquely appropriate introduction to this collection of essays. It was a reply to the abuse, neglect and misrepresentation that MacDiarmid suffered in the 'thirties and 'forties and 'fifties; it was a reply to the anti-cultural and anti-poetic and anti-Scottish forces which flourish in the Scottish climate. Against such forces a poet must use all the resources immediately available to him; 'Arthur Leslie', and his like, was one of the weapons bravely forged by Christopher Grieve in the days before his Established countrymen learned from open-eyed Americans and other foreigners that they had a great poet—and a great man—in their midst.

In his first book, *Annals of the Five Senses*, published by its author in 1923, C. M. Grieve wrote 'In Acknowledgment': 'The old lady described Shakespeare as being "full of quotations". So are my studies.' So also are his essays and, indeed, MacDiarmid's gift for the apt quotation is one of the hallmarks of his prose, but it does mean that in a collection such as this, there inevitably occurs some repetition of quotation. To avoid burdening Dr Grieve with opinions that he may have modified, I have printed with each title the date when the essay was first printed.

DUNCAN GLEN

PART ONE

1

THE POLITICS AND POETRY OF
HUGH MACDIARMID*

1952

Ever since his boyhood 'Hugh MacDiarmid' [Christopher Murray Grieve] has been working towards, and in the service of, that 'first truly human culture', as Trotsky calls it in *Literature and Revolution*, which socialism is eventually to make possible; and his Scottish nationalism is simply his concentration on that task in his own immediate neighbourhood, leaving his comrades in all other countries to do likewise in their own particular spheres, confident that all these will become one—or rather at one—in the era of integrated communism. Like Trotsky too—as his autobiography *Lucky Poet*,[1] makes abundantly clear—he could have said truly of himself at any time after his early teens:

> The leaders of the Social Democracy used the same formulas that I did, but one had only to turn any of them five degrees around on their own axes to discover that we gave quite different meanings to the same concepts. Our agreement was a temporary one, superficial and unreal. The correspondence between Marx and Engels was for me not a theoretical but a psychological revelation. *Toutes proportions gardées*, I found proof on every page that I was bound to these two by a direct psychological affinity. Their attitude to men and ideas was mine. I guessed what they did not express, shared their sympathies, was indignant and hated as they did. Marx and Engels were revolutionaries through and through. But they had not the slightest trace of sectarianism or asceticism. Both of them and especially Engels, could at any time say of themselves that nothing human was strange to them. But their revolutionary outlook lifted them always above the hazards

* This essay was first published under the pseudonym of 'Arthur Leslie' but it is MacDiarmid on MacDiarmid. *Editor.*

of fate and the works of men. Pettiness was incompatible not only with their personalities but with their presences. Vulgarity could not stick even to the soles of their boots. Their appreciations, sympathies, jests—even when most commonplace—are always touched by the rarefied air of spiritual nobility. They may pass deadly criticism on a man, but they will never deal in tittle-tattle. They can be ruthless, but not treacherous. For outward glamour, titles or rank they have nothing but a cool contempt. What philistines and vulgarians considered aristocratic in them was only their revolutionary superiority. Its most important characteristic is a complete and ingrained independence of official public opinion at all times and under all conditions.

Almost all the writers who have appraised MacDiarmid's personality and poetry have realized that that quotation fits him like a glove. Norrie Fraser, for example, wrote twenty years ago in the *New English Weekly*:

'The most persistent and consistent critic of Scottish life in recent years.' The place is Hugh MacDiarmid's whose trouncings of hypocrites and sycophants are the only consistent bright spot in contemporary affairs, and who should play a major part in any realist Nationalist Party who are beyond thinking that a Parliament in Edinburgh, an increased percentage of bare knees in Scotland, and far more Gleneagles would mean anything in the face of a remaining British Imperialist Economics.

About the same time a writer in the Edinburgh University *Student* said:

No fresh idea has entered the nation's head since the Disruption—our Socialism is still Burnsite in spirit—MacDiarmid has splendidly pioneered here. His thought-poetry, besides its criticism of lingering opinions, is a veritable mine of the best European ideas expressed in their relation to our living problems at home. Heir of our Radicalism, he is always a left-wing man, possessed with the idea of Freedom. In thought as in his attitude to language it is for the masses of us that he is working. His poetry is essentially popular. Our inner longings, our inmost resolves, so long inarticulate and half-conscious, find in MacDiarmid's the voice they have lacked since the time of Burns and the great Highland poets. One day his work will be allowed to get across to Scotland.

While so much is common ground to the great majority of those who have written about him, it is necessary (not to point out that his intense Scottish nationalism coexists in him with an almost unbelievably extensive and minutely detailed knowledge and appreciation of a great number of other literatures and languages —that is clear enough in all that he has written; if he is an extreme Scottish nationalist he is also one of the greatest inter-nationalists even Scotland has ever produced) to stress here the way in which he has squared precept and practice in his life. He joined the I.L.P. when he was sixteen, and a little later, the Edinburgh University Fabian Society and took an active part in the formation of the University Socialist Federation. He began open-air speaking, too, in his teens, under the tutelage of 'Jimmy Buchanan', an Edinburgh Corporation scavenger who was one of the stalwarts and pioneers of socialism in Edinburgh. Before he was twenty he had served on a Fabian Research Committee on agriculture on whose behalf he surveyed the whole Scottish aspect of the matter and submitted a series of brilliant memoranda which formed part of the joint volume *The Rural Problem*[2] in which the findings of the committee were embodied. In the preface to that book, the chairman (Mr Henry Harben) paid special tribute to Mr MacDiarmid's work, coupling his name, in this connection, with that of Mr Sidney Webb (Lord Passfield). A little later, MacDiarmid ran a newspaper, *The Monmouthshire Labour News*, for the South Wales Miners' Federation. Living in Ebbw Vale he used to walk over to Merthyr Tydfil to see Keir Hardie and was a contributor to Hardie's paper, *The Merthyr-Pioneer*. Other friends of MacDiarmid's at that time included Vernon Hartshorn, Tom Mann, Victor Grayson, Frank Hodges, and Denis Hird, first Principal of Ruskin College. Since then to the present time he has been continuously actively associated with the working-class movement and has served it as a Town Coun-cillor, Parish Councillor, and Justice of the Peace and in many other capacities. He is a member of the Writers' Group of the

Society for Cultural Relations with the U.S.S.R.; a director of
Theatre Workshop Ltd; President of the Dunedin Society for the
encouragement of the arts in Scotland; a Vice-Chairman of the
British Peace Committee; and his friendships with communist
and near-communist politicians, writers and artists in many
countries, are very numerous—amongst those who should be
mentioned being Nancy Cunard, Valentine Acland, Sylvia
Townsend Warner, Sean O'Casey, Josef Hermon, Norman
MacLeod, Horace Gregory, Muriel Rukeyser, and Kenneth
Patchen. He is one of the most incessant public speakers in
Scotland and there are few places in the country in which his
has not long been a 'ken-speckle' figure now.

*

Hugh MacDiarmid was born in 1892 in the little Dumfriesshire
burgh of Langholm of working-class parents. Writing of his boyhood in *Lucky Poet* he says:

> The main thing about these early days, however—because of
> its bearing on my subsequent literary work and my later life
> generally—is that they made me a man naturally fitted for
> Communism—a man, moreover, who found ready and wait-
> ing in himself by the time he came to write poetry a sound
> relationship between the political thinker in him and the
> artist. I had not to adjust myself in either connexion: above
> all, I had not to scrap or transform any part of myself which
> by education was antagonistically *bourgeois*, because I had
> been on the alert from the very start and had never developed
> any such part. If I came in the end to Communism (that is,
> to membership of the Communist Party, instead of the
> Independent Labour Party, of which I had by then been
> over twenty years an active member) I also *grew* into it
> through a class-conscious upbringing which conditioned but
> did not distort my view of life. My development owed a very
> great deal to my growing-up in a working-class family and
> being fed on out-and-out Radicalism and Republicanism
> when still a child. This was so intense that I was spared
> any out-growing of it by virtue of a *bourgeois* education and

conversion to *bourgeois* manners — and remaining solid with the working-class throughout. Even if I had outgrown the early influence through education and so on, I would have recurred all right to the early standpoint; it was potent enough to have reclaimed me. But in point of fact this was not necessary in my case at all — I had never allowed myself to be drawn away from it; the working-class have always stood, and will always stand, in the relation to me not of 'they' but of 'we' — and so instead of having it recur to mind after the disillusioning lessons of the (First World) War, it only confirmed what from the beginning was my strongest tendency and completed the course I had been pursuing into actual Party membership — a decision that had been implicit in most of my previous reactions to experience. This book, therefore, is not (like the autobiographies of so many fellow-writers of my own generation or thereabouts) the story of a man who came belatedly to Communism, or came rebelling against his temperament, or came — in bitterness of spirit — to save his precious soul. My coming to Communist membership was not the resolution, as it were of a career; no conflict existed except on very minor points — the attitude of the Communist Party to Scottish Nationalism, for example, in regard to which, for a time, I was at variance, not with Communism, but with the unfortunate limitations of certain leading members of the Communist Party in Scotland, and with a deplorable 'twist' given in this connexion to the Communist Party of Great Britain by the circumstance of its inception. For it had never been my aim to rise above the class into which I was born — it had, indeed, been my vigilant determination to see that I allowed nothing to come between me and my class — and my regression to Scots (i.e. the Scots language, in which most of his best poetry is written, instead of English) was, in fact, the counter-process to the usual course; where others were concerned to rise, I, on the contrary, was determined to strengthen and develop my organic relationship to the Commons of Scotland by every means in my power, not to get back to the people — for I had never allowed myself to get away from them — but to get under the skin, to get deeper and deeper into their innermost promptings, their root motives. The tremendous proletarian virtue of the little town I knew as a boy saved me — despite the religiosity, the puritanism, of both my parents, and the ambitious gentility of my mother, and despite my own literary gifts — from the ordeal so many young writers and artists are going through today, of rising again to proletarian integrity, of becoming once more organically welded, to the working-class. From the beginning I took as my motto — and I have adhered all through to it in my literary work — Thomas Hardy's declaration: 'Literature is the written expression of revolt against accepted things.'

Today with over a dozen volumes of poetry to his credit — not to mention about thirty prose works — MacDiarmid might say with the American poet, William Carlos Williams:

> You see, as a writer I haven't even begun to do anything
> Yet all I've been able to achieve so far has been survival.
> My idea of myself as an artist is that of a man running as
> Hard as he could put it from the wolves. I knew what it
> Would be from the first and I was right. I made up my
> Mind that I'd have to live to be very old, like Titian or the
> Jap whose name I have forgotten, before I should be able to get
> Into that peaceful country where I could sit down to the
> Difficult task of composition. All I've accomplished so
> Far is to build up a grand artist's constitution, to be so
> Tough that I could take it on the chin from anybody at any
> Time and be able to come back in the last round and knock
> Them out of the ring.

MacDiarmid has carefully defined his communism in *Lucky Poet*. Here it will suffice to say that the keynote of his whole position is his agreement with the late Ford Madox Ford that:

> The only human activity that has always been of extreme importance to the world is imaginative literature. It is of supreme importance because it is the only means by which humanity can express at once emotions and ideas. To avoid controversy I am perfectly willing to concede that the other arts are of equal importance. But nothing that is not an art is of any lasting importance at all, the meanest novel being

humanly more valuable than the most pompous of factual works, the most formidable of material achievements, or the most carefully thought out of legal codes.

Always anxious to find chapter and verse for his positions in the literature of his own country, MacDiarmid might well have taken as the best expression of his spirit that part of John Ruskin's *The Stones of Venice* in which he compares the three thrones set upon the sand: Tyre, of which only the memory remains; Venice, of which only the ruin; and England, which, if she forgets the example of the others, 'may come to less pitied destruction'. Thus, as Robert Furneaux Jordan has said,

> Ruskin took the step great artists have to take, from intrinsic beauty to social passion, ethics and political economy. It is superficial to regret it. The central work of Ruskin's life is that chapter in the second volume called 'The Nature of Gothic.' The true nature of gothic, it tells us, is the 'dependence of all human work for its beauty on the happy life of the workman … you must either make a tool of the creature, or a man of him. You cannot make both.' That was shattering — in that smug world of academicians and patrons! William Morris said that it was 'one of the very few necessary and inevitable utterances of the century.'

And, again, the reason for his hatred of Anglo-Saxondom, and the essence of his hope for mankind, is clearly discernible in the following passage from the same writer:

> The little society in which D. H. Lawrence moved (i.e. 'all the young people were talking about Nietzsche and Wagner and Leopardi and Flaubert and Karl Marx … and they would discuss the French Impressionists and the primitive Italians and play Chopin or Debussy on the piano … I have never anywhere found so educated a society. These young people *knew* the things that my generation in the great English schools hardly even chattered about') was a microcosm of what the world must come to if it is to be permanent. Its existence foretold to me even then the disappearance of the ruling power of the middle-classes as they then were and even of the class that in England was called the ruling class. The

disappearance of Eton as the educational home of the nation's legislators was there as plainly foreshadowed as the fact England's victories were never again to be won on Eton's playing fields. The one was to go down before the type of education that had produced Lawrence's small coterie and nourished the genius of Lawrence himself just as surely as the other was to disappear before wireless telegraphy, the aeroplane, motor traction and the other wonders of science. You cannot fight an atmosphere of poison gas with the rules of cricket any more than you can expect to rule cultured people —or any people—if you are unacquainted with the highest imaginative thought of the world of your day. This Anglo-Saxondom has never believed. That is why Anglo-Saxondom is crumbling as Rome did to its doom. Even in the Middle Ages they knew that. They used to say:

> When lands are gone and money spent
> Then learning is most excellent.

And the root of MacDiarmid's loathing of the British Empire is certainly to be found in the fact that

the population of the British Empire at that date [1916] was some 250,000,000. For the purpose of the hostilities in which we were engaged it could find seven million men and two or three million women—say one in twenty-five. For its intellectual front line that two hundred and fifty million could find 14,000—one in 17,857. It is not much consolation to say that a large percentage of that 250,000,000 do not read English. If the greatest Empire the world has ever seen cannot induce its subject races to assimilate its highest form of culture its existence seems unjustified. And unjustifiable.

MacDiarmid has stated that his visit to the U.S.S.R. in 1951 has powerfully strengthened all his ideas, since the development of local languages and cultures in the various republics represents just that 'diversity in unity' he has always desired and is the very antithesis of what has always obtained in the British Commonwealth of Nations. He is delighted too by the tremendous educational avidity throughout the Soviet Union and the splendid facilities available everywhere for cultural development. His meetings with leading Soviet writers, including Alexei Surkov, Pavlo Tychina, Konstantin Simonov, Samuel Marshak, and others — as, later, his meetings in the Soviet zone of Germany with Pablo Neruda, Nazim Hikmet, Johannes Becker, Anna Seghers, and other communist writers — have all confirmed his ideas in this connection.

MacDiarmid is tough all right, he has needed to be to survive in Scotland, and there is ample proof of it in the fact that in his fifties, during Hitler's war, being too old for military service, he qualified as a fitter and served two years in a Clydeside engineering works, becoming charge-hand in the copper shell-band department, and then did another year as an estuarial seaman on a Norwegian boat on admiralty service and has since, with an interval as a post-office sorter, had to endure the hardship and ignominy of being unemployed for, although he has had twenty years' experience as a journalist, is generally recognized as the leading living Scottish writer and, as Compton Mackenzie has put it, as 'the most powerful intellectually and emotionally fertilizing force Scotland has known since the death of Burns', and has held all his previous jobs, journalistic and otherwise, with the highest credit and possesses first-class testimonials, he is a 'dangerous man' and there is no job for him in Scotland today. Unemployed or not, however, he is pouring out articles and poems, broadcasting, addressing all sorts of meetings, perpetually engaged in violent controversies with all sorts of people from one end of the country to another, and somehow or other contriving to create an extraordinary impression of ubiquity and omnicompetence.

The present writer once drew MacDiarmid's attention to the following statements made in the *New Statesman and Nation* by Mr Raymond Mortimer:

What one may call the theologians of Communism profess some highly irrational doctrines derived ultimately from the ill-regulated imagination of Hegel. Look, however, for the most active principal of this faith, and you find, combined with patriotism of the most old-fashioned sort, 'a belief in man's ability to conquer nature, to solve the most difficult problems, and to make or create history.' This belief, which every Soviet artist is under an obligation to propagate, is one that has never in history succeeded in attracting any great poet, or, indeed, any mind of the first order.

MacDiarmid expressed his contempt and contented himself with remarking that Mr Mortimer's contention was 'on all fours with the disbelief formerly so frequently expressed in this and other countries that the Russian Revolution was real and irreversible', or again, he said, 'it is just the same frame of mind as led so many people prior to August 1914 to imagine that a modern war could not possibly last more than a week or two. I may not be a great poet or a mind of the first order, but in so far as I am a poet and have a mind, I am certainly — and will continue to be — dependent upon the active principle of that faith which, like every Soviet artist, I certainly regard myself as under an obligation to propagate by every means in my power.'

*

His poetry has always been one of the weapons of his general political fight. It is a mistake to imagine that he came to political poetry late; his poetry was political from the outset, as the 'Ballad of the General Strike' in his *A Drunk Man Looks at the Thistle*,[3] and many other poems there and in earlier books makes clear enough. Not only his work as a seaman and an engineer, but all his life has testified to his complete agreement with his old friend, the late Sir Patrick Geddes, who, addressing a company of distinguished Frenchmen of letters and noted philosophers from Germany and France at Montpelier in 1929, said:

I have the greatest respect for my friend Desjardins as an intellectual and for his colleagues too. But as gardeners they are complete failures. Neither I nor any peasant in the village can have respect for them as men able to do real work. Of course I can't offend my old friend but I say that not until men of learning and of letters can win the respect of peasant or workman *on his own level* will they ever escape from that isolated barrenness which threatens the cultured *élite* of every nation.

He has always been fond of quoting William Dean Howells's remark that 'those who rise above the necessity of work for daily bread are in great danger of losing their right relationship to other men.' MacDiarmid has put this most effectively perhaps in the lines which run:

Above all—though primarily a poet myself—
I know I need as large an area of brain
To control my hands as my vocal organs
And I am fully alive to the danger
Of only grasping so much of the scientific outlook
As is expressed in words or symbols
Rather than actions,
—The common mistake of regarding
The skilful manipulation of symbols
As an activity altogether more respectable
Than the skilful manipulation
Of material objects.
I am organically welded with the manual workers
As with no other class in the social system
Though superficially my interests may seem to be rather
With the so-called educated classes.

Again, in the words of Patrick Geddes, he might say of the spirit that has animated all his work: 'The great need: Intenser life for men and women! Thus in this period of intensest crises in all main lines of life and thought, social and individual alike, I have been seeking life more abundantly. Seeking life first for myself, then others; but now more fully for others, beyond my ageing self. Thinking and doing, seeking for others ... now and beyond ... '

As he has said of himself he is a communist, but *in excelsis* a communist of the kind Lenin described when he said:

Now, for the first time, we have the possibility of learning. I do not know how long this possibility will last. I do not know how long the Capitalist Powers will give us the opportunity of learning in peace and quietude. But we must utilize every moment in which we are free from war that we may learn, and *learn from the bottom up* ... It would be a very serious mistake to suppose that one can become a Communist without making one's own the treasures of human knowledge. It would be mistaken to imagine that it is enough to adopt the Communist formulas and conclusions of Communist science without mastering the sum-total of different branches of knowledge whose final outcome is Communism ... Communism becomes an empty phrase, a mere façade, and the Communist a mere bluffer, if he has not worked over in his consciousness the whole inheritance of human knowledge ... made his own, and worked over anew, all that was of value in the more than two thousand years of development of human thought.

In his fight against ignorance and anti-intellectualism, and the incessant cry of stupid socialists and communists that nothing should be written save what is intelligible to the mass of the people, and that consequently there should be no learned allusions or high-brow difficulties in the work of the writers, MacDiarmid has frequently quoted:

Marx and Engels laid down almost no literary theory as such; profoundly cultivated men both, they merely presented an example of scholarship and cultivation, and trusted to the cultivation and good sense of their followers. Laying the groundwork for the greatest single event in human history as they saw it—the Socialist revolution that would eventually bring in a superperfect harmony and humanity amongst men—they automatically in sketching out the naturalistic and economic foundations of all human experience, subordinated literature and art under the general heading of culture, and studied culture itself as a body of human activity grounded, as they thought all human activity to have been, in the material relations of production. But they did not believe that works of art come into being through mechanized causation, nor did they anticipate that in speaking of culture as the 'superstructure' above the main groundwork of economic relations—a trunk on the central tree—their imagery would be taken to mean that literature, for example, is nothing but a by-product of material activity. 'The economic factor is "not the sole determining factor",' Engels wrote in a letter towards the end of his life. 'The production and reproduction of real life constitutes in the last instance the determining factor in history.'

What this 'last instance' was to mean, Edmund Wilson has pointed out, was confusing enough since it could mean either the last in time or the last in the sense of being the fundamental motive of human behaviour and culture. But it has been confusing only because Engels and Marx took it for granted that their radical insistence on the material foundations of art and literature would not be seized on to confuse the social origins of art with its aesthetic values. Towards the end of his life Engels himself came to deplore the unthinking use so often made of historical materialism and wrote sharply to a correspondent: 'I must tell you from the very first that the materialist is converted into its direct opposite if, instead of being used as a guiding thread in historical research, it is made to serve as a ready-cut pattern on which to tailor historical facts.'

'Marx and I', Engels once wrote significantly to Franz Mehring, 'both placed and *had to place* the chief weight upon the derivation of political, legal, and other idealogical notions from fundamental economic facts. In consequence we neglected the formal side — i.e. the way in which these ideas arose — for the sake of the content.'

For all their understanding of the social origins of art, Marxist critics — if they seek to be critics — begin at that point. What the Marxist critic particularly is faced with — since no field of criticism makes so many demands on the active imagination as the study of literature in its relations to society — is the obligation to show just what those relations are and just what values emerge from a study of them. Condemning the aesthete who seems to believe that art exists in a vacuum, he must yet show that art is something more than the 'idealogical' representation of class forces in society. Patronizing the genteel impressionist who does not know to what extent works of art themselves have often acted as social forces, battlegrounds of ideas, he must yet show that the significance of any art work begins with its immediate success and fulfilment as art, its fulfilments of aesthetic need and pleasure. Fighting the reactionary ideologue, who holds that art is aristocratic and the property of a few exquisite sensibilities, he must yet admit (precisely because he is confident that it is only with the advent of socialism that human energy will be great enough, human fellowship broad enough, to make great works possible again) that without individual talent and humility and discipline, without its immediate origin in exceptional persons, no art is possible at all.

Emerson says that we 'descend to meet'. This is no doubt true of certain kinds of meeting, of the kind that takes place at an afternoon tea, let us say; and Emerson probably did not mean more than this. But the phrase may evidently have another, and, from the humanistic point of view, far more sinister meaning. Instead of disciplining himself to some sort of perfection set above his ordinary self, a man sinks down from the intellectual to the instinctive level, on the ground that he is thus widening his instinctive sympathies. A study of literature in its relation to society is not a feather-bed for minds seeking cosy formulas. It is presumably a rousing-up of the best intellectual energies, and a stimulus to the richest structural imagination that criticism affords.

MacDiarmid, who has quarrelled bitterly with the late Mr Ramsay MacDonald, Sir Hugh Roberton of Orpheus Choir 'fame' and other Scottish socialists with petty cultural pretensions and no capacity for doing anything but darkening counsel and further confusing the issues, has said somewhere in condemning the infantilism of Scottish Socialist M.P.s and commenting on the extraordinary absence of socialist achievement in any of the arts in Scotland that it has been and still is in Scotland as it was in the United States of America when Granville Hicks and other American Marxist critics were rightly characterized as

a race of young men, lost in the tides of change and vaguely hostile to traditional forms, who submitted to Marxism so hungrily that their ambition overreached itself in that spell of the absolute. They had found a new purpose for themselves in the light of the Marxist purpose; but in them one saw the working of the absolute on minds never supple or imaginative enough, never talented or sensitive enough, to write significant criticism. It was this conventionality, aroused and militant in Marxist battledress, a conventionality moving briskly but with metallic ardour through a period of confusion, that betrayed them; their painful limitations all arose from their efforts to apply their seriousness in judgment of sensibilities immeasurably subtler and deeper than their own. Their main gift is seriousness—a quality of moral intelligence —and as a result they fell into a shrewish moralism, a moralism that is conscious of aesthetic differences but has no talent for conveying the necessary discriminations between them.

It is probably socialists of that type, talking down to the people, playing to the gallery, and priding themselves upon just that minimum of culture necessary to differentiate them from the great mass, MacDiarmid has in mind when in one of his latest books (*A Kist of Whistles*)[4] he says that the kind of poetry he wants is a poetry

> That like a wrestling bout on a village green
> Divides the people and wins only those
> Who are honest, strong and true
> —Those who admire the man
> Who has the faster mind,
> The faster, suppler, better-governed body—
> For there is not only a class war
> But a war in the working class itself
> Between decency and self-respect on the one hand
> And a truckling spirit, seeking self-gain, on the other.

MacDiarmid wrote his 'First Hymn to Lenin' for a collection the late Mr Lascelles Abercrombie was editing for Mr Victor Gollancz. Abercrombie was delighted with it and wrote saying that MacDiarmid had done something that was urgently wanted, and had done it in an extremely effective way. Of the 'Second Hymn to Lenin', Dr F. R. Leavis said in *Scrutiny* that it was 'sufficiently a success to deserve inclusion in the ideal anthology (which would be a very small one) of contemporary poetry'. These communist poems of MacDiarmid's were also discussed and highly praised in C. Day Lewis's book on poetry in England,[5] and Miss Babette Deutsch's survey of contemporary poetry in America.[6] The late 'Lewis Grassic Gibbon' (James Leslie Mitchell) said: 'The "Hymns to Lenin" are among the world's most magnificent hymns

3

to the high verities of life. MacDiarmid has shown the Scottish speech capable of dealing tremendously and vividly, with the utmost extremes of passion and pity. All good art is propaganda, and MacDiarmid, *ex officio* or otherwise, is a splendid propagandist.'

Stephen Spender has commented on the extraordinary beauty of MacDiarmid's lyrics and his particular power of achieving great poetry in the exposition of Marxist ideas; Alec Comfort has complained of the difficulty of procuring copies of Mac-Diarmid's 'Hymns to Lenin', and remarking that these are not dull duty-pieces but great poems, refers to the great virtues of character which have enabled MacDiarmid to approach and reapproach this theme in poem after poem without merely repeating himself; and 'David Martin', the former literary editor of *Reynolds News*, has written that

> the magnificent 'Hymn to Lenin' — not published in its entirety even now — is certainly on a par, to say the least, with Mayakowsky's in poetic intensity. He was John Maclean's friend. But like his friend, MacDiarmid has had trouble with the Communist Party. He has had trouble with everybody. He is too big for the nationalists too. Too big. Where there are so many cranks it is easy for the bone lazy to denounce as cranks those who do not fit with a pattern. But in his writing there is nothing ill-organized or haphazard; on the contrary; his works range from translations from the Spanish to topographical surveys of the north, from poetry which is as lyrical and simple as that of Walter von der Vogelweide to literary essays, the brilliance and range of which are certainly not inferior to the best that is written in Britain today. He is as prolific as an iceberg; his throw-offs populate the oceans. And he is as hard, as uncompromising. Yet he is very little known in England, in spite or because of it all. Could it have happened to Swift?

As Mr Cecil Day Lewis has said: 'The "First Hymn to Lenin" was followed by a rush of poetry sympathetic to Communism or influenced by it.' Mr John Lehmann has pointed out that Mac-Diarmid 'stands alone, completely outside the Auden-Spender-Day Lewis group and its particular pattern of ideas'; and says that 'First Hymn to Lenin' was 'a poem much more directly and profoundly Communist than anything that the others had written. In a sense it was the prelude to the whole movement. Though Auden, for instance, had established the corner-stone of his creed with the publication of *Poems* in 1930, he does not show any open and clear Communist leanings until after the 'Hymn to Lenin' had been published, nor do any of the others.' Day Lewis and Orage were among the few who recognized the extraordinary quality of 'The Seamless Garment', about which Miss Vivienne Koch and other American critics have since had a great deal to say, recognizing MacDiarmid as 'by all odds by far the best of the really revolutionary poets'. Mr W. B. Yeats included 'The Skeleton of the Future' in his *Oxford Book of Modern English Verse*[7] and it has already appeared in many other anthologies. Except for a small portion printed in *Lucky Poet*, the 'Third Hymn to Lenin' has not yet been published.[8] Also unpublished in any volume is 'The Communist Discipline'. 'The Glass of Pure Water'[9] and 'Lamh Dearg Aboo' have appeared in the first and second collections of *Poetry Scotland*[10] respectively, but are not yet included in any of MacDiarmid's volumes. 'Auld Reekie'[11] has only hitherto appeared in *Lucky Poet*; and 'Art and the Workers' in *The New Scotland*.[12]

Reading these poems and looking back over MacDiarmid's entire poetic production and his record of active citizenship and of service to the socialist and Scottish nationalist movements it is clear that he has always applied to himself what, in one of his essays, he describes as the touchstone he applied to determine whether any writer today is or is not of any significance, viz.: 'We are living in such a grave, such a dark, such a dangerous epoch and the artist who is not willing to participate in its course, i.e. as a leader of men, seems to me to be feelingless and senseless, and I cannot acknowledge his talent, unless as a formal talent, such as we acknowledge in a good vocalist who can sing well the songs created by a composer some two or three centuries ago.' MacDiarmid's best exposition of his ideas on communist poetry— the role of poetry in the period of transition, and, later, in the integrated communist society—is probably his preface to John Singer's poems *The Fury of the Living*.[13]

As Miss Nan Shepherd has said of him in a critical essay in the

Aberdeen University Review, the vision behind MacDiarmid's creed —
that focuses everything he has written in a point of light —

> never changes. Always he sees man 'filled with lightness and
> exaltation', living to the full reach of his potentialities. In
> that clear world 'all that has been born deserved birth'. Man
> 'will flash with the immortal fire', will

> rise
> To the full height of the imaginative act
> That wins to the reality in the fact.

until all life flames in the vision of

> the light that breaks
> From the whole earth seen as a star again
> In the general life of man.

> The actuality is different. Men are obtuse, dull, complacent,
> vulgar. They love the third-rate, live on the cheapest terms
> with themselves, 'the engagement between man and being
> forsaken', their 'incredible variation nipped in the bud.'
> Their reading is 'novels and newspapers', their preoccupa-
> tions 'fitba' and 'weemen', their thinking 'treadmills of
> rationalizing.' They have hardly issued yet,

> Up frae the slime, that a' but a handfu' o' men
> Are grey wi' still.

> They refuse to explore the largeness of life. This refusal he
> sees as a cowardice.

Like Geddes he holds that 'our greatest need today is to grasp life
as a whole, to see its many sides in their proper relations. But we
must have a practical as well as a philosophic interest in such an
integrated view of life.'

In this book, *Sowing the Spring*,[14] Professor James G. Southworth
says:

> To all classes with their increasing awareness of social pro-
> blems and their revision of their views of life as science has
> pushed back the boundaries of the universe. Mr MacDiarmid
> has much to say, and he says it with force. One may cavil at

individual poems, may disagree violently with specific ideas; but when one lays aside the volumes of his work and thinks about his accomplishment one realizes he has been in the presence of a man of erudition steeped in the best thought of the past and the present; that he has been in the presence of a man who by sincerity of expression, by subtlety and keenness of intellect, and by indomitable energy has sought to fire his readers to an adequate perception of the universe, of our immediate world and its needs, and of their place therein.

2

A RUSSO-SCOTTISH PARALLELISM

1923

It has been said that Professor J. Y. Simpson's new book, *Man and the Attainment of Immortality*,[1] is significant of the changed attitude towards natural science which is to be seen in all Christian communions, since, whereas at the beginning of the present century a Christian teacher who publicly avowed his belief in biological evolution was accounted dangerous, if not heretical, three-fourths of this volume are devoted to a description of biological evolution and the slow development of primitive man, and, in the concluding quarter, the whole process is related to the Christian doctrine of immortality. It also illustrates in a most interesting fashion the way in which, in theology as in every other sphere of human speculation, identical conclusions may be independently arrived at, often along entirely unrelated lines, by workers in divers countries. Almost every new idea of world moment manifests itself sporadically in contemporary consciousness; and its various appearances have no other relation than approximate contemporaneity. Superficially it would seem improbable that Professor Simpson and that most remarkable of Russian thinkers, the late Vladimir Solovyov, could have a great deal in common. Yet as a matter of fact their conclusions are practically identical. It would be ridiculous to call Professor Simpson a disciple of Solovyov. Despite the wide and ever-developing influence of Solovyov's philosophy since his premature death in 1900, it is extremely unlikely that Professor Simpson owes any conscious debt to it. In the field of literature, charges of plagiarism are frequently based upon similar and much more slender grounds; but there can be no question of the intentional appropriation of a previous thinker's ideas by the Professor of Natural Science at New College, Edinburgh, although, as a matter of fact, his book is largely a restatement, in terms intelligible to those who have been bred in similar traditions to his own, of the

38

essence of Solovyov's philosophy which, as stated by him, in the terms of a culture entirely different from ours, is for the most part quite outwith the comprehension of the great majority of Professor Simpson's audience of readers.

In his early youth Solovyov became convinced that perfect and exhaustive truth had been revealed in the Christian faith, and he made it the supreme task of his life to show, by disclosing greater depths in Christianity, that it contained a complete and sufficient answer to the demands of reason; or, as he put it, to prove that this ancient faith coincided with eternal and universal truth. In a sense, then, it is true to say that for Solovyov philosophy was preeminently the handmaid of theology. But nothing could be further from Solovyov's mind than to maintain that philosophy should be guided in its development by the demands of theology. Philosophy was for him the expression of an essential characteristic of the human spirit, in virtue of which it refuses to submit to any external limitations or to be enslaved by any creeds, traditions, or institutions. All values accrue from the inner life and become a part of our conscious being. The spirit of man is always seeking a greater fullness of life; and in rejecting ancient idols it formulates a demand for a more perfect embodiment of truth.

The conclusion reached by Professor Simpson, equally a creative iconoclast, in his chapter on the 'method of evolution', is that 'the only way in which the future progress has been successively and triumphantly secured has been by conformity to some as yet dimly appreciated but higher element revealed in the unmasking environment, which in its ultimate aspect is God.' He rejects the idea that man is inherently an immortal soul—an idea that is not a Christian idea if the unambiguous witness of the New Testament is accepted as conclusive, and, moreover, one that does not cohere with our present knowledge of man's origin and development. He suggests that with the origin of man there emerged the possibility of some new relationship, 'a moral linkage' with God; and only in so far as this possibility is realized does man attain the true 'individuality which is immortality'.

These sentences contain a paraphrase—and a simplification which sacrifices a great deal that is essential to a full realization of the position taken up—of the metaphysical argument exhaustively developed in Solovyov's *La Russie et l'Eglise Universelle*—

an epoch-making book, the power of which is now beginning to pervade European thought in unmistakable fashion. According to Solovyov there is no opposition between the universal and the individual.

Reality is one living system, each part of which, while remaining unique and individual, enters at the same time into the composition of a wider whole. And the whole, which includes the limitless multiplicity of forms, may itself be regarded as an individual entity; and just as the particular forms that enter into it require for their explanation to be related to the Absolute Being or God, so, too, the perfect whole — tout dans l'unité — can only be conceived as dependent upon God as the eternal object of the divine thought and love. The whole as an object of God's thought is not a mere lifeless image in God's mind, but a conscious and living entity — the Wisdom of God, Sophia. In the words of the Old Testament Sophia plays before God, evoking before God images of possible extra-divine existence, shapes of chaotic multiplicity, and reabsorbing them again into herself.

Sophia is not only the perfect unity of all that is *sub specie aeternitatis*, but also the unifying power in the divided and chaotic world, the living bond between the Creator and the creature. Sophia is for ever seeking to bring back to herself the existence that has split off from the original whole, and by becoming incarnate in the lower world, to attain complete and perfect realization of the ideal union between God and the universe.

Similarly regarding the world process as a means whereby God designed to communicate himself to beings which should come into existence, Professor Simpson's opposition of freedom and individuality to bondage and dissolution and his contention that creation involved a definite self-limitation of God, a surrender in part of his freedom, is obviously a transposition of Solovyov's conception into the terms of a different tradition of thought.

Since there cannot be any real existence without God, the extra-divine world can only be a distortion of the divine reality. This is, Solovyov maintains, what we find to be the case. The medium of distortion he terms the 'world-soul'. Being purely negative and indeterminate, it has a double and variable character; it can strive to assert itself outside of God, and, in its blind desire for chaotic and anarchical existence, attempt to produce a world discordant, aimless, and irrational. But it can also surrender itself to God, and by bringing all creation to perfect harmony identify itself with Sophia. Drawn in all directions by blind forces making for exclusive possession, broken into fragments and pulverized into an innumerable multitude of atoms, the world-soul becomes conscious of a vague longing for harmonious being, and thus attracts the action of the Logos, that gives the chaotic universe the form of an indefinite space, the form of one time — past, present, and future — and binds together the *disjecta membra* of the terrestrial world by the law of universal gravitation. Yet the world-soul aspires to a more perfect unity; it disengages itself from the earthly mass, and transforms its power into a new and subtle form of matter called ether.

This matter is used by the Logos to create another cosmical unity still more perfect — the dynamical unity, expressed by light, heat, electricity, etc. It envelops the material mass in all its parts, but does not enter into it, does not regenerate it. The soul of the world, 'the Earth', recognizes in the luminiferous ether the ideal image of its heavenly prototype, but attains no real union therewith. Yet it absorbs the light, transforms it into vital fire, and brings forth the creatures that have life — plants, animals, men. The new organic unity is objectively manifested by plants in the very form of their existence; it is subjectively felt by animals; it is conceptually understood by man. The earth at last concentrates itself, enters into itself, and puts on a form in which it can meet God face to face and directly receive from Him the breath of spiritual life. The sensitive and imaginative soul of the physical world becomes the rational soul of man. The essential unity of all that is becomes now for the first time recognized by the world-soul through the reason and conscience of man. The Divine Wisdom finds at last the conscious subject that can enter into conscious and reciprocal union with her and raise up to her the whole of the material world. She finds this conscious subject and rejoices. 'My joy', she says, 'is in the sons of man.'

This conception of 'conscious and reciprocal union' is what Professor Simpson is endeavouring to express when he suggests the possibility of some new relationship, a moral linkage, with God, and just as from that point Solovyov proceeded, recognizing the two-fold nature of man, to ask how man was to overcome his chaotic state and to obtain realization of the ideal unity which he conceptually grasps through reason, so Professor Simpson, regarding evolution as the winning of freedom, suggests that man, 'in the earlier stages of humanity out of which we are just beginning to emerge', has been a passive participant in his evolution, though of course in a considerably less degree than his animal predecessors, and, recognizing that 'neither science nor philosophy, intelligence, nor any form of human power necessarily carries with it mastery of the self, or has the ability to set man free from bondage to the physical and mental characteristics that he has inherited', holds that as man enters a moral world his individuality becomes perfected in so far as he establishes harmonious relations with God. Man becomes perfect when his freedom and God's freedom are harmonized. There is unity 'in perfect mutual spiritual experience, free from all limitations', and that unity is 'Eternal life.'

In conclusion, Professor Simpson contends that so far from the universality of law negativing any such uniqueness as Christians find in their Lord, 'in an evolutionary process, once it is proved to be a progressive process, there is more reason to consider everything unique: there is no duplication, no repetition': and he urges that 'in the perfect manhood of Jesus Christ the creative spirit of God came to full and perfect expression as a revealing, energizing, and saving power.' In terms of Solovyov's philosophy the same conclusion has been set down thus:

Christ was not the last word of the human kingdom, but the first and all-embracing word of the Kingdom of God. By His teaching and the work of His whole life, beginning with the victory of the temptations of moral evil and ending with His resurrection—that is, His victory over physical evil or death— Christ revealed to humanity the kingdom of God. Yet from the nature of the case revelation cannot here coincide with attainment. Christ finally conquered evil in the true centre of the universe—that is in Himself—but the victory over evil in the world's circumference—that is, in the collective whole of humanity—can only be attained through the personal experience and free choice of each individual, each member of the collective whole being a rational agent. Hence the necessity of the historical process after the appearance of Christ. The Kingdom of God, or the perfect moral order, can no more be revealed to a horde of savages than a human being can be born from a mollusc or a sponge. Just as the human spirit in nature requires the most perfect of physical organisms, so the spirit of God in humanity requires for its actual manifestation the most perfect of social organizations, and that is being evolved in the course of history.

It is significant that new theological conceptions of so comprehensive a character should be beginning to enter into Scottish thought at a juncture so rich in promise of national renaissance in other directions.

3

ART AND THE UNKNOWN

1926

Comprehensibility is error: Art is beyond understanding.* The function of art is the extension of human consciousness. Art is therefore the most important of human activities; all others are dependent upon it.

The highest art at any time can only be appreciated by an infinitesimal minority of the people—if by any.†

The ideal observer of art at work would be one conscious of all human experience up to the given moment. (The ideal observer of art—as against art-at-work—is God, conscious of all that has been and *will be* achieved.) If consciousness be likened to a cleared space, art is that which extends it in any direction.

The ideal specialist as compared with the ideal observer is conscious not of the whole of human experience up to a given moment, but of its entire development in a particular direction up to then.

The ideal observer alone can appreciate the value, in relation to art as a whole, of any further achievement.

The ideal specialist can only appreciate an advance made in his particular direction. Artistic experience within the cleared space is only possible in so far as one's range is less than that of the ideal observer and, in any particular direction, than that of its ideal specialist.

---

* Cf. Edwin Muir. 'The unnecessary and the inconceivable have been greater friends to man than the necessary and the reasonable. This enigmatical character of art, this ultimate impossibility of making it turn any moral mill, has been noted occasionally in the last two centuries, etc.' (*Latitudes* [Melrose, London, 1924], p. 143.) The ultimate impossibility of making it turn *any* mill is what is here affirmed.

† Cf. Denis Saurat. 'The more complicated beings become, the more subdivided and subtle their desires, the smaller is the group of beings they can collaborate with, until the subtlest artists create, *on the basis of the common languages*, a personal means of expression which we have to learn in order to understand them.' (*The Three Conventions* [Nott, London, 1935] p. 89.) The emphasized clause should be excised.

Capacity for artistic experience increases in so far as one is making progress in any direction towards the confines of the cleared space.

Ground covered in any direction ceases to be art for those who have covered it, and, for them, lapses into education or entertainment for those who haven't.

However ponderable from other points of view, from the standpoint of art, those bogged in what has lapsed (for those who have passed any given point) into education or entertainment cease to exist. Only those who are further ahead than themselves are of consequence to those who are making artistic progress. Any relationship with others is a waste of time, of life—a betrayal of art.

To halt or turn back in order to try to help others is to abandon artistic progress, and exchange education for art. There is no altruism in art. It is every man for himself. In so far as he advances, the progress of others may be facilitated, but in so far as he is conscious of affording any such facilitation his concentration on purely artistic objectives is diminished.

From the point of view of the ideal observer nothing has value as art which does not add to the area of the cleared space. For him, everything coming within the cleared space automatically lapses into education or entertainment upon its inclusion.

From the point of view of the ideal specialist nothing in any given direction is of value except its furthest point.

All dicta on art are therefore to be judged in relation (a) to omniscience of human experience, or (b) to the appropriate specialism or specialisms.

All that claims to be art therefore is of value *in inverse ratio* to its comprehensibility and to the extent to which it falls into any particular category.

Artists of any degree whatever are recognizable by their intolerance of what they have surpassed.

Art is incapable of repetition.

No artist is great (or really an artist) unless he reaches some point in the unknown outside the cleared space and then adds to the cleared space.

The total addition made to the cleared space is the measure of greatness as an artist—*at the time the addition is made.*

No achievement in art is permanent—as art.

Great artists of the past diminish in so far as the point or frontier of their particular addition recedes from the latest confines of the cleared space.

They cease to be great artists from the point of view of the ideal observer or any ideal specialist, and acquire compensatory importance in the history of art (the highest kind of knowledge).

They remain artists or great artists only in proportion to the appropriate ignorance (i.e. incapacity for experience) of those for whom they are so.

If great art is compatible with a big popular appeal, it can only be so in so far as it contains elements unthinkable to the public.

In direct ratio to its popularity (i.e. its comprehensibility) it is not art.

The greatest art at any given time is that which is comprehensible to the fewest persons of competence and integrity, whether as approximations (a) to the ideal observer or (b) to the requisite ideal specialist. For an artist or critic to pride himself on his knowledge of art is to boast—not of his achievements, still less of his powers—but of his tools.*

II

The greatest artist at any given time is the creator of the greatest art as just defined in proportion as it defies ideal specialists and demands the ideal observer.

As the cleared space increases the relative importance of each ideal specialist to the ideal observer decreases. The greatest artist is the greatest critic.

Neither his art nor his criticism need be expressed.† The greatest (non-artist) critic is he who feels most intensely the necessity of overcoming the incomprehensibility in question, and that the more intensely in proportion to his intuitive, and correct, realization that the resolution of it calls for the ideal observer rather than for any ideal specialist or any series of ideal specialists.

* 'La mémoire et les sens ne seront que la nourriture de ton impulsion créatrice.' Rimbaud.
† 'Kunst ist Gabe, nicht Wiedergabe.' Herewath Walden.

It is impossible for the artist to achieve the incomprehensible to him, but he may not know how he knows.

The critic may show him that; but that has nothing to do with art.*

The critic's function is to make art comprehensible, and so transform it into education and/or entertainment.

His ability to demonstrate his greatness as a critic, therefore, depends upon the extent or difficulty of the supply of art available for his purpose.

A subsidiary function is, therefore, to stimulate an increase of either of these.

His value lies in the rapidity with which he can perform his function for the most incomprehensible art; his greatness on the extent of the circumference of the cleared space upon which he operates.

His value as a critic is not, however, determined in any way by the number of people for whom he makes the art with which he deals comprehensible. The intimate association of the most important criticism with advanced art precludes more than an extremely limited public for either.†

Both operate beyond the farthest limit of education, although the ultimate achievement of both is to advance it.

'Popular art' is a contradiction in terms.

'The educative value of art' is a confusion of functions.

Criticism is inferior to art because art is for it a means to an end — the end of the art to which it is applied.

This inferiority is least discernible when criticism confines itself most to the subsidiary function referred to above; or when it co-operates indissociably with the creative spirit in the artist himself.

Herman Bahr quotes Goethe as pointing out, in his *Data for a History of Colour*, that there are sciences which must transcend themselves and become something higher — that is to say, art.

---

* 'It is terribly difficult to accept influences which are necessary, and yet use them only as a means toward the end of shaping one's own being from within, and not to keep on carrying these elements as foreign bodies in one's system, however enthusiastically one may have accepted them at first.' Otto Braun.

† 'A new synthesis of intellect and spirit has become necessary. A synthesis which is directed towards establishing a new balance of the various parts of man, not with he backward, but with the most highly-developed elements.' Hermann Keyserling.

Since nothing whole can be created either out of knowledge or out of reflection, because the first is lacking in Inwardness, and the second in Outwardness, we are forced to think of Science (*Wissenschaft*) as Art, whenever we expect a sense of entirety from it ... But in order that we should be able to fulfil such a demand we must exclude no human force or faculty from scientific participation. The profundity of intuition, a firm contemplation of the present, mathematical depth, physical accuracy, the acme of reason, the keenness of intellect, the phantasy moving and full of yearning, a fond joy of the sensuous—none of these can be omitted in order to seize the propitious moment, and exploit it in a live and fruitful sense, that moment which alone can give birth to a work of art, no matter what its content may be.

Appendix. Types of nonsense in criticism. Cecil Gray's contention that poor poetry suits composers better than great poetry. James Agate's statement that Duse's talent 'must be deemed less than supreme in that it needs masterpieces to feed on'.

4

PAUL VALÉRY

1927

'The intelligent man must finally reduce himself knowingly to an indefinite refusal to be anything whatsoever.' Valéry.

The whole point of the neo-classical tendency which is increasingly manifesting itself in all the arts is being ludicrously missed by those who are confusing it with a return to any 'classical' formalism instead of to fundamental form and are welcoming the apparent volte-face of most of our advanced composers—e.g. Stravinsky, Bartok, Casella—as a repudiation of their 'wild oats' instead of a far more intensive cultivation of them.

The meaning of the effort to 'depersonalize' music—to rid it of its literary, personal and humanistic element, and to hail the time when all instrumental music will be played by mechanical reproducing instruments as a means to this end—is akin to that of Mallarmé when he said, 'Ce n'est pas avec des idées qu'on fait des vers, c'est avec des mots', or to Valéry's own call for a 'language machine'. All the arts must disencumber themselves completely of the moral and ethical clichés, the dreary literalism, the empty bombast, the democratic insistence on 'more meaning', the messianic illusion, by which they are presently confused and confounded. All kinds of eloquence are having their necks wrung with a thoroughness as unprecedented as it is vitally necessary. Let us regard all the arts altogether technically. Let us, in particular, disabuse ourselves of the idea that art becomes great in direct ratio to the number—and consequently relative ignorance —of those to whom it appeals. Let us get rid of all the solemn awe-struck nonsense about genius, all the high-falutin about 'poets being born, not made', and the like, and all the brainless rhodo-montade about 'architecture being frozen music', music 'volatilized architecture', and the rest of the fatuous journalese. Let us acquire some such sane and self-respecting attitude to ourselves and our

4

readers as Valéry's. 'M. Valéry would at once concede that neither in his choice of themes nor in his treatment of them is he concerned to stir the common heart of man.'

*

Mr Fisher's essay[1] is an attempt, with the inevitable reservations and caveats, to explain such a position as Valéry takes up (which is even more antipathetic to the English spirit than any other in Europe) to a wider public than that small section of our intelligentsia who are constitutionally fitted to receive it. An amusing instance of the difficulties of Mr Fisher (who shares most of the less obvious disabilities of the majority of those he is presumably addressing) may be cited. He complains of the effects of bathos experienced in connection with work of this kind by the ordinary reader who 'cannot altogether succeed in divesting music from meaning', or live in that 'light from a solitary wing' which permits the undiverted pursuit of a poet guided solely by considerations of euphony. And he instances the closing lines from 'Le Sylphe'. 'Then comes the bathos. A rhyme must be found for *promises*. M. Valéry lights upon *chemises,* and so we have:

> Ni vu ni connu
> le temps d'un sein nu
> Entre deux chemises!

Clearly the sylph has made a precipitate retreat. The *deux chemises* may be euphonious, but they are not inspired ...

What amuses me (as a result of this fatal association of ideas) is that a little earlier Mr Fisher translates from Valéry a passage in which the concluding sentence is rendered as follows: 'This singular angle of vision prevents me from forming a reasonable judgment on ... any kind of work which takes man as he appears to us, as a unit or element *in its combination.*'

*

Instead of accusing Valéry of 'having set himself an impossible task', whilst himself attempting in a public lecture the impossible task of explaining an author who is professedly inexplicable save, perhaps, to the few, Mr Fisher would have done better to have used some such terms as Prince Mirsky's concerning Blok: 'A large part of his work will seem to the uninitiated nothing better than verbal and phonetic play; *it must joyfully be accepted as such,* and as such it is very exhilarating.' Or he should have pointed out the bearing of Valéry's work to kindred work in all the arts throughout Europe today, e.g. his relationship to such a poet as Khlebnikov.

Rather a conjuror playing with the language than what we understand by the word 'poet'. All things were only a material for him to build up a new world of words, a creation of genius but obviously not for the general. He is not, and probably never will be, read except by the poets and philologists. The poets have found him an inexhaustible mine of good example and useful doctrine, a granary whence they take the seeds for their harvests. His work is also of great interest to the philologists, for he was a lord of language. He knew its hidden possibilities and forced it to reveal them. His work is a microcosm reflecting on an enormously magnified scale the creative processes of the whole life-story of the language.

Infinitely rarer and more important phenomena, poets such as these, than what Mr Fisher would have preferred Valéry to have been! In the face of all that has happened since Rimbaud, he exclaims: 'Let it not, however, be imagined that the symbolist movement was wholly barren'! This masterpiece of ineptitude — a howler raised to the nth — reminds me of the canny Scot who, when Professor Legouis made his shocking disclosures of Wordsworth's French liaison, took it upon himself to assure M. Legouis that 'nevertheless they in Great Britain would continue to regard Wordsworth as a great poet'!

*

What Valéry says — and practises so marvellously — of his 'comprehensive exclusions', of his object 'being in a certain sense to eliminate life', and of his inability to give all sorts of phenomena, popularly believed to constitute it, any place in poetry at all, reminds me of Shestov, who abandoned his religious immoralism and irrationalism and fell back on the most ordinary common sense whenever he had to deal with anything so unimportant as the world of ordinary experiences, the conduct of men, and the facts of history;—or of Rozanov who wrote conservative articles in the *Novoe Vremya*, and radical articles in the *Russkoe Slovo*, but, when charged with moral insanity, 'did not regard this inconsistency as anything outrageous. Politics were to him a very minor business that could not be brought *sub specie aeternitatis*. What interested him in both parties were only the various individualities that went to form them, their "taste", their "flavour", their "atmosphere".'

As Valéry says: 'Learned poetry is a profoundly sceptical art.' No doubt Mr Fisher is satisfied that he was competent—and has efficiently discharged the task he set himself. But the relation of that task to the subject 'Paul Valéry' is different in degree, but not in kind, to that relation between what Shelley meant by 'love', and that passion of the butcher-boy for the kitchen-maid with which he was rightly afraid it might be confounded. M. Valéry will have no difficulty in refusing to be what Mr Fisher has made him.

5

MY NATIVE PLACE

1931

After journeying in recent years over most of Scotland, England, and Central, Southern, and Eastern Europe, I am of the opinion that 'my native place'—the muckle toon of Langholm, in Dumfriesshire—is the bonniest place I know, by virtue, not of the little burgh in itself (though that has its treasurable aspects, and on nights when, as boys, we used to thread its dim streets playing 'Jock, Shine the Light' and race over the one bridge, past the factory, and over the other, with the lamp-reflections wriggling like eels at intervals in the racing waters, had an indubitable magic of its own), but of wonderful variety and quality of the scenery in which it is set. I have not been there for years; and years before that I felt that I had completely outgrown the place. My interests lay along lines no one else in the place seemed to share, and I seemed to share none of theirs. In all my published poetry there is, I think, but one lyric in *A Drunk Man*[1] and a few lines of allusion in *To Circumjack Cencrastus*[2] devoted to it. And yet, within the past year or two I have found myself increasingly caught up in happy recollections of it and speculations as to what divided me so early and so completely from all the tastes and tendencies of my relatives and other early friends. One of the main reasons for this, probably, is the fact that my own children are domiciled in London, and that I cannot but compare the quality of the childhood available to them there with my own childhood's happy playground. The delights of sledging on the Lamb Hill or Murtholm Brae; of gathering 'hines' in the Langfall; of going through the fields of Baggara hedged in honeysuckle and wild roses, through knee-deep meadowsweet to the 'Scrog-nit' wood and gathering the nuts or crab-apples there; of blaeberrying on Warblaw or the Castle Hill; of 'dookin' and 'guddlin' or making islands in the Esk or Ewes or Wauchope and lighting stick fires on them and cooking potatoes in tin cans—these are only a few

of the joys I knew, in addition to the general ones of hill-climbing
and penetrating the five glens which (each with its distinct
character) converge upon or encircle the town — Eskdale,
Wauchopedale, Tarrasdale, Ewesdale, and, below the town
Carlisle-wards, the 'Dean Banks'. As we grew up, too, we learned
to savour the particular qualities and rites of Langholm in comparison with other Border burghs — the joys of Langholm Com-
mon-Riding compared with those at Selkirk or Hawick, for
example; the peculiar shibboleths of local pronunciation; the
historical associations of our corner of the 'ballad-land' rife with
its tales of raidings and reivings and with the remnants of peels;
the wealth of local 'characters' who were still about but seem now
to have almost died out — Jenny Spells, Jimmy Moniplies, and the
like. As I grew into my early teens I ranged further afield, and
soon all the Borders were within my ken. Many places had their
special beauties or points of interest and advantage; but none had
the variety of beauty centred round Langholm itself — none
seemed so complete a microcosm of the entire Borderland. I
knew nowhere to find not only the common delights of hill and
forest and field and waterside (and chiefest of all these to me were
the chestnut trees at the sawmill — even now it thrills me to remember the beautiful chestnuts, large and lustrous as horses' eyes,
which so surprisingly displayed themselves when we cracked open
the prickly green shells, and I remember many huge 'strops' of
them I strung and many a fierce competition at 'conquerors'),
but the various kinds of orchises, and butterwort, sundew, and the
like; the various nests — including Terrona crags where ravens
nested; how to deal with adders and smoke out wasps' 'bikes', and
much other lore of that sort. In short, a boyhood packed full of
country sights and sounds — healthy and happy and able to satisfy
its hunger with juicy slices of a big yellow 'neep' stolen from an
adjoining field. Apart from the most radical mental and spiritual
divergence, and the circumstances which sent me first to school
and thence to work in other parts of Scotland and furth of
Scotland, ties which might have drawn me back more frequently
were broken with my father's early death, and again, 'the men
who were boys when I was a boy' — my old school chums and
playmates — suffered the sudden dispersal of the war generation.
Many of them made the supreme sacrifice: and I myself was on

active service for nearly four years, in Salonika, Italy, and Marseilles, and of all the men I met in the Army, only one, I think, was a Langholmite. These war years interposed a barrier like that set up by a serious illness; it is difficult ever to take up again threads broken in that way: and now, while I have many a vignette of rare beauty, many a memory of pure and enriching experience — while at times I am positively haunted by some of the curious place-names; Baggara, Kernigall, Tarras — as the result of the early years I spent in Langholm, to which, however, I have only returned once, and that for a mere flying visit twelve years ago — it is not for myself that I crave any renewed experience of its delights, but for my children, whose city-sted lives seem to me attenuated and glamourless in comparison. I would have their lives enriched by a similar colourful and diverse contact with nature in turn, even if they too, must needs break with it as radically as I have done. But for myself — and perhaps for them, if a return to Langholm or any like spot (and there is no like spot — no spot quite like) is impossible — if I ever go 'out of the world and into Langholm again', it will only be in dreams or in my poet's craft in which, perchance, I may yet find words for some of the felicities I remember and to which (despite all my subsequent divergence of interest and effort) the texture of my spirit must owe incomparably more than I can ever repay or acknowledge.

6

THE CALEDONIAN ANTISYZYGY AND THE GAELIC IDEA

1931–2

I. THE KELPIE IN THE DORTS

The kelpie in the dorts owre lang has lain
Drooned in the heedlessness o' men,
Owre idle or owre ignorant to ken
The glories that it micht ha' ha'en,
Till in its hingin' fupple's dreich lines nane
Can weel be blamed for dootin' they remain,
Nor lippen to see't uncurl its blazin' train
And, louch nae mair, through a' the lift be gane.

There is nae height that ony leid can gain,
You canna match wi' ferlies o' your ain,
Nae height unreached but you may first attain;
Faurer than the laverock's soars your sweeter strain.
Only to earth the laverock sinks again,
But you plunge deeper faur than ony brain
'S yet gane, or aiblins can till you unchain
                         Poo'er's yours alane.

Then up and skail your maikless fires again,
And multiply new shades o' joy and pain
Kittle and mony-shaped as licht or rain.
Tak' nae fixed shape. Nae suner kyth in ane
Than to anither 'yont belief you're gane
Until you show in sicna sequence plain
A' that we'd tine if you s'ud halt and hain
This form or that, that silly folk are fain
To fix—oh!, *recta ratio factibilium* reign
                         In a' we're daen'.

Banish oor beliefs for they are a' in vain,
Whummle oor sanctities in quick disdain,
Licht vulgar words wi' glories that contain
Nocht that to human life can appertain,
Glories denied, or understood, by nane,
Like new stars lyin' in the faur inane,
Brichter and bigger and to ootlast oor ain,
Or glorify oor beliefs afore they've gane,
Honour oor sanctities, let laich life feign
New stature frae you—shed on us bliss or bane;
But oot and aboot; nor in the dorts be lain
But wax a hundred-fauld abune your wane.

II. FREEDOM

Freedom is *inconceivable.* The word
Betrays the cause—a habit o' the mind,
Thinkin' continually in a certain way,
Generation after generation, till it seems
This is Thocht's fixed, unalterable mode.

It is a wise critic who has seen that the attacks made by the new movement in Scottish arts and affairs are 'frequently directed against persons and institutions more because they have come to hinder appreciation of other merits, or development in other directions, than because they offend in themselves'. This reaches right down to the root of Scotland's distinctive function in the world ('which partakes not of fairyland, but of the enchantment of life itself—indescribable as a sea of changing colours touching all the shores of possibility'); its essential contribution, past and potential, to civilization. A friend recently asked me to define the Scottish genius, and I answered, 'Freedom—the free development of human consciousness', and in the course of the argument I cited the misconceptions and difficulties that have arisen through successive attempts to force Scottish history, with its incomparably chequered character, into the mould of English constitutionalism; the radicalism of Scotland in politics versus the conservatism of England; the typical production in Scotland of a philosopher like Hume and an economist like Major C. H. Douglas (a particularly good example, with his demand for the abandonment of the whole system of 'rewards and punishments' and the removal of all limiting factors in the interests of 'life and that more abundantly'); the extent to which the religious genius of Scotland had sought freedom until it became stultified and subverted and an apt illustration of the fact that eternal vigilance is the price of freedom and that, as Dostoevsky says, in his Legend of the Grand Inquisitor, all human organizations become conspiracies to short-circuit the development of human consciousness:

> A' men's institutions and maist men's thochts
> Are tryin' for aye to bring to an end
> The insatiable thocht, the beautiful violent will,
> The restless spirit of Man ...*

And, most apt of all, the many profoundly penetrating phrases in which Professor G. Gregory Smith describes[1] the prime quality of Scottish literature—phrases such as these: 'Almost a zigzag of contradictions; a reflection of the contrasts which the Scot shows at every turn, in his political and ecclesiastical history, in his polemical restlessness, in his adaptability'—' "Varied with a clean contrair spirit" '—'Oxymoron was ever the bravest figure, and we must not forget that disorderly order is order after all'—'There is more in the Scottish antithesis of the real and fantastic than is to be explained by the familiar rules of rhetoric. The sudden jostling of contraries seems to preclude any relationship by literary suggestion. The one invades the other without warning. They are the "polar twins" of the Scottish Muse'†—'This freedom in passing from one mood to another'—and so on. Professor Smith traces this 'Caledonian antisyzygy' clearly through the whole course of Scottish literature. I spoke not only with a lively awareness of the extent to which my own work has continued to exemplify it, but with a satisfying recollection of the

---

* Hugh MacDiarmid, *To Circumjack Cencrastus* (Blackwood, Edinburgh, 1930), p. 191. *Editor.*

† Splendidly exemplified in Sir Arthur Keith's recent Aberdeen rectorial address, stressing the two sides always in the affairs of men: nature and reason, separatism and integration, individualism and co-operation, nationalism and internationalism—a flow of the one succeeded by a flow of the other, the problem of civilization to ride upon the flux and reflux of these forces—the differences between person and person, country and country, race and race, give life a pattern and a colour without which it would be an infinitely dreary and uniform affair.

fact that Professor Smith did not confine himself to Dunbar, Burns, and others usually claimed as specifically Scottish authors, but roped in Byron, too, whose tremendous reputation on the Continent and comparative neglect in England is largely explained by the extent to which this element in his work—in Scottish work generally—is antipathetic to English tastes. But my interlocutor, while conceding the interest and value of these points, said that they were perhaps more convincing in relation to creative artists than to the history and nature and tendencies of the Scottish people as a whole. I do not think so—except in so far as the latter do simply remain the undifferentiated mob because they have not 'found themselves': but (and this is the main point in this essay) it scarcely matters. What is of consequence is what the determined and determining minority do. This being so, there is no need for me to stress here how a failure to entertain or recognize the antisyzygy—what Professor Whitehead emphasizes as incomparably important today as a counterbalance to over-specialization and single-track mentalities in the phrases 'organic appreciation—variety of aesthetic appreciation'—underlies what Willa Muir in *Imagined Corners*,[2] calls, dealing with Scottish life, 'the hotch-potch' of absurd notions which still almost incredibly imposes itself on most people; the stupidities of 'democracy'; the false 'internationalism' of the labour movement; the importance attached to the views of the 'man in the street', and to the 'consensus of opinion' and all the other conventional attitudes with which as, *inter alia*, essentially un-Scottish the Scottish renaissance movement is at this or that point and on this or that plane joining issue.

It is because of this—a carry-over from the un-Scottish politics they have professedly abandoned—I conflict sharply with the great majority of the members of the National Party of Scotland.* I welcome for what it is worth—for however little it is worth—the very superficial stirrings of Scottish national consciousness in various directions. The National Party of Scotland is better than most of these, but I stand very loosely to it too, for the reason involved in the following pregnant sentences which I read somewhere recently:

* Dr Grieve was one of the founders of the National Party of Scotland in 1928 but was expelled from it in 1933. *Editor.*

The modern habit is to create a political organization and then evangelize. This is like building a cathedral, consecrating a bishop, formulating a creed, and then seeking converts. Great movements have not been born in such a way. They begin with the Word; the plant and paraphernalia of organization are a by-product made inevitable by the lusts of the believers. Indeed one of the great advantages of a new movement is precisely its lack of any kind of organization. Those who join it do so for its own sake alone. No hope of office tempts the unscrupulous; no possibilities of advancement bring in adventurers whose mere association with a cause is its undoing. These modern parties which establish a secretariat before they have a rank and file and whose headed notepaper precedes their appearance in the market-place are not likely to contain the principle of growth. Posters and loudspeakers and novelty will collect an audience, but permanent allegiance comes only as a result of genuine convictions—a real message. Truth is like corn; it must be constantly replanted, and its harvest is its own rich decay.

The National Party of Scotland is too apt already to give the impression of being ready for the harvest—already quarrelling over the crop. But has it laboriously prepared the soil and planted seed? The answer is in the negative. It has only scratched the surface—it has not dug down nearly far enough. As for the seed of creative ideas it is far too content—owing to its pusillanimity and lack of ability to 'distinguish and divide'—with intellectual seediness, with the common sense which is unfortunately only too common and that avoidance of lunacy advocated by the Duke of Montrose [the sixth duke], which is perhaps the worst form of it.

A revival of true Scottishness is to be found in the active part the Scottish P.E.N. have taken at Oslo, Warsaw, Vienna, and The Hague in promoting 'the decentralization of literature' (an action which incidentally necessitated the formation of a Gaelic section of the Scottish P.E.N. and led to an Irish centre)—a question which, since Mr William Power first raised it at Oslo by insisting upon Scotland's title to representation and voting power independent of England, has become one of the most vital issues in European literary politics. Scotland has incurred French opposition in particular, but if the French who may have a genius for centralization not found, nor desirable in, other countries attempt to suppress cultural minorities in the international P.E.N. organization they must be prepared to find the Scottish P.E.N. invading the enemy's field and using the relationships they have already established with the Bretons and Provençals to secure the establishment of autonomous, or, at least, subordinate centres at Rennes, Bordeaux and elsewhere, with incalculable consequences to the future of French literature. This is a matter which goes far beyond a mere revolt against standardization. It is positive—not negative—and represents a definite contribution by Scotland to European literary development. The role played has already been far-reaching in its effects, if not decisive, but I do not wish to exaggerate its importance, save as a real manifestation of Scotland's purposive re-emergence in the European field, and to point to Professor W. J. Entwistle's recent address to the Scottish P.E.N. on 'Some Spanish Experiments in the Decentralization of Literature' and my own long essay on 'English Ascendancy in British Literature' in the current issue of the *Criterion*[3] as further developments in this direction of a renewed Scottish plea for diversity as against uniformity in keeping with our essential national genius.

The latter essay reflects not only the literary—but political—aspects of this issue in so far as Scottish and English relationships in particular are involved. Who shall say what makes nations rise and fall and alters the balance of their respective contributions to the arts and affairs of the world at divers junctures? They move towards the unconscious goal of history and as long as they have failed to realize any fraction of their distinctive function in that great process, they will and must continue to strive for it, however they may seem at any particular period to forget it or neglect it or however they may seem to be dominated and absorbed by some other nation with a different nature and a different historical function to fulfil. I believe that Ireland during its long struggle not only set a magnificent example of 'following the gleam', but that it had a prescience of the wider implications of the necessity of doing so—its bearing upon world-affairs and upon British and imperial affairs in particular—in short, that the true interpretation of its achievement in regaining a measure of autonomy was a deep intuition of the ruination a continued English ascendancy was enforcing on these islands by its blind prejudice, and the extent to which it has been betraying European civilization by pandering to colonials and Yankees and coming down to their level. Just as in British arts and letters we have lost incalculable strength and variety by putting all our eggs in the basket of the main English tradition—excluding the great Gaelic literatures of Ireland, Wales, and Scotland, Scots vernacular literature, and literature in the diverse English dialects— extirpating their racy native dialects from the speech of our children in a psychologically outrageous and culturally sterilizing fashion in the interests of snobbish convention—so in politics the position in which England finds itself today, and must increasingly find itself, is just retribution for the selfish imperialism which in these islands particularly and in the organization and policy of the empire generally has insisted by the most unscrupulous means on English ascendancy rather than on that synthesis of the potential contributions of the various elements, the fostering of which would have added so enormously to the vitality, variety, and breadth of a truly *British* tradition. A section has been consistently preferred to and exalted above the whole; stupendous possibilities have been sacrificed to the English public school type; and the extent to which this pig-headed and callous policy has imperilled the economic future and political power of these islands cannot today be exaggerated. Ireland's breakaway—its power to sunder itself in the teeth of the entrenched English power—is one of the happy signs that all may not yet be lost. I welcome like tendencies in India, Egypt, South Africa and elsewhere, and think it is high time Scotland in particular was realizing what it is all about in terms not only of the crucial and immediate problems of our own country but in terms of world politics.

III. A LESSON FROM DOSTOEVSKY

The insistence on freedom has played a special and significant role throughout the whole course of Scottish literature from Barbour's

A! fredome is a noble thing,
Fredome mayss man to haiff liking;
Fredome all solace to man giffis:
He levys at ess that frely levys!
A noble hart may haiff nane ess,
Na ellys nocht that may him pless
Gyff fredome failzhe ... ;

through Burns's *Jolly Beggars* to Lewis Spence's

My heart shall never sleep,
Nor shall my soul be free
Of shadows till our Scotland keep
Her tryst with liberty.*

Literature is, of course, 'the written expression of revolt against accepted things', but the particular meaning of the recent long-overdue developments in Scottish poetry is revolt against a dreary rut of imitative versifying and a new freedom in vocabulary, in subject-matter, in angles of expression, in technical means, in experimentation of all kinds. It has not gone far yet—the shackles have been loosened but not broken away. But as Alexander Webster points out in his *Theology in Scotland*:

Tannahill, Aird, Cunningham, Hogg, Joanna Baillie, Jean Adams, Robert Nicoll, Ballantyne, William Miller, Alexander Smith, David Gray, William and Robert Leighton, Blackie, James Nicolson, Alexander Anderson, James Smith—the hundred and one Scottish lyrists, are all distinctly anti-Calvinistic ... The rising of a distinctly Scottish literature which was destined to be cherished throughout the ages of Scottish life as a source of spiritual refreshment is a remarkable phenomenon. The literature has its source in human nature as reflecting and thrilled by the divine movements in earth, sky, and sea. It consists mainly of expressions of emotion in view of natural things or as touched by social sympathies. It contains an analysis of emotion and direction for it. The source of it is not Biblical; it is not technically pious in its character; it is unconnected with the Kirk. In its spirit it is wholly opposed to sectarianism and stationariness. When we

* 'Claymore.' *Editor.*

compare the influence of the poetic literature of Scotland, which reached its highest watermark in Burns, with that of the literature produced in the sphere of orthodoxy, we see a power and permanency in the former far exceeding that in the latter. Experience has shown which of the two classes of literature — the Calvinian or the anti-Calvinian — is the more congenial to the Scottish soul ... If we take the period of dogmatic dominance from 1649 till 1843, we find the manifestation of the native mind in Hume, Burns, and Carlyle, rather than in any of the leaders in the orthodox field. The deeper sincerity and more vital thought came out in expressions which were treated as heretical. We trace the line of spontaneity and verity from one reprobated man to another — the daring thinkers and sayers who stood forth against dogmatic dictation and the shams of conformity.

Mr Webster did not follow his own principles far enough. The literature he thinks destined for the ages is already obsolescent or properly very poorly regarded. We are less conscious today of Burns's freedom that of his eighteenth-century conventionalism, his spoiling by bowdlerization of fine old bawdy models, his crass Hildebrandism, his anti-intellectualism, his narrow range, the poverty of his aesthetic sensibilities. But substantially Mr Webster is right, and the process to which he refers is being stupidly betrayed instead of furthered by those 'religious leaders' amongst us in Scotland today who are trying to repopularize their churches with a little silly hypnotism derived from a scrappy acquaintance with Otto and Barth, just as (tardily forced to admit the desperate plight of Scottish trade and industry) most of those associated with the Scottish Trade Development Council, in their panic-stricken desire to avoid the painful process of thinking (for which, admittedly, they are wretchedly, if at all, equipped) profess to hope to reconstruct our collapsed economy with a little American Couéism, while others in lieu of attempting any genuine economic reconstruction, are advocating the Switzerlandization of Scotland.

To return to literature — which is my main concern here — we should be guided, not by the special pleading of the heretical Mr Webster, right in essence however grotesque in example and lacking in critical faculty he was, but by Allan Cunningham's remark when writing to Sir Walter Scott about his *Songs of Scotland, Ancient and Modern*: 'I have not been very sensitive about our free old songs. I have not excluded all that is overfree and glowing. I wished to preserve an image of the livelier moments of the Lyric Muse when she sang without fear, without scruple, and without sin', or by Joanna Baillie when she wrote to the same correspondent that she wished to include a copy of Howieson's 'Polydore the Robber' in a collection, 'for it is good strong stuff such as School Boys and Country Lairds will like to read as well as fine Ladies, and I must not have my volume too much filled up with what is called *pretty* poetry'.

Them's my sentiments! But on the wider issues of my theme I must commend to my countrymen, not only these robust views, but Goethe's 'Earn it anew, to really possess it' —

> He only earns his freedom and existence
> Who daily conquers them anew,

and his hatred of single-track mentalities; Schiller's declaration to Goethe that 'it is a very important advantage that you consciously advance from the (artistically) pure to the impure, instead of seeking a method of soaring from the impure to the pure, as is the case with the rest of us barbarians'; Leontiev's profound contempt for mere morality, passionate hatred of the democratic herd, violent assertion of the aristocratic ideal, and love of the imperfection of earthly life, with all the variety of forms implied in it; Shestov's accounting the things of this world as an inferior reality, indifferent, *adiaphora*, so that religious standards can in no way be brought down to measure them, and so that, when he has to do with the world of ordinary experiences, with the conduct of men and the facts of history, his religious immoralism and irrationalism become inapplicable and unnecessary and he falls back on the most ordinary (except in Scotland) common sense; and, above all, Dostoevsky. I am not referring only to 'Improvement makes straight roads; but the crooked roads without improvement are roads of genius' (of which, and its opposite, I have suggested that we in Scotland have a higher synthesis in the Gaelic saying: *Is cam's is direach an lagh*; Crooked and straight is the law), or to his extraordinary appreciation of the stratification of the human mind and its power of entertaining all sorts of

5

irreconcilably opposed beliefs at one and the same time—all
of which, like my previous references to other writers, represents
only a carrying further than, owing to our long national misdirection, we in Scotland have carried our essential national
principle of 'antisyzygy'—but to passages such as these:

> Science and reason have, from the beginning of time, played a
> secondary and subordinate part in the life of nations; so it will
> be to the end of time. Nations are built up and moved by
> another force which sways and dominates them, the origin of
> which is unknown and inexplicable; that force is the force of
> an insatiable desire to go on to the end, though at the same
> time it denies that end. It is the force of persistent assertion
> of one's own existence and a denial of death. It's the spirit
> of life, as the Scriptures call it, the river of living water, the
> drying up of which is threatened in the Apocalypse. It is
> the force of persistent assertion of one's own existence, and a
> denial of death. It is the aesthetic principle, as the philosophers
> call it, the ethical principle with which they identify it, 'the
> seeking for God', as I call it more simply. The object of every
> national movement, in every people and at every period of its
> existence, is only the seeking for its God, which must be its
> own God. It has never happened that all, or even many,
> peoples have had one common God, but each has always had
> it's own. It's a sign of the decay of nations when they begin
> to have gods in common. The stronger the people the more
> individual their God. Every nation has its own conception
> of good and evil, and its own good and evil. When the same
> conceptions of good and evil become prevalent in several
> nations, then these nations are dying, and then the very dis-
> tinction between good and evil is beginning to disappear.

And again:

> There is no going against facts. The Jews lived only to await
> the coming of the true God and left the world the true God.
> The Greeks deified nature and bequeathed the world their
> religion, that is, philosophy and art. Rome deified the people
> in the State and bequeathed the idea of the State to the
> nations. France throughout her long history was only the

incarnation and development of the Roman God ... If a great
people does not believe that the truth is only to be found in
itself (in itself alone and in it exclusively), if it does not believe
that it alone is fit and destined to raise up and save all the
rest by its truth, it would at once sink into being ethnographi-
cal material and not a great people. A really great people can
never accept a secondary part in the history of humanity,
nor even one of the first, but will have the first. A nation
which loses this belief ceases to be a nation.

I cite these Russian names and use these Russian quotations
advisedly. We in Scotland are at the opposite side of Europe. The
old balance of Europe—between North and South—has been
disrupted by the emergence of Russia. How is a quadrilateral of
forces to be established? England partakes too much of Teutonic
and Mediterranean influences; it is a composite—not a 'thing-in-
itself'. Only in Gaeldom can there be the necessary counter-idea
to the Russian idea—one that does not run wholly counter to it,
but supplements, corrects, challenges, and qualifies it. Soviet
economics are confronted with the Gaelic system with its repudiation of usury which finds its modern expression in Douglas
economics. The dictatorship of the proletariat is confronted by
the Gaelic commonwealth with its aristocratic culture—the high
place it gave to its poets and scholars. And so on. It does not
matter a rap whether the whole conception of this Gaelic idea is
as far-fetched as Dostoevsky's Russian Idea—in which he pictured
Russia as the sick man possessed of devils but who would yet
'sit at the feet of Jesus'. The point is that Dostoevsky's was a great
creative idea—a dynamic myth—and in no way devalued by the
difference of the actual happenings in Russia from any Dostoevsky dreamed or desired. So we in Scotland (in association with
the other Gaelic elements with whose aid we may reduce England
to a subordinate role in the economy of these islands) need not
care how future events belie our anticipations so long as we polarize
Russia effectively—proclaim that relationship between freedom
and genius, between freedom and thought, which Russia is
denying—help to rebalance Europe in accordance with our
distinctive genius—rediscover and manifest anew our dynamic
spirit as a nation. This Gaelic Idea has nothing in common with

the activities of An Comunn Gaidhealach, no relationship whatever with the Celtic Twilight. It would not matter so far as
positing it is concerned whether there had never been any Gaelic
language or literature, not to mention clans and tartans, at all.
It is an intellectual conception designed to offset the Russian
Idea: and neither it, nor my anti-English spirit, is any new thing
though the call for its apt embodiment in works of genius is today
crucial. It calls us to a redefinition and extension of our national
principle of freedom on the plane of world-affairs, and in an
abandonment alike of our monstrous neglect and ignorance of
Gaelic and of the barren conservatism and loss of the creative
spirit on the part of those professedly Gaelic and concerned with
its maintenance and development.

The essential point is that all fixed opinions—all ideas that are
not entertained just provisionally and experimentally—every
attempt to regard any view as permanent—every identification of
Scottish genius with any particular religion or political doctrine—
every denial of the relativity and transience of all thought, any
failure to 'play with' ideas—and above all the stupid (since self-
stultifying) idea that ideas are not of prime consequence in their
qualitative ratio and that it is possible to be over-intellectual—
are anti-Scottish—opposed to our national genius which is
capable of countless manifestations at absolute variance with
each other, yet confined within the 'limited infinity' of the
adjective 'Scottish'.

But the Saxon folk? I have never wist them
In the ways of chivalrous chance,

Rachel Annand Taylor sang before me; and boasted that

Poverty hath the Gaelic and Greek
In my land,

and praised our country in which

Amber rivers wind
Through magic and strangeness enough to drown
The pitiful madness of London Town.

I have said that, from the point of view of the Gaelic idea, knowledge of, or indeed even the existence of, Gaelic is immaterial. It is not for nothing that Mrs Taylor cries:

It is unfair that I have not the Gaelic although I be a Gael
And to the sweet and intricate inflexions that prevail
In that proud language dances my heart,[5]

and that William Power and others who 'have not the Gaelic', with a few who had it not but have since acquired it, have led the way in insisting upon its major importance to creative Scottish endeavour, while almost all the Gaelic speakers have been hopelessly false or unequal to their trust.

It is along these lines that we must discover this God of our own — that we must, in consonance with our natural genius, meet the Russian Idea at every point. A parliament bringing back Tom Johnston and his like from Westminster to Edinburgh is like Habakkuk 'capable de tout' — et de rien! Cut and dried-schemes — so-called practical proposals — the 'cursed conceit of being right' — we can, if we choose, use to operate behind and through; but they have no real relation to our purpose, and we can only deploy very minor impulses on such planes. Our real task lies on the level I have indicated.

IV. SCHROEDINGER AND HUME

In conclusion here,* however, to illustrate the leeway we have incurred in the promulgation of our essential national spirit in one particular, but vitally important, direction, I may quote the following passages from a recent interview with Professor Schroedinger.

The eighteenth century [he said] introduced doubt as an essential element into the philosophical theories of that period. David Hume, the boldest and most radical among the sceptics of his time, extended his scepticism even to the law of causality—in the estimation of traditional philosophy the root of human cognition—stating that the dogma of the inevitable necessity by which a cause is taught to produce its respective effect, is merely a convenient facility, but that no logic can prove that law to be binding for all times and under all

* This was the conclusion of the first part of this article in *The Modern Scot. Editor.*

circumstances ... David Hume never denied the general order ruling in nature which we, for facility's sake, are wont to reduce to the law causality. He would be astonished to learn that recently scientists who can claim weight as theoretical physicists, go far beyond his scepticism.

So must we.

V. *BLUTSGEFÜHL*

Scottish nationalists—especially in view of the ascendancy in Anglo-Scottish politics of a Labour-cum-socialist electoral majority in Scotland, or, at all events in the more densely populated and commercially and industrially important centres, and the particular hatred which Scottish nationalism inspires in Labour-cum-socialist circles—ought to consider carefully the principle which Hitler and his National Socialists in Germany oppose to Marxism. Hitler's 'Nazis' wear their socialism with precisely the difference which post-socialist Scottish nationalists must adopt. Class-consciousness is anathema to them, and in contradistinction to it they set up the principle of race-consciousness.

Mr Wyndham Lewis in his book on Hitler brings out this essential difference excellently when he writes that the National Socialist 'says that the fact that a man is a sorter at the Post Office, or a metal-worker, is not of such importance as that he is English, German or French—or Chinese. Take a Chinese metal-worker and a German metal-worker, for instance. The fact that both were metal-workers would not be so important as that the essential nature of one came out of all the past of China, and the essential nature of the other out of all the past of the White Northern Races'.

This is the perception and principle which is expressed in *Blutsgefühl*, the keyword of the Hitler movement, and Mr Lewis analyses it into a reiteration of the necessity for men acting on nature's principle that like mates with like, or, as he says: 'It desires a closer and closer drawing together of the people of one race and culture, by means of bodily attraction. It must be a true bodily solidarity. Identical rhythms in the arteries and muscles and in the effective neural instrument—that should provide us with a passionate exclusiveness, with a homogeneous social framework, within the brotherly bounds of which we could live secure from alien interference, and so proceed with our work and with our pleasures, whatever they may be.'

The importance of the fact that we are a Gaelic people, that Scottish anti-Irishness is a profound mistake, that we ought to be anti-English, and that we ought to play our part in a three-to-one policy of Scotland, Ireland, and Wales against England to reduce that 'predominant partner' to its proper subordinate role in our internal and imperial affairs and our international relationships (not to go further for the moment and think of a Gaelic West of Europe as essential to complement the Russian idea which has destroyed the old European balance of north and south and produced a continental disequilibrium which is threatening European civilization, and, behind that, white supremacy) are among the important practical considerations which would follow from the acceptance of *Blutsgefühl* in Scotland.

Those in the Scottish Nationalist Party who are attracted to Douglasism as the only economic policy for the party may also be recommended to peruse with care Mr Lewis's chapters on Hitler's economics which naturally follow from this principle of social solidarity. 'How,' asks another commentator on Lewis's book, dealing with these particular chapters,

can a people be homogeneous when it is divided into debtors and creditors, particularly when the burden of debt is so great that it makes the producers too poor to sell and the consumers too poor to buy? The mechanism of exchange is out of gear; buyers and sellers cannot come into touch with one another; they strive to approach but are held back by their chains and their debts. The root of the trouble, then, is not, as the Marxists falsely pretend, capitalism as such, but only a particular form of it. According to the Hitlerite, productive capital is not merely tolerable but virtuous, whereas loan capital is damnable. We are, in fact, hearing again in the twentieth century the old cry of *novae tabulae*, which we have been taught to think of as having been silenced with the disappearance of the economics of antiquity. It has, however, now become an international cry, for the whole world is clogged and hampered by War debts. There is universal debt; there is consequently universal scarcity. Wipe the whole score off the slate and we shall all be able to prosper again.

That this doctrine of national socialism, which by uniting Moscow and Paris in a common anathema has appealed at once to the quiet, steady man and to the boisterous patriot, should have originated on German soil is not more natural in view of Germany's geographical position and economic circumstances than Scotland's failure to produce a variant of it appealing to the majority of the Scottish population is unnatural in view of the progressive denudation of Scotland, the extent to which even relatively to England it is disproportionately taxed, and has all its interests systematically and ruthlessly sacrificed to English interests, and the falsity of an abject acceptance of such a position.

It is some such variant that is tardily and still very tentatively emerging in certain elements of the Scottish nationalist movement, but, whereas Hitlerism, being German, has developed both a philosophy and an organization, in the Scottish case the latter is still embryonic and immune to anything in the nature of the former.

VI. *SCOTIA IRREDENTA*

Scotia Irredenta is another realization upon which a creative Scottish nationalism must be erected, and by this phrase here I do not mean the reclaiming of that part of northern England which forms a true economic unity with southern Scotland (which, joined together, correspond to the old Brythonic kingdom and are the economic centre of the United Kingdom) — a project which many between the Humber-Mersey line and the Border, who realize the vast cancerous excrescence of London and the extent to which it has distorted our true economy, must favour; nor the effective linking-up of Scottish elements overseas with their mother-country again; nor the revival of our old European connections. By *Scotia Irredenta* here I mean the realization of the extent to which our national accomplishments have been restricted and our potentialities inhibited by the identification of minor and transitory manifestations with the terms 'Scotland' and 'Scottish'

—terms like Protestant, canny, Gaelic, Lowland, and the like. And at the same time I am protesting against the idea that a scheme for developing the poultry industry in Ayrshire or reafforesting part of Sutherlandshire, or re-establishing a parliament in Edinburgh, or, in short, any scheme to do anything at all, political, economic, commercial, or industrial—except to rouse a distinctive and dynamic spirit in Scotland again *and without any cut-and-dried scheme let that spirit find its own forms* no matter how impredictable and how unrelated to anything in our past history may be—has anything whatever to do with Scottish nationalism.

The curse of post-Union Scottish psychology has been its insatiable itch to domesticate every issue with which it has been concerned; and the curse of the National Party today—as of the English-controlled political parties—is its desire to foresee and guide the course of events. Nothing that can be so foreseen and guided is worth a curse; Scotland needs a great upwelling of the incalculable.

'As for living,' said Villiers de L'Isle Adam, 'our servants can do that for us.'

'I shall be told,' wrote A. R. Orage years ago,
that events like the rise of China, the Russian Revolution,
the discovery of the North and South Poles, and the invention
of the aeroplane, not to mention the great social movements
of labour and capital, are as great as any that ever inspired
a dramatist. And I shall reply that there is not a shadow of
hopeful wonder, of awe, of grandeur, of beauty, of mystery,
or even of intelligent human power, in one of them. Go into
the wilds of Africa, and be out of reach of newspapers for a
month or two, and the whole cosmic show fades into trivial
gossip.

And he condemned modern art as in no respect 'more defective than in precisely this and because of precisely this; that its standards and aims have ceased to be impossible.'

Scotland's worst disease is its appalling love for, and dependence on, the calculable, and our movement will only be worth-while in precise proportion as any of its achievements are the by-products of a striving toward what can never be produced—the unattainable, the unrealizable, the impossible. And, in this connection, it is equally true that restoring a Scotland like 'restoring art that has lost its unattainable aim is like attempting by reason to restore the youth of a religion. The source can be affected only by a fresh source, not by any of its own issues.'

VII. CLASSICAL STANDARDS AND THE GAELIC SPIRIT

Where is this fresh source? Let us keep in mind here, amongst other things, *Blutsgefühl* and Henri Massis' *Defence of the West*,[6] and Daniel Corkery's perception[7] that the national art of Greece had, via the Renaissance, whitened the cultures of all other European countries and prevented them doing in turn what Greece did, or, in other words, that we must 'get back behind the Renaissance' and realize that classicism is concerned with Ur-motives and is precisely the opposite of neo-classical formulations.

My friend Orage is useful to us here in one passage, and we must join issue with him in regard to another. Orage pointed out that Clutton-Brock, 'while rejecting the philosophy that accompanied Germany to war, accepted in its entirety the philosophy of Croce who approved of it; that is, he rejected the master but followed the disciple', and insisted that this must be wrong. Let us beware that we are not the disciples of the master-ideas which have brought Scotland to its present plight—we cannot accept the traditions and tendencies responsible for our pass, and effectively deplore that pass.

But Orage is wrong where, speaking of England, France, and Italy—the three great European cultural nations—he says: 'I am hopeful myself of the possibility of a new renaissance, but without a fresh antiquity from which to call up and revivify an old spirit, I see no source of novelty in all or any of the three Western cultures. None has any longer so much to give that a pooling of our resources would amount to more than a new fashion. A renaissance without a spirit to be reborn is impossible.' But he goes on to direct us to India—'if the rediscovery of Greek culture gave us mediaeval and modern Europe, the rediscovery of ancient Indian culture will give us the Europe of tomorrow,' he says. 'Nothing else will!'

What a pity he learned Sanskrit and not Gaelic!

7

CHARLES DOUGHTY AND THE NEED FOR HEROIC POETRY

1936

Only in the U.S.S.R. today is the trend of poetic effort towards epic — in keeping with the great enterprise afoot in that country, and as a natural consequence of the linguistic experimentation in recent Russian literature, the liberation and encouragement of minority languages and literatures, and the de-latinization and de-frenchification of the Russian language. For the condition of any language which has deserted its native basis and over-adulterated its vocabulary, and been devoted to all sorts of tasks save only the expression and elucidation of the Ur-motives of its people, must unfit it for any effort of like magnitude — for, that is to say, in other words, a form equal to the perspectives of modern life and the horizons now opening before us. That was why Charles Doughty — his genius lying in the direction of epic — had to abandon modern English and use a large infusion of Anglo-Saxon words and native syntactical forms. Robert Graves and others went 'back to Skelton' and used the old native rhythms, and Auden and other young poets today [1936] are following that lead, and that accounts for their communist tendency. But the far greater enterprise of Charles Doughty has gone unrecognized or obstinately opposed. It is dismissed (in *The Times Literary Supplement*) as a 'reversal of language' — which is on all fours with the fact that Wagner's *words* are generally dismissed as of no consequence. Yet Wagner was right, not wrong, when he spent years studying word-roots. He knew (as Charles Doughty knew) that we were coming to another of the quantitative — as against accentual — periods in culture. It is that lack of historical knowledge which disables no Marxist that is wrong with our mere impressionist commentators on such a phenomenon. (It is this question of quantity as against accent that distorts to most Scots the nature of our pibrochs of the great period. These knew no 'bar'. They were

75

timeless music—hence their affiliation with plainsong, with the neuma. Barred music—accented music—finds its ultimate form in symphony. Unbarred music—quantity music—expresses itself in pattern-repetition; hence the idea that the Celt has no architectonic power, that his art is confined to niggling involutions and intricacies—yet the ultimate form here is not symphony; it is epic.) It is epic—and no lesser form—that equates with the classless society. Everything else—no matter how expressly it repudiates these in the mere logical meaning of what it *says* as against what it *is*—belongs to the old order of bourgeois 'values', to the nebulous entities described by terms like 'spiritual' and 'soul'; in short, it stands for the old romantic virtues, which is to say, pragmatically, for nothing. Doughty, as against Auden and Day Lewis, say, is the only English poet who belongs to the new order, that is to say, to our own time. His significance today dwarfs all the other English poets since Elizabethan times into utter insignificance, and the failure of contemporary English literati to recognize that is only another confirmation of the communist diagnosis of the present phase of English literature (it is significant that D. S. Mirski had no difficulty in recognizing the overtowering quality of Doughty) as being thoroughly in keeping with the imminent fatal crisis of a degenerate capitalist society. To those of us who are concerned about a Scottish renaissance, Doughty's unique preoccupation with—and marvellous imaginative penetration into— ancient British (Celtic) consciousness* is as convincing a 'pointer' as Wagner's devotion to the study of word-roots. '*The Dawn in Britain*[1] is a great storehouse of the history, fact, legend and romance of the Celtic peoples', truly observed one of its earliest reviewers. That sealed its fate. How the English ascendancy policy treated Irish Gaelic literature, Dr Douglas Hyde shows us. How then could it tolerate Doughty's attack from inside—from within the English language itself? Never!

When two new books on Doughty recently appeared,† all the

---

* A complete account and examination of Doughty's sources is now [1936] under way. Until that is published we will not know in any detail the means whereby Doughty came to this extraordinary understanding of the ancient British element.

† Anne Treneer, *Charles M. Doughty: a study of his prose and verse* (Cape, London, 1935); *Selected Passages from* The Dawn in Britain *of Charles Doughty*. Arranged, with an introduction, by Barker Fairley (Duckworth, London, 1935). Readers should also consult Professor Barker Fairley's *Charles M. Doughty: A Critical Study* (Cape, London, 1927).

host of contemporary little English reviewers hastened to deny that Doughty is a great poet and to dismiss his work as hopelessly archaic, mere obstinate linguistic pedantry and a 'reversal of language'. Despite these, Doughty will yet come to his own:

> For while the tired waves, vainly breaking,
>   Seem here no painful inch to gain,
> Far back, through creeks and inlets making,
>   Comes silent, flooding in, the main.
>
> And not by eastern windows only,
>   When daylight comes, comes in the light.
> In front, the sun climbs slow, how slowly,
>   But westward, look, the land is bright.

It is not through the English that due recognition of Doughty can come. It is significant that the authors of these two new books on Doughty are a Scotsman (a Shetlander) and a Cornishwoman. The trouble with all the little English reviewers is their inability to realize that 'the stone the builders rejected' may well 'become the cornerstone'. The whole development of modern English literature has gone hand in hand with an ascendancy policy that has belittled and discouraged literary effort in its own dialects, done its utmost to stamp out Irish, Scottish and Welsh Gaelic and the Scots Vernacular, thinks (with Sir John Squire) that 'it would have been much better if Burns had written in English'. As I pointed out in *At the Sign of the Thistle*,[2] 'it must be remembered that it was only with the utmost difficulty—and against precisely the same sort of opposition and arguments as we are now contending—that Elizabeth Elstob succeeded in preventing England treating its own Anglo-Saxon background (and where would English studies be without that now?) in precisely the same way as it has treated the other minority elements in our midst.' Doughty was a great English national poet in the same sense as Björnson was a Norwegian one—'to name the name of Björnson is like hoisting the Norwegian flag'. As Björnson put it:

> A poet's is the prophets' call:
> In times of need and travail-throe
> His faith the gleam they seek can show

To those who strive, and striving fall.
Now ringed by champions from of old,
Now marshalling the new-enrolled,
Mid whispering hopes, he hears the cry,
He sees the dreams, of prophecy.
In song the spring-sap of his nation
Breaks forth, and is its inspiration.

As a writer on Björnson has said:

> In the lines in which he pictures himself appealing alternately
> to the heroes of old and the contemporary generation, as well
> as in the metaphor, to which he was so fond of recurring, of
> the spring renewal of life, he discloses one of the key-points
> in his philosophy—his ever-present sense of the continuity
> of national existence, which viewed future and past with a
> correlated faith and pride, and looked upon the great figures
> of Norwegian history as collaborators in his task no less than
> his contemporaries ... It was with a just appreciation that
> Ibsen saw in his rival the model for King Haakon in his
> *Pretenders*, the character in whom this ideal of union is so
> central.

What English poet but Doughty could be cast for any similar role
in a drama of English history? And assuredly it is of prime importance at this great crisis, this watershed, in English history that
we should have Doughty sending Brennus and young Sigamer
and Caradoc and all the rest of his great characters out into our
streaming streets today instead of letting English poetry leave it
to Blake to send Albion's Angel, driven howling from Westminster
by the fires of Red Orc, to go

> Grovelling down Great George Street, and
> thro' the Park Gate.

It must be realized that one cause for his countrymen's repudiation of England's most comprehensive understander—the
only English poet of whom, in Matthew Arnold's famous
phrase (criticizing Byron as 'so empty of matter, Shelley so incoherent, Wordsworth even, profound as he is, yet so wanting in

completeness and variety') it cannot be said that 'he did not know enough' — is the fact that Doughty was not 'a prophet of easy things', but came with what their misguided spirits regard as bad news. English literati are still babbling about English as a 'world language', and following the 'pure English' lead of the B.B.C. Doughty alone foresaw and understood it all thoroughly and realized that the English ascendancy policy must go — that England must relapse on its native basis and let its dialect and minority language elements at long last resume their proper function after the tremendous misdirection of a policy by which England had gained the whole world and lost its own head. Great Britain, or better still, England might inspire an epic, but not the British Empire. And so, just as, during the war years, it was government policy to represent Ramsay MacDonald (destined for the highest political honours) as a dangerous man in order to hide the fact that John Maclean was really the dangerous man, we have today all sorts of little rhymsters hailed as revolutionary poets (as if real revolution would not involve far greater technical changes than any they affect) and Doughty, the real revolutionary, ignored. Doughty and Wagner; real revolutionaries — Wagner with the *Nibelungenlied*, Doughty concerned to give the ancient British (Celtic) the due they are denied in the official story and in the consciousness of the vast majority of Britons today. Wagner 'wasting his time' among word-roots, and Doughty emphasizing aspects of English history generally and best treated as non-existent and dragging out hosts of obsolete words too — sad spectacles both for contemporary 'common sense'! The sinister opportunism which prevails amongst us is in significant contrast to the spirit of Lenin's admonition: 'We do not know and we cannot know which spark — out of the innumerable sparks that are scattering around in all countries as a result of the political and economic world crises — will kindle the conflagration, and therefore the most seemingly hopeless, musty and unfrequented directions are not to be taken for granted and overlooked but diligently explored.'

The general rejection of Doughty by these English reviewers is only a ridiculous belated insistence on a poetic diction — on the employment of a certain English and not any other. It is the same 'quaint survival' of an idea that dismisses my 'synthetic English' experiments in *Stony Limits*[3] as 'unfortunate,' that denies, not only the urgent and unescapable necessity of the poetic use of the full range of modern scientific terminology, but the experiments in linguistics of James Joyce, and Ezra Pound's use *as a language* of multifarious references to all periods of history and all phases of human activity. This is the great stumbling-block which compels every modern creative writer in English to use lots of unfamiliar and often technical words—and compels each of them (Meredith, Hardy, Patmore) to use different ones. It is this stumbling-block, too, which is responsible for the failure to incorporate in the canon of our speech the ubiquitous out-of-the-way words constantly being used, not by such creative writers, but in the ordinary course of contemporary English journalism and conversation (e.g. from one recent newspaper, snickersnee, finnimbruns, and ipsissimosity). Yet Edward Garnett, in the *Sunday Times*, had to take severely to task for his egregious utterances Mr Basil de Selincourt, the *Observer* reviewer of the recent books on Doughty. This provided the only refeshing feature of a dreadful exhibition of ineptitude, prejudice, and the complacency of reviewers so immersed in the cataract of current tittle-tattle and coterie disputes that they are completely incapable of any objective view. Forgive them; they do not know what they are talking about. As a friend of mine writes: 'In this hopelessly introverted world you can't expect any response from the gang-leaders to a great *out-going* spirit. They blink like owls in the strong sunlight.' And the most owlish blinking of all was not even de Selincourt's but Geoffrey Grigson's—and that is the right measure of *New Verse* and its young hopefuls. Montagu Slater, in *The Left Review*, clearly understands the 'back to Skelton' movement and the partial return to a native basis in rhythms and words of Graves and Auden and others, but I have not yet been able to study the effect of Doughty's 'strong sunlight' on any communist critic; I eagerly—and confidently—await the spectacle. My friend writes to me: 'How little sense there is anywhere of his (Doughty's) being in any way a new vision, a radical genius, something to approach from the inside, not the outside ... What needs rubbing in strongly now is the importance of this heroic poetry for the new ideal in Europe. England, being the least progressive country at present, has the sort of poetry that goes with it: Eliot, Auden, etc., all ironists, using the old forms and calling themselves revolutionaries. But there has been no revolution yet. A real revolution would affect technique more.'

I ought to make it clear that in referring especially to Doughty's significance for communists I do not mean that he belonged to the Communist Party. I remember the following passage from the obituary notice in the *Cambridge Review* by his friend G. G. Coulton: 'Once or twice Alfred Ollivant, the novelist, made a third with us; but his rather extreme socialism met Doughty's extreme conservatism without the least friction. Doughty with his characteristic slight turn of the head, but far more definite sidelong turn of the eyes towards the man he was talking with, would blast Socialism and all kinds of Liberalism in a single Elizabethan phrase, but with such impersonal detachment, or even personal cordiality, that Ollivant would appreciate the utterance almost as much as I did.' And I think of how Professor B. Ifor Evans says that Bridges, in his poem 'To a Socialist in London', expounds 'a sort of spiritual *laissez-faire*, which is not unsavoured with self-complacency', and how Mr R. L. Megroz says: 'Only a long succession of academic praises of Bridges by people suffering from very similar mental restrictions derived from the old-fashioned English class educational system could have culminated in the extraordinary chorus of excited eulogy which greeted this scholarly minor poet's verbose *Testament of Beauty*. What was said about this prosaic and rhetorical but skilful metric exercise in unoriginal uplifting thought in the English Press, if exhibited in a collection, would supply a most damning illustration of the meaning of "middle-class culture".' The people who hailed Bridges in this egregious way are the same people who are now denouncing or rejecting Doughty at the same time as they are belatedly revelling in the slight achievement disfigured by exaggerated Marianism and other unpleasant and singularly untimely and undesirable traits of Gerard Manley Hopkins (whose technical achievements are all to be found equalled and excelled in Doughty, as Professor Fairley pointed out in an admirable article in the *London Mercury*, June 1935). They are the same people, too, as those who are now reviewing Thomas Lovell Beddoes favourably and at great length apropos the three new books which have just appeared about him and his

6

work. Hopkins and Beddoes accepted; Doughty rejected. 'It's a mad world, my masters.' *And they chose Barabbas.*

I feel sure that it will be a long time before any of these little writers — even those of them plying most assiduously such catch-words as 'a sense of one's own time' and 'economic awareness' — achieve or find any better passage to their professed purpose than this of Doughty's:

> I saw the travail-stained hammer-men stand;
> Sons of the daily labours of their hands:
> Idle, at corners now of shot-crazed streets:
> Toilers, for whom, those daylong murky hours,
> The vital air was a pernicious breath;
> An headstrong, handstrong, hungered, impotent
> Pale multitude, with thick curses on their lips.
> Cumbered dejected wretches the town paths.
> Some were, that only shades of manhood seemed.
> (Those startle, at the coming of a Stranger!)
> Their joyless mills, and chimneyed factories,
> Blackened by fire; be broken down and waste.
> Shut were the iron gates, behind their backs!
> Drudges of steel! that giant, ere few days were,
> Reciprocating stride of wheeling engines;
> Which wrought, with panting breaths, for human livelihood
> Hath ceased!

As Miss Treneer says: 'I can think of no modern picture of a machine which surpasses this of the giant drudge. A line like 'Reciprocating stride of wheeling engines' makes a reader wish that Doughty had more often tried to write in this condensed and pregnant way. Metaphor is exciting. The leap of our imagination gives something of the same satisfaction to the mind, as speed to the body; it is exhilarating, and daring and dangerous. Simile is more sedate.' And this, in this particular connection alone out of the immense range he establishes (one of the greatest of English poets alike in range and mass, in concentration and variety, in historical imagination and proleptic power) is the poet they are dismissing as a dull pedantic archaicizer!

There are precedents in literary history for the precise position in which Doughty has been placed — and precedents of special interest to us Scots at that.* But let me quote Miss Treneer's admirable passage on this archaic business:

> Recently we have been able to hear the voice of Gerard Manley Hopkins, who did not live to see Doughty's verse, and probably tasted the prose only in extracts, raised emphatically against the principle of archaism. While admitting that Victorian English is a bad business, he 'cannot away with any form of archaism' or any diction 'sicklied o'er' with Elizabethan English. 'But come now,' he writes to Bridges who had recommended *Arabia Deserta*, 'is it not affectation to write obsolete English? You know it is.' What Hopkins could not realize was that Doughty was engaged on a process for which the word 'archaism' as applied, say, to the poetry of William Morris, is unsuitable ... Of the diction of Doughty's poetry it is hard to say a final word. For myself the words rejoice me, and I do not think this is merely because I am, to use a phrase of Hopkins, weathered to the style. Doughty's language accords with what he says in his *Notes* language should be; 'wine of a good vintage', 'words of a good stock', of 'honest ancestry', 'hale'. 'It is rich of a golden simplicity, antique, of singular efficacy, distinct'. I have examined numbers of his words in relation to the sources from which he drew them, and have lingered to admire the rightness of his usage of forgotten words, and, even more, his skill to re-brighten known words by calling to the surface their overlaid tones. The work he did for words often corresponds to what a new owner will do for an old room; he will strip off layers of shoddy paper or plaster to show the genuine panelling beneath. In addition Doughty was able to make his words carry the force of his conviction in a way which annuls Hopkins's objection to the use of obsolete words as tending to 'destroy earnest'. Earnest is only destroyed if a writer is concerned preciously with words instead of with what he has to say. Doughty was not thus concerned; though he sometimes uses his old words

---

* See 'Sixteenth-Century Humanism as illustrated by the life and work of George Buchanan', *George Buchanan: Glasgow Quatercentenary Studies* (MacLehose, Glasgow, 1907), where the same charge of 'archaicism', on similar entirely superficial grounds, against this great Scottish revolutionary are brilliantly repelled in terms that almost without alteration would equally stand for Doughty's case.

merely for colour as in the Saxon episode in *Mansoul*, or for glee as in the faerie poems, or for rusticity as in the pastoral scene in *The Titans*, or for pageantry as in some parts of *The Dawn*. To criticize his diction as though it were everywhere alike and always 'quaint' is like applying a common measure of criticism to Spencer's *Hymnes*, to his *Shepherd's Calendar*, and to *The Faerie Queen*. Thenot may ask Hobbinol what 'garres him greete,' with perfect fittingness, but this 'rustical rudeness' would not be fitting to *The Four Hymnes*. So in Doughty, Goodfellow Pipit may 'play pluck-buffet in the hazel scrogs,' but the diction is very different in the loftier parts of *Mansoul* or of *The Dawn*. The 'eclectic' used by Doughty in these parts is merely an extension of common practice, not what he called 'a whisteling, windy singularity.' All speech is an eclectic; Doughty merely extended the bounds of choice, while at the same time making the conditions of choice more rigorous.

We Scots ought to remember with pride how Doughty was influenced by a Scottish book— *The Effect of the Mis-use of Familiar Words on the Character of Men and the Fate of Nations* (1856), by David Urquhart. Like David Urquhart, says Miss Treneer, Doughty

held that the English of his day and the mode of thinking which the preponderant use of abstract terms implied was thoroughly bad. Urquhart, who had been much in the East, praised the concrete qualities of Turkish, and contrasted with it unfavourably the generalities too current in English ... Doughty studied words no less as a moralist than as a poet, believing that the right use of vital language was essential to the health of individuals and nations. 'Words are almost the elements of human thoughts,' he wrote in his *Notes*; and on another page he jotted, 'The old manly English, full of pith and stomach.' One of the duties of a poet was to preserve the elements from decay, and keep the notation clear, warring against loose use of words as a thing perilous to thought and feeling, and as an insidious means to undermine the integrity of individual persons and finally of whole peoples.

Charles Doughty was advanced, generally, far ahead of his times. Professor Fairley is right in claiming that in inner chronology Doughty is later than T. S. Eliot. As the following note appended to *The Dawn in Britain* puts it: ' ... it is the prerogative of every lover of his country to use the instrument of his thought, which is the Mother-tongue, with propriety and distinction; to keep that reverently clean and bright, which lies at the root of his mental life, and so, by extension, of the life of the Community: putting away all impotent and disloyal vility of speech, which is no uncertain token of a people's decadence.'

Doughty's idea was to make a fresh channel for English direct from the upper reaches, from the vernacular as it was before the Renaissance, and so freshen and purify the corrupt main flood ... Not that the revival of obsolete words is of main importance in Doughty's experiment. Much more important is his scrutiny of known words, and his close fitting of word to sense. He did not fall into what Bacon calls the first disease of learning, that men hunt words rather than matter; but neither did he neglect the warning of his favourite Ascham, 'Ye know not what hurt ye do to learning, that care not for words but for matter, and so make a divorce betwixt the tongue and the heart.'

I have only space left in which to say that Professor Fairley's book is a model of selection and arrangement—an invaluable introduction for 'weaker brethren'—and that Miss Treneer's study is beyond praise in its tact and thoroughness. They should be carefully read by all who are concerned with the problems of the Scottish renaissance, as showing in detail how all the difficulties involved in the reintegration and full modern use of Scots were solved to great poetic purpose in a kindred medium; and bearing no less effectively on the issues involved in the future use and development of Scots Gaelic as a literary medium.

8

JOHN SINGER

1942

> ... the tangible working,
> of which need is *ourselves burning*.

But for the unfortunate associations of the word 'God', perhaps no better motto could have been placed on the fly-leaf of this first selection of Mr John Singer's poems[1] than that sentence which Aristotle wrote in the *Metaphysics*, which has been translated: 'The occupation of God is intelligence.' 'Intelligence', like 'God', alas, is a very questionable word. As that wise writer 'M. B. Oxon' says in his *Cosmic Anatomy and the Structure of the Ego*:[2]

> Probably the translation which has hidden the meaning of Plato and all Greek philosophy more than any other is that of 'Intellectual,' or 'Intelligible' world for νοητος τοποδ, for with our present use of the word, it would be more rightly translated the 'Unintelligible World.' It might be called the 'World of Intelligence' (not intellect). It is the reason that governs all things, ἐν πολλα. The only *comprehension* of it is by γνωσιδ, and it is related to knowledge, noumena and essence, just as hypostasis, the brilliant Sun and Intellect, is to sight, phenomena and existence.

Mr Singer, in other words, is a poet of 'mental fight', in William Blake's sense of the phrase; a communist of that only authentic kind (Lenin himself insisted that all the others who fall short of this are not really communists at all but 'mere bluffers') of whom it has been rightly said that it would be better to call them 'mentalists' instead of 'materialists'. He is a champion of the acid that will eat through all falsity. His purpose is that what can be shaken shall be shaken, till only the unshakeable remains.

'M. B. Oxon' also says:

It appears that the true function of psycho-analysis is to produce the fusion of *Kritam* and *Kratu* on the upward road, or to
change faith to understanding through the medium of analysis,
whereby we reach knowledge. But it is more than questionable whether this is what many psycho-analysts are doing.
For there is the other road, very similar in appearance, by
which the fusion of faith and belief results in intellect, and
where the birth is into the lower instead of the higher world.

Just as, during the last war [1914–18], the authorities represented Mr Ramsay MacDonald (destined for the highest political
honours) as a dangerous man in order to divert attention from
the fact that Mr John Maclean was really the dangerous man
(since he alone was not of the type denounced so forcibly by
Macbeth 'that palter with us in a double sense; that keep the
word of promise to our ear, and break it in the hope'), so in
recent developments of British poetry there has been a great deal
of fuss about the leftward tendency of many writers, and the near
communism of Auden and others, and the alleged intellectualism
and 'difficulty' of many of the younger poets associated with these
developments. Mr Singer, for me, is rather more truly 'apocalyp-
tic' than many of the younger (and some not so young) practi-
tioners of the art of literary prospecting. And the 'new frontiers'
he outlines have a much more satisfying smack about them than
those fog-enshrouded horizons which merely hide ramshackle
reconstructions of the 'ivory tower'.

The pseudo-progressive movements of the past two decades,
surrealist and other psychologizing developments, undoubtedly
represent a 'birth into the lower world'. When my friend, Mr W.
B. Yeats, died, *The Times Literary Supplement* denounced his
intellectualism as something rather apart from the tradition of
English poetry. All the reactionaries everywhere are on the qui
vive against developments along that line (wrongly, of course,
attributed to Yeats). Poetry, they hold, must remain bogged in
infantilism; must keep to the 'other road'. Hence the alacrity
with which the exciting character of the 'communist' trend of
poets like Auden, Day Lewis, Spender, MacNeice and others has
been trumpeted despite the appreciation in many quarters of the
inability of these poets to remain at the height of consciousness

for more than a couple of words at a time, and their consequent
continual relapses into 'boy-scout communism', philistine 'hearti-
ness', and emotional obscurity, together with their recourse to
'private jokes', their parade of personal neuroses, the obvious
shallowness and superficiality of their learning, the orderless
heterogeneity of the influences obvious in their work and the
claims made for it. And hence, too, the reason why a poet like
Mr Singer, who really does what these others are falsely supposed
to have been attempting to do, is still little known and sparsely
published; despite a volume of work of which the contents of this
volume are but a small first selection. While the group I mention,
falsely (but conveniently) represented as 'truly significant', as the
literary radicals and creative 'mentors!' of the 'thirties and 'forties,
have had a world vogue, and have been the subject of detailed
and solemn discussion in books like Professor J. G. Southworth's
Sowing the Spring,[3] Mr John Lehmann's *New Writing in Europe,*[4]
and Mr Francis Scarfe's *Auden and After.*[5] The parallel here is
close between Mr Singer and these over-publicized and finally
insignificant adolescents on the one hand, and Mr Ramsay
MacDonald, premier, and Mr John Maclean, prisoner in Bar-
linnie Jail, on the other; those two about whom Lenin himself
discriminated so sharply! Mr Singer is the poet who above all
others in this country really presents those revolutionary developments (dynamic integrity) which have for reactionary reasons
been falsely attributed to Auden and his associates, and the
younger poets, now at their creative last gasp before they had
really begun! Mr Scarfe, indeed, gives the game away when
again and again in his studies of these younger poets, he is compelled to complain and show their incapacity for sustained
thought, their inability to work out any idea fully in their poetry,
instead of just raising it and passing on to raise another and
another in the same merely nominal and impenetrative way, until
their work resembles an idealogical rag-bag rather than any
constructive (let alone creative) utilization of the materials in
question. All of which is, of course, dismally illustrative of a
further degenerative trend, even from a traditionally literary
apart from logical aspect; so that to find the occasionally valuable
creativity in their outpourings of mental and emotional onanism
becomes increasingly hopeless.

Much of this was realized by Matthew Arnold, who, in another age, wrote:

It has long seemed to me that the burst of creative activity in our literature, through the first quarter of the century, had about it in fact, something premature; and that from this cause its productions are doomed, most of them, to prove hardly more lasting than the productions of far less splendid epochs, and this prematureness comes from its having proceeded without having its proper data, without sufficient material to work with. In other words, the English poetry of the first quarter of this century, with plenty of energy, plenty of creative force, did not know enough. This makes Byron so empty of matter, Shelley so incoherent, Wordsworth even, profound as he is, yet so wanting in completeness and variety.

The English poets of the last twenty years have known a great deal less. John Singer's poetry has no such inadequacy, indeed there is much evidence in it of a power of perception and a philosophic range, which, if disciplined and shaped, may achieve permanent distinction. Nor has his poetry to struggle as with fly-paper with those clinging attributes of the poetry of the past from which most of his contemporaries even yet can only free one of their legs now and again, for a short period of frantic wriggling, before they have to let it fall and be trammelled again. In his splendid straightforward work, immediately comprehensible to every reader, and not merely to a specialized public exclusive of the working class, Mr Singer has won completely free of all that, and addresses himself to his proper tasks with no diversion of his energies to other purposes, however time-honoured.

In one of his letters to Clough, Arnold went further and predicted that the poetry of the future, the poetry which would really prove capable of discharging the great tasks looming up in the modern world, would be bare, spare, devoid of ornamentation and all unnecessary verbalism, direct, stripped for battle, sinewy and strenuous. In a word, that *the poetry would be in the dialectic*, that it would stand and fall by the intellectual level taken by the poet, and the power shown by him in conceiving and working out his 'plots' or 'arguments'. This prediction of Arnold's may be related to the welcome Yeats extended in his *Oxford Book*

of Modern Verse, 1936, to the 'naked' poetry of some of our younger
writers (without endorsing Yeats's choice of the latter!)

In my opinion this dialectical poetry has nowhere yet in any
European literature (least of all in recent Soviet literature itself,
perhaps), or in American poetry, or in the work of any of our
own leftist poets in England, Scotland, Ireland or Wales, manifested itself with the clarity, the adequacy, existential 'doubling'
(to use Kierkegaard's term), the capacity for sustained development, the absence of immaturities and such sniggering schoolboy
defects as have disfigured the work of the Auden-Spender school,
as in these poems of Mr Singer's, with their great scope and yet
perfect consistency, their intellectualism that nowhere abates
their impassioned quality, and above all that they are in keeping
with Mr Singer's objective affiliations. Not only in that Mr Singer
has squared his precept and his practice in never being far away
from, and usually in the thick of the workers' *permanent battle*, and
the complete absence in his case of those suspect influences such
as a large private income and a reactionary public school–varsity
education, but that his communism is thought out, fought out,
and lived out in personal life.

The leftist poets of the comfortable classes have, with a few
inspiring exceptions such as John Cornford and Christopher
Caudwell, been 'debunked' since Spain, and especially in the
present war, in a manner which can only call for criticism and
satire—anything but faith! 'Debunked' intrinsically by the utterly
irrelevant semi-mystic and hotch-potch labyrinths of their
thought and work, and more obviously in the growing gap between the coteries and 'new schools' they are feebly fermenting,
and the implacable unity and identity of interest that the peoples
today need more than at any period in history.

Events can lead to no similar exposé of lurking weaknesses in
Mr Singer's work. Its integrity is complete. Here, indeed, is a
'man speaking', a whole man, and the level he takes is everywhere
worthy of the great tasks with which human consciousness is
charged at this greatest turning-point in human history. I have
not, in this brief preface, condescended on particular poems, but
there can be no gainsaying the quality of poems like 'Love is the
Flower of our Wandering', 'Some on the Battlefront', 'To be
Alive', 'French Soldier, 1940', 'The Poets' (a magnificently and

burningly clear statement of the poet's own position in relation
to his art and society), and those extracts from 'Journey to
Triumph', which must surely whet the appetite of every reader
for the publication of the whole of that great and most timely
poem. It is in keeping with the spearhead role Scotland has
played in the development of socialism in Great Britain that these
poems of Mr Singer's should have been, many of them, written,
and now published in Glasgow, where he is working. They
represent the reality for which so much inferior stuff has already
been hailed under the cry of a leftward tendency in British literature—and they are blessedly free of left infantilism or any of
those handrails which would be welcome to poetry readers who
would fain appear 'progressive' and yet dare not for various
unworthy reasons (from various unworthy *causes*, rather), accept
the position (intolerable to all mere demagogues) established so
unchallengingly in Count Alfred Korzybski's *Science and Sanity*,[6]
or Professor James Harvey Robinson's *Mind in the Making*.[7]

Mr Singer's work, however, can take all that in its stride, just
as an incoming tide takes up rock-pools along the shore, and
floods on irresistably 'without variableness or shadow of turning',
and above all with that simplicity and directness which calls for
no exaggerated 'expressiveness' and little or no ornamenting, no
poetic diction of manner or matter, but achieves its effect at the
conversational level, one man speaking to his fellow, but speaking
with natural unforced eloquence of the things that matter, and
matter above all; 'not snared by words, but urged by love of life.'

9

WILLIAM SOUTAR

1944 (published 1948)

The time has not yet come, although I write this introductory essay to his *Collected Poems*[1] nearly eight months after his death (which took place on October 15th, 1943), for a definitive biographical and critical study of the personality and poetry of the late William Soutar, for the simple reason that he left a great body of as-yet-unpublished poems, and, in prose, a long sequence of diaries, and of journals kept concurrently with the diaries and in which he was wont to expand the more important ideas he hit upon in the course of his daily diary-entries. Extracts from these extremely detailed and voluminous diaries and journals (written up with unfailing regularity for over twenty years) are now being prepared for publication, and I am indebted to the Reverend David Stevens of Auchterarder,* who is handling this matter, for my own knowledge of the extent and tenor of these writings, which in many ways invite comparison with Amiel's *Journal*[2] even more than with 'W. P. Barbellion's' *Journal of a Disappointed Man*.[3] His literary remains also include a collection of aphoristic writings and a unique series of notebooks which, in contradistinction to his diaries, may perhaps be called his noctuaries, in which, over all the years of his bedfast state, he kept a record of his night-thoughts and his dreams which will undoubtedly be of singular psychological value. Despite the fact that he was bedfast for so many years, his demeanour generally evoked tributes to his amazing serenity of spirit, the fineness of his character, and his freedom from the slightest trace of rancour or repining. That was undoubtedly the impression of himself he disengaged continuously; but the truth of the matter is now known to be far from so simple. The serene acceptance was only the polish on the surface of the steel. Under

* Now of Kirtlebridge. [A selection from Soutar's diaries was issued as *Diaries of a Dying Man*, ed. Alexander Scott (Chambers, Edinburgh, 1954); see also Scott's biography of Soutar, *Still Life* (Chambers, Edinburgh, 1958). *Editor.*]

the bland appearance he always maintained, there was a very
tough and very tortured character indeed. An excruciating fact
which I have nowhere seen mentioned by writers about him is
that the illness which struck him down in early manhood, and
kept him bedfast for the remainder of his life, would almost
certainly have been cured—or its consequences made much less
serious—if recourse had been had to a competent specialist a little
sooner than was the case. When Soutar first saw Sir John Fraser
(not then knighted) about it, it was already too late. Food poisoning contracted on war service aboard ship was the cause, but the
germ had penetrated the spine before Dr Fraser was called in,
and nothing could be done. Soutar made the best of a desperately
bad job. The general demeanour and appearance of patient and
even contented acceptance he always maintained were genuine
enough. That is to say, they were a genuine product of two factors
—his own high courage, determination and devotion to, and deep
satisfaction in, the practice of poetry, and gratitude to his parents
and his adopted sister and other friends for all they did to make
the bedroom, to which the whole world had suddenly contracted
for him, as attractive and convenient to the helpless man as they
possibly could, and for all they did for his happiness, and the
promotion of his literary work, all these years. It was not in his
nature to inflict any pain he could possibly avoid on those who so
helped him, even if only by the expression of ideas which might
be painful to them. But the doubts and fears and certain under-
standable bitternesses and frank statements regarding the difficulties, intellectual and psychophysical, which inevitably beset
him from time to time were all written out and discussed in his
diaries and journals, and it is only when these are available that
it will be possible to make a final estimate of his character, life,
and work which is not at variance with the complex and in many
ways cruel facts of which some of us are already partly aware.
Apart from this tragic element, the diaries and journals for the
most part only confirm, and greatly amplify and enrich, the
evidence as to the main elements in his personality conveyed
by his poems—his rich humour, his wide interests and ever-
developing thought, his amazing memory, the exactness of his
powers of observation even of the most minute things which came
under his notice (and lying in bed all he could see, apart from the

contents of his room, were a little flower-garden and, beyond it,
the summit of a hill—but not a leaf stirred, no bird or insect
moved, no colour of sky or flower changed hue or tone without
his noticing it and describing it in his diary. His friend Severn is
reported as saying of Keats—and the same can certainly be said
of William Soutar—that 'nothing seemed to escape him, the song
of a bird and the undernote of response from covert or hedge, the
rustle of some animal, the changing of the green and brown lights
and furtive shadows ... '). He permitted nothing personal to enter
his poetry, but kept it always impersonal, objective, classical. It
is all to the good then that he should have revealed himself so
completely, in such well-nigh incredible detail, in his diaries and
journals, and certainly if the false impression so generally entertained of his resignation and serenity cannot stand against the
painful revelations of these extremely intimate writings, the gain
of exchanging for that false conception a fully human personality
is one by which his reputation will not suffer but he greatly
increased. The publication even of a selection from these diaries
and journals, which may be all that is possible in the lifetime of
any who knew their author in the flesh, will be a great event for
Scottish literature. Another fact that emerges most powerfully
from these writings is his devotion to his work, his unremitting
productivity, the remorseless system upon which he organized all
his writing and reading activities, and, towards the end, his
anxiety to complete and see through the press himself the works
that he had by him nearing publishable condition. (His attitude to
his own work, and his shrewd clear sense of the problems of
literature, and especially of Scottish literature today, emerge
plainly enough from such passages in his diaries as these:

> It gave one rather a startled feeling when the other day,
> having noted down the hope that I might be remembered as a
> poet, Jim Finlayson produced a short notice of *But the Earth
> Abideth* in which I am referred to as 'probably the greatest
> living Scottish poet': nonsense, of course, so long as Mac-
> Diarmid breathes. If it were true—what a queer position for
> a leading poet—to have been sending out poetry for twenty
> years, and still compelled to issue it in book form at his own
> expense! And as regards his verse in English—to remain after

twenty years almost wholly unknown, so that, apart from exceptions, he has appeared in none of the anthologies published during that lengthy period! We had better gang cannily.

That was written on September 28th, 1943. He returns to the matter over and over again. Here is a typical example, dated September 8th, 1943:

... Proofs of *Seeds in the Wind* will be ready at the end of the week: how much fun, one sometimes feels, might have been given to Scottish children by these rhymes if our language had been wholly active and alive. I cannot keep down the presumptuous thought that I am a better writer of verse for bairns than Stevenson, and even De la Mare—but there are so few to listen ...

On August 18th, 1943 he wrote:

The various tasks were in the main completed: a sufficiency of bairn-rhymes, a sufficiency of riddles, lyrics sufficient for an ample collection, enough whigmaleeries for a fair-sized book, *Theme and Variation* already in MS., *Local Habitation* and *Yon Toun* all but completed, and, in English, all my best lyrics gathered together in *The Expectant Silence*.[4]

And on September 13th, 1943 he wrote:

To be beyond all effort in, say, six months would mean the difference between a modified fulfilment and a collection of oddments without co-ordination. I should like, if possible, to see my final collection of lyrics in English, the jottings *from a Notebook* and a large selection of Scots lyrics in print, or at least, assured of appearing in print—but many things must remain unattempted.

Finally, a passage in his diary for September 26th, 1943 reads:

... I hope I shall be remembered as a poet, if for no other reason than that my folks may not be forgotten, nor the fact that they had done so much for me, and had received so little in return ...

He was, indeed, all along bitterly conscious of neglect and of the difficulties of literature at the present stage of capitalist society, and typical of frequent entries in his diaries on such matters is the following poignant passage dated December 11th, 1941:

A further communication from X—— and Y—— today, in which they propose to issue *The Signature of Silence* in brochure form if 300 sales can be assured. Again we meet the conflicting values—the gesture of faith and the economic limitations; the impasse between quality and quantity which is the doom of our age. Here is a MS., according to their reader's report, in which there are poems better than the best of Housman, poems that transform the war-revulsion of Sassoon into revelation, poems of Blakean vision, etc. etc.—in short, a book most needful to our time of conflict. And here are the monetary qualifications—curtailing expenditure to £27 plus a guarantee; for after all, there is no certainty that a most needful thing will be recognized by the needy. We have knocked at publishers' houses for nearly twenty years and still await more than the half-open doors; we'll continue to knock ...

In particular he was anxious to put together and edit his collected poems himself. Indeed he worked steadily to the very end. He knew his death was imminent and this compelled him to do his utmost to complete certain things. He was so intent upon this, so anxious to put 'his house in order' before the end, and so diligent, methodical, and meticulously careful in all his work, that the present writer feels all the more keenly his great responsibility in taking over and carrying through the task Soutar himself was not given time to discharge, as he intended, himself ... *

Soutar's life was his work, and the dates of appearance of his various volumes are the stage-marks of his biography. Apart from these, and visits from, or correspondence with, friends his life was singularly devoid of 'events' other than those which took place in his own mind and spirit—and these form the subject-matter of his diaries and journals and can only be mentioned in passing here. By way of biographical particulars, therefore, it must suffice

* With the permission of Dr Grieve I have deleted a section in which he discusses his selection for *Collected Poems*. Editor.

to say he was born in 1898, the only son of Mr John Soutar, master joiner, Perth. He entered the navy from school in 1916, and served in home and foreign waters. In 1919 he matriculated at Edinburgh University, and in 1923 graduated M.A. with honours in English. Afterwards his health broke down and he became bedfast for the remainder of his life. But of Soutar's long years of enforced inactivity and premature death one may well say, as has been said recently of the American poet, Stephen Benet, who, after a long and painful fight against arthritis, died in 1943 aged only forty-four:

> We are living in a time of death for young men. Steve would have asked us to pay homage to those who meet death in action. Yet somehow he so perfectly symbolizes what other boys are dying for, that we ought to pause for a moment, in our struggle, to remember him. Steve became a part of three wars—the Civil War (in *John Brown's Body*), and World Wars I and II. He had to fight with the spirit, not as a soldier. But in each one he performed a miracle: he gave it meaning.

In the same way, what Soutar's life teaches us, in this confused and dangerous moment of history, is that the objectives of free men are, ultimately, to be found in their arts and letters—the expressions of their inmost nature. However bloody and carnal the war, our hearts must transcend the horrors, in song and colour, in rhythm and in line. It was Shelley who pointed out that, had Locke, Hume and other philosophers never lived, the loss, while great, could be calculated: but that 'it exceeds all imagination to conceive what would have been the moral condition of the world' without Dante, Chaucer, Shakespeare, the Hebrew poets, the Greek sculptors. 'Poetry', says Shelley ,'creates for us a being within our being.' It is that being which Soutar's work so lucidly reveals. Soutar's war was not fought with bullets, but with Scottish intimations. His signal corps was not concerned with laying telephone wires but with the 'authentic tidings of invisible things'.

Soutar's work is almost equally divided between poems in English and poems in Scots. Many critics have pointed out in relation to modern Scottish poets writing in both languages that Scots invariably proves their happier medium, and that, through it, they were able to liberate faculties of their personalities for

7

which their English work afforded no outlet. This general rule was as applicable to Soutar as to all the others: but he applied himself to Scots verse far more systematically than almost any of his predecessors since the death of Burns, with the exception perhaps of 'Hugh Haliburton' (James Logie Robertson), and, indeed, his output in Scots, and the extent of the Scots vocabulary he used, were greater than are to be found in any other Scots poet since Burns, except for two or three poets still living. Mass tells, and the cumulative effect of Soutar's work in Scots — the impression of his steady devotion to this medium, the range of his work in it to include not only poems but riddles, epigrams, and, as he called them, 'bairn-sangs' and 'whigmaleeries' — is far more important than any particular poem or group of poems he produced in it. His *Seeds in the Wind* (Poems in Scots for Children),[5] for example, is not poetry on the same high level as some of his other Scots poems, but it met a felt need, not only among Scots children themselves and among their parents and teachers, fills a unique place, and is likely to be increasingly used in our schools; in short, *The Times Literary Supplement* was right in declaring on its appearance: 'In its own country the book should assuredly become at once a minor classic.' Alas, that is not the way things happen in Scotland. Recognition is slow. Soutar got little encouragement during his lifetime. *Seeds in the Wind* is winning appreciation slowly but surely. I have no doubt that it *is* a minor classic of our literature, that the reality of the Scottish literary renaissance movement can hardly be better exemplified than just by the difference between these poems for Scots children and the previous sentimental trash designed for this purpose from the days of the *Whistle Binkie School* to our own time, and that it will yet win due esteem as such; but 'at once' — or even 'soon' — is not to be looked for in our all-too-grudging and graceless land.

A minor classic! The adjective 'minor' must be stressed. I think that the lack of longer poems in Soutar's work, the extent to which he devoted himself to extremely short poems, and to trifling oddments like his riddles and epigrams, was a consequence of his bedridden state — that, and the disabling doubt expressed in a letter to myself (June 1934) when he says:

Do you think it is possible to write great poetry to-day? I

very much doubt it when the whole world system is rotten
and going to bits. Isn't it very possible that your present
sense of frustration is the most natural condition for a poet of
any magnitude; and nothing more (though disturbing enough
to the individual) than an indication that there are many
things which poetry cannot do today until the social life is
reorganized.

Even more serious—and due, I think, to the same causes—was his
inability to take 'the mad leap into the symbol', and the infre-
quency with which his muse takes wing. He was a whimsical and
reflective poet—very Scottish in his insight into our national
psychology, and in his humour—and idiomatically authentic in
his use of Scots, but the movement of his verse is almost always too
tame—the Scots Muse has a wilder music and a far more complicated and unexpectable movement. And nearly all the Scots
poets (unlike the English poets) have been song-writers. It is
strange that so genuine a Scots poet as Soutar should sing so
seldom. A sympathetic composer, and friend of Soutar's, like Mr
Francis George Scott, has only been able to set two or three of his
pieces. Soutar, however, had much to set against these defi-
ciencies. His work abounds in acuities and felicities of observation
of the Scottish scene and of the humours of the Scottish psyche.
Despite the small formal range of his work and its lack of musical
variety, he rings the changes most adroitly, and in poem after
poem dealing with substantially the same or very similar themes
displays a wonderful resource in showing a new facet here, vary-
ing the emphasis there, and, in brief, always has a new angle of
approach, a new aspect to present, a fresh comment to make. (In
this respect Soutar reminds me of Mr Irving Berlin, who has
managed to remain entirely objective, too, towards his work,
and sometimes startles people by pointing out that although he
has written more than eight hundred songs, he has actually done
nothing more than rewrite some seven or eight of his best ones over
and over again. 'White Christmas', for example, is nothing more
than 'Easter Parade' in thirds; 'Easter Parade', in turn, is based
on 'Smile and Show your Dimple', a tune he wrote in 1917. 'All
good song writers', he says, when mentioning his borrowings from
himself, 'have no more than half-a-dozen good tunes in their

systems, and if they have that many, they are liberally blessed.')
Yet his work generally is too pedestrian; it takes all his skill in
minor variation to prevent the weight of repetitiveness in it, and
the unexciting jog-trot of his verse, from drowning out the vivid
details and turns and twists of whimsicality with which he offsets
that sameness. But the vivid, various and vital in his work barely
suffice to rescue it from the dangers of mere platitudinizing and
sententiousness which continually threaten to engulf it. It will
be observed that he wrote most of his Scots work, and his best work
in Scots, fairly early in his literary life, and in his later work wrote
more in English. The faith that was in him was expressed in one
of his few longish poems, 'The Auld Tree', dedicated to myself,
which appeared in his *Poems in Scots*.[6] And here the exultant use of
Scots evokes a far livelier music than he usually achieves. It may
be that in his condition he was unable to sustain demands on his
energy that would have been inevitable if he had continued to make
a more intensive — and extensive — use of Scots. But certainly, in
so far as he *was* able to indulge this, it led to his best work. As a
writer in *Alba Nuadh* (New Scotland) said of him away back in
1935:

> To read Mr Soutar's poems is to become aware that in the
> hands of such a master Scots is meet to express the widest
> rangings of thought and inspiration. These poems reveal, too,
> how much more adequately Scots conveys the intimacies of
> our native outlook than English. Mr Soutar gets far ben to the
> spirit of Scotland and one cannot help feeling that for a true
> and irresistible awakening of that spirit the reading and
> understanding of such poems will do far more and act more
> effectively than all the political and economic arguments
> from now to the crack of doom. Mr Soutar has long since
> established his right to be regarded as one of the authentic
> poets, not only of Scotland, but of New Scotland, and all
> who aspire to the pursuit of the high purpose involved in the
> creation of New Scotland should lose no time in procuring
> his *Poems in Scots* ... a few more such makars and Scotland
> will assuredly 'wauk frae her souff'!

However little general recognition Soutar won, other Scots poets
were not tardy in acknowledging his pioneer work and their

indebtedness to him, and it may prove that his greatest service to Scotland was just in the way his example called into being a whole succession of younger poets in Scots—men like Douglas Young, Sydney Smith, Maurice Lindsay, and 'Robert Garioch'.

It has been remarked that his latest work showed an increasing preoccupation with Marxism and left-wing politics; and he prefaced *In the Time of Tyrants*[7] with 'An Introductory Note on Pacifist Faith and Necessity'. In a later entry in his diary, however, he cautions that this should not be taken too seriously. The fact of the matter is that his thought was evolving—he entertained changing ideas, but was very worried about the war and about political problems—what matters in these poems is the extent to which they manifest that deep anxiety and not the temporary positions his mind took up, for he had not come to final conclusions. Only one thing is certain. His heart was always in the right place. It will always be true of his poetry—and his place in relation to Scotland—as he himself sings in 'Birthday'—

> There cam a flaucht o' levin
> That brocht nae thunner ca'
> But left ahint a lanely lowe
> That wadna gang awa'.

And it is true of all his best work that it manifests a many-sided knowledge and love of Scottish life and landscape that calls to mind, though unfortunately it scarcely rivals the movement of, that 'Wren o' Tibbermuir' of which he writes:

> She breisted like a puddy-doo;
> She tirl'd upon her tipper-taes;
> And, in a whup, her whurlywas
> Breel'd owre the caller braes.
>
> Up steer'd the cock and gien a craw;
> Up steer'd the coo and gien a croun;
> Up steer'd the sin—and there was a'
> The bricht world birlin' roun'.

The story of his life and work provides us with a wonderful example of endurance, high courage, devotion to poetry, love of Scotland, and it will be largely due to him, indeed, if the prophecy Mr William Power wrote nearly twenty years ago comes true yet (as I have no doubt it will), viz.: 'For a potent spirit lies within those volumes of Scottish poetry, a spirit that, when liberated, will prove stronger than industrialism, latifundia, and the sporting system. We shall see "a dead man win a fight". The makars will remake Scotland.'

Vivian H. S. Mercier, writing in *The Dublin Magazine* on 'The Verse Plays of Austin Clarke', has said: 'The most immediately obvious way in which Clarke has enlarged the scope of verse drama—as Yeats understood the term—is by introducing humour into it. Any humour in Yeats's plays is confined strictly to prose; verse is for more serious things. Clarke, on the other hand, is not afraid to call his *Black Fast* "a poetic farce".' Soutar was equally unafraid to associate poetry and the comic—not, however, by lapsing into the witless jocosities of so many of our post-Burnsian rhymesters and debasing the poetic currency, but by such utilizations of the *vis comica* which is so potent and pervasive an element in Scottish life as draw the very essence of the poetry from the important achievement; a comic poetry—at once really comic and really poetry—is urgently desirable on many grounds, and it may eventually be regarded as one of Soutar's most important achievements that in many of his poems, if only on a very small scale, he effected this most unusual combination which Plato approved and 'the humour of the saints' in Catholic tradition has always exemplified, and of which Professor Gregory Smith in his book on *Scottish Literature*[8] has so well said:

> This mingling, even of the most eccentric kind, is an indica-
> tion to us that the Scot, in that mediaeval fashion which takes
> all things as granted, is at his ease in both 'rooms of life', and
> turns to fun, and even profanity, with no misgivings ... For
> Scottish Literature is more mediaeval in habit than criticism
> has suspected, and owes some part of its picturesque strength
> to this freedom in passing from one mood to another. It takes
> some people more time than they can spare to see the absolute
> propriety of a gargoyle's grinning at the elbow of a kneeling
> saint.

PART TWO

10

THE SCOTTISH RENAISSANCE:
THE NEXT STEP

1950

In his deplorable article on 'Scottish Literature in the Universities' in the *Scots Review* of March, Professor W. L. Renwick has unfortunately forgotten what he wrote in the first volume of *Introduction to English Literature*,[1] when he drew attention to Sir David Lyndsay's verse and said: 'It's comic inconsequence is part of the Scottish birthright ... Some day Scotland may remember the art and the music that those generations made, and may set this part of her tradition in its place when she rebuilds.' Elements in Scotland have been trying to do just that during the past twenty-five years. The universities might, and should, have done a great deal to help them.

I think it may be said of my own best songs, which Francis George Scott has set to music, as Peter Monro Jack (himself a Scotsman, and former student under Sir Herbert Grierson at Aberdeen) has said in the *New York Times Book Review* of Garcia Lorca:

The specific recurrent imagery of olives, jasmine, fig trees, salt pits, the smell of the Sierra, the little squares of the towns, the ponies in the mountains—all this will be for most of us a dream landscape. What makes it *seem* so real to us is that Lorca, without being a storyteller, constantly gives the sense of life in his pictures: men riding, women on the balustrade, gipsy girls dancing. In effect it is what Burns does so easily and simply in his Scots poems, as in 'I'll aye ca' in by yon toun, and by yon garden green again'—and the feeling of Scots life is there. So Lorca will write 'Through the arch of Elvida ... I want to see you pass', or 'Although I know the road ... I'll never reach Córdoba', or 'You leave us singing ... in the little square', and in the same way he savours and sweetens a people and landscape that he loved deeply and intimately. But though like Burns in his realism and his nature-sense, and like him also in his musical knowledge (he composed, sang his own songs, had the respect of de Falla), Lorca is *far beyond in linguistic sophistication*. [My italics. I stress this as the principal requirement of further development in Scots poetry.] He uses every effect of symbolism, fantasy, super-realism, and he has the astringent difficulty and corresponding pleasure of solution that most modern verse has, and that Blake, rather than Burns, had.

It was for such a development of Scots song that F. G. Scott was waiting, and supremely fitted to deal. If circumstances had allowed us to live in the same town and be constantly in touch over a considerable period, we would, I think, have performed the necessary long-overdue audit and working-over of the whole corpus of Scottish popular song which would at once have been most beneficial to our respective gifts and would have enabled us to carry with us the great mass of the Scottish people.

What I am thinking of is such a procedure of study, analysis, imitation, and adroit variation as the young Maurice Chevalier carried out on the repertoires of the then popular café-singers and music-hall artistes in Paris and elsewhere — as when he tuned in, for example, to Dranem's supreme success, 'Ah, les p'tits pois, les p'tits pois', watched Mistinguett tackling such songs as 'Coeur en feu' and 'Mon Petit Watman', music by Lestac — picked up new physiognomical and grotesque tricks and sang 'Les foies gras', 'Sale voyou bonsoir', and on to 'Allume, Allume !', 'L'omnibus', 'Le beau mome'; proceeded to Marseilles and sang 'J'aime les fleurs, j'aime les fleurs parce qu'elles ont un bouton', and then sang the same number in the style of Mayol and Dranem, singing it as they would have sung it and mimicking their mannerisms; on to 'Ta bouche' and 'Il faut savoir tout prendre avec le sourire'; and later, showed himself 'quick to perceive that there was too wide a gulf between the popular American songs of, say, Winnie Lightner, and the free-and-easy ditties of the essentially French 'Dédé'; then, back to France again, sang 'La petite bête qui monte', 'La chanson du Rugby', and 'T'en fais pas pour le chapeau de la gamine' — songs that were 'just street incidents transferred to the stage, complete with words, twists, and gestures. That is what made them so successful. The market-place and the Champs-Elysées were portrayed with equal felicity. Maurice was quite as much at home in the one as in the other ... Dressed up as a Breton peasant, Maurice asked his audience naïvely, 'Savez-vous planter les choux?' He said it in a way to make them feel as if they had never heard of cabbages before, let alone how to plant them ... Then even the great establishment of which Maurice had become the rage, when he introduced his world-famous song, 'Valentine', proved too small for the crowds that crushed to see him.

By means of those songs, which seemed to have been transferred straight from the streets of Paris to the stage, Maurice could stir the hearts of the crowd. The fundamental reason of his success lies in that his listeners, especially those of simple heart, get the impression that this popular singer is the interpreter of their own feelings. So sincere and realistic are his renderings of those typically Parisian songs that most of those present think they could express them just as well if they took the trouble. Of course, that is only an illusion on their part, for it takes a sort of genius to succeed in this difficult art.

What I commend to younger Scots writers is the patient hard work, the acute analysis, based on a thorough knowledge of popular types, local dialects, slang, and a profound love of the streets and all sorts and conditions of people, which are necessary for success of this sort.

Scottish life has never been studied to artistic purpose in this way. Our Scottish music-hall artistes have no wit whatever to put an edge on their native humour. But to re-achieve a body of popular Scottish song that will really capture the public is the great task confronting Scottish poetry today, and apart from lively affection for the Scottish people, and a good background of knowledge of the Scottish popular tradition down the centuries, few studies would help anyone tackling this great task better perhaps than a study of French popular songs, and of the training in observation and the methods of artistry whereby such singers as Chevalier secured successful additions to their repertoires. That F. G. Scott and I have been unable to do a great deal more in this direction is a great pity, since it is seldom that a poet and a composer with so much community of insight and capable of such an exceedingly close collaboration come together, and the things that have prevented our much more effective conjunction have been so exasperatingly unnecessary. Still, that we came together as we did at all has been a bit of supreme good luck.

> He analyzed [we read of Chevalier] the talent of fat Vilbert, that bluff actor from the south who invaded the Paris stage with his wit, his mocking jokes, and his badinage, his breath still smelling of garlic, he having overlooked the fact that he had left Marseilles. Maurice had studied his effect on the spectators. Some shouted with delight; one of them managed to insert a spicy wisecrack in the accent of the south, which made the audience rock and which revealed that the spectator was a compatriot of the artiste. Maurice studied the moment when Vilbert's jokes extracted the maximum of laughter from the audience. He analyzed him, just as he had previously analyzed Mademoiselle Polaire and Paulette Darty, and as he had analyzed the anatomy of his recent colleagues, the crowd-workers, appraising their make-up and the different angles of their legs when at work. Always very observant, he made great strides ...

The Scottish movement will make great strides too when our young writers begin to study Scottish life, and the work of our Scottish comedians and other artistes, with a like thoroughness. And not till then!

The only good essay towards beginning an effective analysis of this sort I have so far encountered is that on 'The Glasgow Comedians', by Colm Brogan, in the symposium *Scotland 1938*,[2] edited by John R. Allan. And, as he says,

> The stoutest fortress of a grand tradition (i.e., among the Glasgow theatres) is not the Princess or even the Metropole but the Queen's. The Queen's is in Watson Street, behind Glasgow Cross ... The pantomime is a twice-nightly show, and its principal comedian is Sam Murray. By instinct and tradition the pantomime is unrefined, and it would be foolish to pretend that Sam Murray does anything at all to raise the general tone ... Next to Sam Murray in distinction is Doris Droy. She is full of life and fire and she is as honest as the

day is long. Her voice is wonderfully strong. Her top notes are a punch on the ear. She is never tired ... The pantomime is one solid chunk of 'Glesga'. But even the Queen's is threatened with danger. Treachery is unthinkable; the danger comes from outside. It is impossible to imagine Sam Murray keeping right on to the end of the road or Doris Droy being winsome in the steamie. But they are in danger of having their audience diluted. Half the enjoyment of a Queen's pantomime is the simple but Aristotelian pleasure of recognition, and it is impossible to guess how much encouragement the performers derive from a perfect community of thought and feeling with the audience. That is in danger of being lost, because the clients of more fashionable houses are beginning to discover the Queen's. The Queen's may become a fad. If it does, genius and Art will take wing and they will not perish in flight. There are haunts as yet unsuspected by the bourgeois. Somewhere or other honesty will find a home.

Instead of adopting a Kelvinside snobbishness and despising its 'atrocious garble' of a dialect, it would say a great deal more for Glasgow if it threw up a poet of the kind of Jehan Rictus (who, indeed, lived for a time in Edinburgh), or, still better, Jean Richepin, of whom, apropos his 'La Chanson des Gueux' (1876), 'Les Blasphèmes' (1884), and other poems, it has been said: 'Il n'y reculait ni devant la grossièreté, ni devant le cynisme ... Richepin a chanté les loqueteux, les chemineaux, les misérables ... Sanguin et bruyant, mais ayant a son service un vocabulaire extrèmement riche, aussi pittoresque et aussi varié que celui d'un Rabelais, il possède à la fois la couleur et la force.'

But Glasgow, alas, has produced no such poet *au tempérament fougueux*; its bards have all been backward-looking ruralists, spineless triflers, superior persons insulated from the life of the city in petty suburban snobberies, all utterly incapable of catching the real rhythms of Clydeside at all and all hopelessly at variance politically and in every other way with all that was really significant, really alive , in their area, or, indeed, elsewhere. A Richepin among the members of the Glasgow Ballad Club would truly be a cat among the sparrows, or, rather, the budgerigars. All these Glasgow singers—and, indeed, all the Glasgow intelligentsia—are shut away behind a thick frosted-glass wall of respectability and at the farthest possible remove from realizing joyfully (at any rate in respect of Glasgow itself) with Maurice Chevalier that in this life 'Faut pas s'en faire'. What an accumulation of hypocrisy, affectation, claptrap, hooey and anti-vital rubbish of all kinds would be blasted away if ever the dynamite of this realization is put to work by any Glasgow writer!

The problem of 'getting across' F. G. Scott's work is precisely the problem of the entire Scottish movement. Every Scotsman is faced with just the same position as in Russia confronted Chaliapin. It was Dmitri Andreivitch Ousatov, who at Tiflis gave Chaliapin his first insight into musical characterization, and he did so through examples from Moussorgsky's *Boris Godounov*. 'Now,' he would say, 'you see how music can react on the imagination? You see how silence and a pause are able to give the subtle effect of characterization?' This was the lesson which invoked in Chaliapin the qualities which made his art unique. 'Don't take any notice,' the other singers of Ousatov's class said, 'all he says may be true, but "La donna e mobile" is the right stuff for singers. Moussorgsky with his Varlaams and Mitiouks is literally poison for the voice and singing.'

Chaliapin declared that he was torn in two. 'Sometimes I was so racked with doubt that I lay sleepless. Which would I choose— "La donna e mobile" or "In the big town of Kazan"?' This was the one critical moment in his career, the one moment when he had to choose his party. Beside it all the later adulations of the great, the angling for his adherence, the fawning of the crowds, and the police warrants out against him, were of no importance whatsoever.

If he had chosen 'the right stuff for singers' there would have been, no doubt, one more highly successful singer in a world full of them, but there would have been no Chaliapin—none of that secret of his art, a secret which everyone knows but no one else can possess. So far Scotland, in every connection, has chosen 'the right stuff for singers', and the whole influence of all our M.P.s, all our ecclesiastical leaders, all our educationists, and even of the National Party of Scotland and the Scottish Convention is on that side.

The future of the Scottish renaissance depends on those who choose as Chaliapin chose and work as Maurice Chevalier worked.

11

THE QUALITY OF SCOTS
INTERNATIONALISM
1950

An essayist writing on John Knox in *The Times Literary Supplemen* recently put the matter very well by observing that:

Scotland, a small but ancient kingdom of Europe, had always occupied a larger place in events than her population, or — let us be frank — her earlier achievements, wholly justified. She lay, a hard nut to crack, in the hinge between the cultures of the Baltic and of the Mediterranean. She was always conscious both of the negation of the ice (her northern coast looks out towards no further shore) and of the fruitful southern lands, with which she also had kinship. Her merchants traded, and her clansmen fought, in both cases for a bare livelihood, all the way between Leith and Russia. Yet her kings and queens also inter-married with the blood-royal of France; before that, her soldiers had charged with Joan of Arc and one of her craftsmen had emblazoned Joan's banner. Before that, long before that, the Orkney-men had sailed to Constantinople, and returned to build the beautiful cathedral at Kirkwall. Scotland was a microcosm of Europe, in a sense the great fenced, fertile self-centred metropolitan country of England, to the south, never was. The traditions and the origins of Christianity in Scotland differ radically from those of England.

And the article ends by quoting 'McAndrew's Hymn' and reminding us that its author, Rudyard Kipling, was himself (as was Mr Stanley — afterwards Earl — Baldwin) 'half a Macdonald, though this is usually forgotten'.

The fact of the matter is, of course, that Scotland's dispersion of her people and their influence is not confined to Europe, but is world-wide. There are over twenty million people of Scots extraction abroad, and only about five million in Scotland itself. There are great numbers of Scots especially in Canada, the United States, Australasia, and South Africa, and in all these lands there is a flourishing network of Burns Clubs, Caledonian Societies, Clan Societies, St Andrew Associations and other Scottish organizations and the ties between them and Scotland itself were never closer perhaps than they are today, nor visitors from them to the old country more numerous. It is an old joke that if you go to the unlikeliest places in the world—the North Pole, Tibet, Tierra del Fuego—you are sure to find Scots living there. And it is true. Mr H. L. Mencken in his book on *American Language*[1] tells of a Scottish-Gaelic-speaking community of Negroes in one of the Southern states; a correspondent of *The Scotsman* the other day told how he found a little pocket of Gaelic-speaking descendants of Scots in Georgian Caucasia; and Mr Peter Fleming—himself a Scot—in his *News from Tartary*[2] tells how he and Miss Maillart on that wonderful journey found hosts in Tangar—five weeks after leaving Peking—in Mr and Mrs Marcel Urech. He was Swiss, she was Scots. They had previously lived at Tatsienlu, on the borders of Tibet and Szechwan.

Such cases could be drawn in hundreds from every part of the globe. We read in the press in rapid sequence continually paragraphs like the following:

> Chief of Staff of the Brazilian Air Force, General Gervasino Duncan de Lima Rodrigues, has arrived in London by air from Rio de Janiero. He is paying a formal visit to the Royal Air Force and will study British civil aviation. A Scotsman by birth, he hopes to visit Scotland during his stay in Britain.

Or again:

> Scotsman Major-General Frederick Franklin Worthington, 'Fighting Frank of the Tanks,' retires from the Canadian Army this month at 57. He organized and took overseas the Dominion's 1st Armoured Division, and began his 35-year Army career as a soldier of fortune in Nicaragua and Mexico. In the second world war he earned the nickname of 'Fighting Frank' while training his division—the 4th Armoured—in Britain. During the first world war he enlisted as a private in

the Black Watch in Montreal and served at the front from 1915 until the war's end.

Or again:

Strolling through Glasgow yesterday—and noting 'the very underfed-looking children here'—was a native of Scotland for whom the six years of the war have changed the world fantastically. Eight years ago Robert Jack was a city-bred student of Glasgow University. To-day he is no longer even a Scotsman. He is the Rev. Robert Jack, a naturalized subject of Iceland, a minister of the Icelandic Church, a farmer who feeds his Icelandic wife and two small children by his own working of a 100-acre 'estate' on the Arctic Circle, a doctor and dentist and who attends to the sick among the 190 people on a small island (Grimsey, eight miles long and forty-five sea-miles from the mainland of Iceland) that is an Icelandic St Kilda—and a centre-forward in the island football team!

Let us have a look at just one more typical Scot before we cease these quotations from the current press:

Rising 84, Major H. L. Fleming is by no means satisfied with his golf handicap of 10. It is, of course, the result of two years of serious illness, but now that he's fit and strong again he hopes to get it down to 4, which is where it stood when he was in his late 70's. Allowing for being, in the course of nature, a little short with his drive, he feels that nowadays his golf is improving every day. He's learning more and more about the game at which, in the past, he was a formidable competitor in the Amateur Championship. He hopes to be really good one of these days. Is golf Major Fleming's favourite game? Looking back and chewing things over with the deliberateness of the typical Scot, Major Fleming ponders and fails to make up his mind. His favourite game—well, that is not so easy? Golf?—yes, possibly. If it isn't golf, it's lawn tennis or cricket or rugby or billiards; but, of course, anything to do with horses really interested him most in youth, whether breaking in and training ponies or playing polo or riding winners on the Flat or piloting steeplechasers home over four and a half miles of ferocious country at gymkhana meetings in the Punjab or on the North-West Frontier. You see, Major Fleming has stood head and shoulders above his challengers at all these sports. And for a makeweight you can throw in big game shooting and pig sticking as well. As a polo-player he was a tireless No. 2, on the ball from the first whistle of the first chukka to the final hit of the game. He was good enough to play for Burma, when he commanded a battalion there during five years out of the quarter-century he spent in the East.

A great all-rounder, indeed!

It has been this way all through the centuries and Scotland stands where it did in this respect, if in no other, today as always. It is no use attempting to catalogue even the more interesting travels of famous Scots. I think as I write of Tobias Smollett in Jamaica, Italy, and France; of William Lithgow meeting in Cracow in 1616 'with divers Scottish merchants ... especially the two brothers Dicksones, men of singular note of honesty and wealth'; of Sir Thomas Mitchell, one of the best-known Australian explorers; of Sir Pulteney Malcolm, the admiral who guarded Napoleon on St Helena; and scores upon scores of others. Let me drive to the heart of the matter and ask what is the secret of the Scot's universal acceptability and success, so different from the attitude evoked by the Englishman. It can be illustrated perhaps by what Miss Freda White has said in discussing Margery Perham's and J. Simmon's book, *African Discovery. An Anthology of Exploration,*[3] which deals with the ten great African explorers, namely Bruce of Abyssinia; Mungo Park, Clapperton, Lander, Baikie, all four explorers of the Niger; Burton, Speke, Livingstone, Baker and Stanley, travellers in East and Central Africa. Professor Joad, says Miss White:

> once madly committed himself, on the Brains Trust, to the opinion that the Scottish Nation had contributed little to the foundation of the British Empire, even in exploration. What about Livingstone? I would recommend to the Professor's notice the fact that five out of these ten—and by far the greatest one—were Scots ... Livingstone towers above this very considerable company. It is not easy to define why. His

writing in his journals is plain to dryness. He has no charm, and is indeed terrifying in the ruthlessness in which he pursued his object, and which he himself admits with shame. Other missionaries have served God as faithfully, and loved humanity as well. It may be his extraordinary honesty, wedded to the statesmanship which planned not only the abolition of the slave-trade, but a happier future for the Africans; it may be the regard which to the end saw every man truly as a person, not as a type or a race. There is all that, but it does not in itself constitute greatness, and no one can read his writing without knowing that this was a great man. Stanley felt it, and his skin was thick enough. The passages where he shows his reverence and love for Livingstone redeem his usual assurance, and render him momentarily likeable. Next to Livingstone, in my estimation, comes Bruce. Partly because he writes excellently well, in the easy graphic prose of his date (he is the only definitely eighteenth-century member of this volume). Partly because he is a man with whom one would love to travel. He preserves his own standards—the cruelty of the Abyssinian warfare sickens him—but he does not expect isolated African communities to share European habits, as some travellers do even today, and he is entirely free from race snobbery. It does not enter his head that he should not regard himself as a guest of the Ethiopians, and there is not even any deliberate thought in his acceptance of their customs. He prostrates himself before the king as is fitting, stands his long and weary watch as a chamberlain when he is appointed to office, and in consequence wins a liking which allows him much closer insight and much more liberty than any assumption of superiority could have gained. He was given every facility to visit the source of the Blue Nile, and indeed only found difficulty in gaining permission to leave the country. When his patron was defeated in civil war and he met the queen, his friend, in exile, he recorded the meeting as 'one of the happiest moments of my life'. This capacity for liking people, and his natural proper behaviour, are in sharp contrast to Burton's constant sneer and in utter opposition to the ill-breeding of Speke who wrote: 'Now I have made up my mind never to sit upon the ground as the

Arabs and natives are obliged to do, nor to make my obeisance in any other manner than is customary in England ... I felt that if I did not stand up for my social position at once, I should be treated with contempt during the remainder of my visit, and thus lose the vantage-ground I had assumed of appearing rather as a prince than as a trader, for the purpose of better gaining the confidence of the kings.

As Miss White says: 'It is clear, through all the conceit of the narrative, that this nonsensical pretentiousness earned the dislike it invited. But how typical it is of the sort of English traveller who has made the whole nation unpopular abroad.'

It is really astonishing to comb through the files of the newspapers for the last three or four years to find the unanimity with which foreigners of all kinds have expressed their preference for Scotland over England and praised Scottish hospitality and kindness as against the snobbery and social stratification of the English. Sir Ronald Ross, who discovered the cure for malaria, describes an interview with Joseph Chamberlain:

Neither he nor his officials had understood in the least what we meant. As usual with politicians, he deprecated expenditure, not recognizing that sanitary expenditure is an insurance against the much greater expenditure caused by sickness, as that on fire-engines is against fires. On the other hand, he was 'prepared to consider' a travelling commission of three business men and one scientific expert, all of whom would have to be paid by the Chambers of Commerce for doing the business of the Colonial Office. This proposal was characteristic of British administration. Instead of doing cheap and necessary work it spends large sums on expensive and worthless talk. The proceedings now closed with more compliments. Chamberlain had done some good (and won much political capital) by suggesting the schools of tropical medicine; but, in my opinion, his refusal of a proper sanitary organization for the colonies largely cancelled, then and since, the benefits which might have accrued. I suppose I was the only one present who had any real knowledge of tropical sanitation; and I remember thinking to myself angrily as I left stately

Whitehall: 'These people are no longer fit to hold the hege-
mony of the world.'

If we turn to a very different personality, Ross's great co-
worker, Sir Patrick Manson, we find again and again—more
quietly stated—the same complaints against the stupidities of
officialdom and the freemasonries of mediocrity, and see again
the Scottish rebellion against the British system. Manson, like
most of the better type of Scotsmen abroad, had a very much
better attitude to the 'damned foreigners' than is usually found
in the Englishman abroad—the Bruce of Abyssinia attitude
versus the Speke attitude—and was animated by a very different
spirit than that of the typical empire-builder. This different spirit
in regard to such matters of the Scotsman as compared with the
Englishman finds magnificent exemplification again and again
in Manson's biography. Dr Abraham in *The Surgeon's Log*[4] depicts
a Scot far more typical in his attitude than the English care to
recognize, when, discussing, the treatment of the Kling porters in
Malaya, he tells of a Scotsman, Guthrie, who looked at him and
said, ' "You think it very high-handed?" I nodded. "Man," said
the Scotsman, "if you come to think of it, our mere presence in
the country is the most insufferable high-handedness, we haven't
a moral leg to stand on!" '

This Scottish spirit, so utterly different from anything English,
was never better shown perhaps than in the character of Sir
William MacGregor, of Fiji. Captain C. A. W. Monckton, in his
Some Experiences of a New Guinea Resident Magistrate,[5] tells how Sir
William MacGregor came to be appointed on New Guinea:

Sir William, at that time Doctor MacGregor, was attending,
as the representative of Fiji, one of the earlier conferences
regarding the proposed Federation of Australasia; he had
already made his mark by work performed in connection with
the suppression of the revolt among the hill tribes of that
Crown Colony. At the Conference, amongst other questions,
New Guinea came up for discussion, whereupon MacGregor
remarked: 'There is the last country remaining, in which the
Englishman can show what can be done by just native policy.'
The remark struck the attention of one of the delegates, by
whom the mental note was made, 'If Queensland ever has a

say in the affairs of New Guinea, and I have a say in the affairs of Queensland, you shall be the man for New Guinea.' When, later, New Guinea was declared a British Possession, Queensland had a very large say in the matter, and the man who had made the mental note happening to be Premier, he caused the appointment of Administrator to be offered to MacGregor, by whom it was accepted.

Another tremendous advantage the Scots have over the English is in their flair for languages. That is why all through our history we have thrown up great linguists like Sir James Grierson, who compiled the dictionary of Indian dialects, and Sir Edward Denison Ross, and scores upon scores of men who have done far more for native languages and literatures than any of their English colleagues. Katherine Tynan in her *Twenty-Five Years; Reminiscences*[6] has several delightful paragraphs about the then Chinese professor at Oxford — a very dear, charming old man, with snow-white hair, bushy eyebrows and side-whiskers, the blue eyes and pink and white complexion of a child. 'Lovely as a Lapland night.' Well on in the seventies, he used to rise at four o'clock every morning, make himself a cup of tea, and work away through the quiet hours at his Chinese folios. His study, hung with Chinese scrolls, was walled about with his lifework in the shape of Chinese classics which the Oxford wits used to say might or might not be genuine, since none but the Professor himself knew anything about them. And she mentions his 'strong Scottish accent', his 'appalling moments of frankness', and the fact that he was 'justly proud that he had refused a chair at a Scottish University in his young manhood because he would have had to conform in some way'. Another typical Scot in fact! And I think next of E. J. W. Gibb of Glasgow, who devoted the whole of his life to the study of Ottoman poetry. When Gibb died, only one volume of his monumental *History of Ottoman Poetry* had appeared, if most of the matter for the other five volumes had been gathered in; as a labour of love Professor E. G. Browne took upon himself the onerous task of seeing the whole work through the press, completing the unfinished parts, and this involved an immense amount of research, for every quotation had to be verified, and the originals of many poems translated by Gibb had to be traced to their sources, often in rare manuscripts, and copied for the printer. It fell to Browne, too, to establish with five other scholars and Gibb's widow the 'E. J. W. Gibb Memorial', founded with a sum of money given by the scholar's mother. This Trust has published upwards of thirty texts and translations of Turkish, Arabic, and Persian authors.

The Scottish gift of languages was held in high measure by Sir William MacGregor too, and Captain Monckton, after showing Sir William's ability to deal with surveyors, engineers and others on their own ground and surpass them, says:

The same sort of thing occurred with Sir William in languages; he spoke Italian to Giulianetti; German to Kowold; and French to the members of the Sacred Heart Mission. I believe if a Russian or a Japanese had turned up Sir William would have addressed him in his own language. Ross-Johnston, at one time private secretary to Sir William, once wailed to me about the standard of erudition Sir William expected in a man's knowledge of a foreign language. Ross-Johnston had been educated in Germany and knew German, as he thought, as well as his own mother tongue, Sir William, while reading some abstruse German book, struck a passage the meaning of which was to him somewhat obscure; he referred to Ross-Johnston, who, far from being able to explain the passage, could not make sense of the chapter. Whereupon Sir William remarked that he thought Ross-Johnston professed to know German. Ross-Johnston, feeling somewhat injured, took the book to Kowold, who was a German. Kowold gave one look at it, then exclaimed: 'Phew! I can't understand that. It's written by a scientist for scientists.'

It is this flair for languages that accounts for the fact that Scottish translators have introduced many important European writers to the English-reading world from the time of Urquhart's *Rabelais* onwards. Nietzsche, Rilke, Kierkegaard, Kafka, Leontiev, and Martin Buber were being translated and written about by Scottish writers before they began to be mentioned in England, great as their vogue has been there since. *The Times Literary Supplement* recently commented on the very small proportion of important European literature yet available in English translations. In the late C. K. Scott-Moncrieff in respect of Proust, and in Edwin and Willa Muir in respect of Kafka and many other modern European writers, Scotland has supplied some of the very best translators English literature has had. And it is significant that contemporary Scottish poets like Douglas Young, George Campbell Hay, J. F. Hendry, Sydney Goodsir Smith and others have rendered into Scots or English poems from a score of different languages.

When Scotland's premier contemporary wit, Mr Harold Stewart, wrote recently about the preparations for MacSiccar Week going forward at Glenbrochan, he added: 'Mr Duncan Ban MacSiccar (Fair Duncan of the Aspirates) will be host to the visitors in the unavoidable absence of the Chief who, as the venerable bard explained yesterday, "iss a cannibal shentleman in the South Seas and not fery keen on missing his favourite diet. There is nothing much in that line we could be gifing him to eat here, except maybe an occasional MacSnoover, and, och, man, but they would be wersh, wersh!"'

12

THE SIGNIFICANCE OF
CUNNINGHAME GRAHAM

1952

In view of the centenary of the birth of the late R. B. Cunninghame Graham which occurs in May I have written a centenary
study[1] which gives a full biographical account of this great Scotsman, my impressions of his personality, and a description and
discussion of all his books in the order in which they were published. There is therefore no need to recapitulate here any of that
material. My purpose in this article is a different one — to consider
in the light of Cunninghame Graham's career and reputation
the place of the artist in Scotland today and the proper relation
that should obtain between the political and cultural sides of the
great national awakening now in progress in our midst.

'C'est magnifique, mais ce n'est pas la guerre.' The same sense
of their unreality, of their failure to engage with the hard facts
which had to be accurately geared into if the machine was to be
got going at all, afflicted me all along in Cunninghame Graham's
case, and, to a lesser extent, Compton Mackenzie's, while two
other distinguished Scots, Sir Patrick Geddes and Pittendreigh
MacGillivray in their different way seemed also to 'speak a
different language altogether' and to be incapable of taking a
realistic grip of the problems of Scottish arts and affairs. Except
Mackenzie they were all much older men than myself, of course,
and in Mackenzie's case religion was another difficulty (he is a
convert to Roman Catholicism) while MacGillivray was deeply
dyed with Eastern Mysticism (Sufi-ism). The interests, the objective affiliations, of all these men, except MacGillivray, were
largely outside Scotland. Cunninghame Graham's subject-
matter was drawn from Spain, Morocco, Spanish America,
Iceland — only in a few cases from Scotland itself — and he was
virtually unread and unknown in Scotland. It was this that
turned the scale against him when he so nearly defeated Earl

Baldwin for the lord rectorship of Glasgow University. The
students had no real sense of his significance at all. The astonishing measure of support that accrued to him did so because of his
picturesque appearance, and the hard work of the substantial
body of Glasgow students who had become aware of Scotland's
acute problems and urgent need of self-government—but appreciation of Cunninghame Graham's work, or even the barest
acquaintance with it, was almost non-existent, while, of course,
the Anglo-Scottish press were dead against him, as were the
stuffy yes-men of the status quo of the university authorities. He
was never given his due in Scotland.

Mackenzie, who at the next time of asking was successful in
securing the lord rectorship, was in different case—he was a
popular novelist, and his work did not fall under that disabling
suspicion of highbrowism which attached itself so adversely to
Cunninghame Graham's because of its exotic subject-matter, and
still more because it was cast for the most part in forms—the short
story, the sketch, the essay—which have never taken on in Great
Britain and against which there is a very deep and widespread
prejudice.

Mackenzie, too, is a picturesque figure—but Cunninghame
Graham was picturesque to a literally incredible degree; and his
over-romantic appearance actually operated against him, whereas
Mackenzie's physical graces were sufficiently in keeping with
modern standards to serve as an asset. But neither of these men
were able to pull anything like the weight they should have been
able to pull, because they were both more or less exotic figures,
and their very gifts and graces made them hated and distrusted
by a Scotland overwhelmingly devoid of culture, hopelessly
provincialized, and full of a 'bad conscience' towards arts and
letters. Both of them were socialists (like myself, Mackenzie was
on the I.L.P. panel of parliamentary candidates at the time the
National Party of Scotland was formed—and we both withdrew
our names on the strength of pledges by the other leaders of that
party; pledges which were not redeemed—by no means the only
instance of gross betrayal to which both Mackenzie and I were
subjected by the same people), but they had no organic relationship to the Scottish working class, their interests were almost all
'caviare to the general', their idealism was not supported by any

real grasp of the essential facts and figures of Scottish social and economic conditions, and they had not the effective help of the socialist and Labour Party organizations, while the National Party organization was still hopelessly inadequate and its propagandist literature had scarcely begun to scratch the surface of the problems with which it purported to be concerned.

I have said elsewhere[2] of Cunninghame Graham:

A somewhat similar, if not identical, combination of qualities to that which constitutes Cunninghame Graham and differentiates him so completely from the great masses of the Scottish people today, has been the recurring agency in the production of almost all Scottish literature worthy of the name. That explains the dichotomy between Scottish literature in its most distinctive forms (exemplified in, say, Herman Melville's *Moby Dick*) and the reading public in Scotland today, which regards as exclusively Scottish all that is most completely destitute of those peculiar qualities which any careful study of our literary history will reveal as characteristically Scottish ... For a Scot so significantly and unmistakably aligned with those elements which throughout our history have always revealed themselves as the most peculiar and essential elements of our national genius (albeit, in their practical artistic bearing, at all events, so utterly at variance with the 'ethos' of our nation as a whole, so diametrically opposed in 'direction') is thus transformed into an incredible figure, the antithesis of everything that is accepted as Scottish ... Had Scotland been his prime concern, Cunninghame Graham's declarations would have largely had to paraphrase Miguel de Unamuno's of Spain: 'the poisonous wells of what Menendez Pelayo called clerical democracy are re-opened, and now the terrible cancer of Spain is visible—envy, envy, hatred of intelligence!

One who knows Scotland well, knows how well-nigh hopelessly it is bogged in mediocrity and platitudes in the last stages of decomposition, may have the true measure of indignant regret that circumstances compelled one of Scotland's greatest sons to apply his genius otherwise than to his native country—and less effectively, since that which is more truly nationalistic is also

most universal in its appeal. It is lamentable to find Scotland still
so largely preoccupied with what is conventionally regarded as
Scottish literature, the mindless vulgarities of parochial poetasters
and the cold-haggis and ginger-beer atrocities of prose kailyaird-
ism, and presenting an inaccessibility (of which the general
puritan conspiracy of silence, the bourgeois blindness that won't
see, and the incorrigible *suppressio veri* and *suggestio falsi* of commercial journalism are only parts) to the genius of such a great
contemporary as Cunninghame Graham, the essence of whose
philosophy—calculated to open the windows of most of his
countrymen's minds for the first time and let in pure air—is
expressed more succinctly perhaps than anywhere in his own
writings (all of which it bracingly informs and in all of which it is
magnificently, if less quotably, illustrated) in the following
passage from George Santayana:

> What a despicable creature must a man be, and how sunk
> below the level of the most barbaric virtue, if he cannot bear
> to live and die for his children, for his art, or for his country!
> ... Nothing can be meaner than the anxiety to live on, to live
> on anyhow and in any shape. A spirit with any honour is not
> willing to live except in its own way, and a spirit with any
> wisdom is not over-eager to live at all!

George Scott Moncrieff put the matter very well when he said:

> The basis for any consideration of Cunninghame Graham,
> the artist, is in his nationality to a degree applicable to the
> work of no other Scot of his generation. Here, unfortunately,
> some definition is necessary. There are many Frenchmen; but
> there are, in the true sense, comparatively few Englishmen:
> the majority of Englishmen are, all unconsciously, imperialist
> in their outlook, which factor, more than their insularity, has
> given them their Lord-God-Almighty reputation on the
> Continent. Those Scots who are not Scotsmen, and they
> represent the majority, are for the most part in a humbler
> state than the English imperialist, they are imperialized
> rather than imperialist. But from time to time amongst the
> ruck you find the real Scotsman, kenspeckle in a dozen ways
> that relate him, in terms of literature, with Dunbar, with

Andrew Fletcher, with Lord Cockburn. He, and the real Englishman, alone in the two countries are capable of being cosmopolitan. Such English critics as Mr Malcolm Muggeridge, who would probably claim to be an internationalist, but who is in fact merely denationalized, are overcome with an outlook whose roots are deep set in the imperialism of their forbears: imbued with an essential belief in centralization, in progressive (either happy or otherwise) social evolution, and an irascible tendency to dub all other outlooks romantic. 'That dangerous spirit of nationalism', of which we hear so much from Imperialists, bespeaks enthusiasm. Cunninghame Graham's capacity for enthusiasm was unbounded: it never lessened and was not daunted by the apparent hopelessness of right causes that jaundices the view of the uninspired humanitarian. The value that he found in failure, implicit in the majority of his best stories, was a product of his realism and faith. If to Mr Muggeridge he seems a romantic, that is an error natural to those to whom lost causes represent lapses in human efforts, and to whom the substance and the shadow of life are perpetually confused. To Mr Muggeridge Cunninghame Graham appears to have been less shocked by slums than by advertisements of life insurance policies. This was because Cunninghame Graham did not see a slum merely as something to be cleared, but saw in it a comminuty of fellow human beings condemned to many sufferings owing to the attitude of mind that begat the life-insurance policy; because he was a lover of Mankind instead of a social reformer; and because, to paraphrase his own words, he was less concerned with the hallucinatory rights of the poor than he was sympathetic with them, and their champion, on account of their wrongs. Compared to a mean and tortured generation of grub-streeters it was perhaps natural that the figure of Cunninghame Graham should appear romantic; but his style, whatever its extravagances, is never artificial. If he used a *cliché* it was not, as with the poor writer, a scantily appropriate stop-gap: he used it because it fitted what he wished to say, and he had no time to grope for a more novel expression. He unashamedly liked the picturesque, and was the more immune from its deception.

He was consistently honest and clear in his thought. The sense of place and of character was keen in him and he has conveyed it in more than a score of the finest short stories written by any Scot.

Or, as Compton Mackenzie put it:

Call him Don Quixote if the facile epithet pleases you, but if you call him Don Quixote you must recognize counsels of prudence for the cornless windmills they are, and salute the Scottish electorate as sheep driven down hill by English shepherds. If to believe that Scotland is potentially as prosperous a country as Holland or Norway or Belgium or Denmark is to be a Don Quixote; if to believe that Scotland is strong enough and brave enough and wise enough to choose her own destiny is to be a Don Quixote; if to believe that Scotland has a political future in Europe comparable to the glorious future which lies before Ireland is to be a Don Quixote; if to ride and dream and plan and speak and act like a gentleman, a patriot, and a scholar is to be a Don Quixote, then let him be called Don Quixote. Yet for a visionary who looked so fearlessly into the cold eyes of truth I should prefer an epithet less suggestive of an outlived chivalry. If in Scottish history he be doomed to remain just another of our picturesque failures, the blame and the shame will rest upon a Scotland which allows some thousands of Scots bleating round London in comic tam-o'-shanters that a Hottentot would spurn, to be accepted as a more representative expression of the nation's life and the nation's pride.

I and most of my most active friends in the Scottish movement were in precisely the opposite case with regard to Cunninghame Graham to that of James Joyce with regard to Yeats. Joyce regretted he had not met Yeats twenty years earlier, since Yeats was now too old to be influenced by him. A Cunninghame Graham restored to the pristine vigour of his youth again would have been a godsend to Scotland. He was too old to give the movement of which he was titular head the impetus and guidance it needed. Yet it was astonishing what tireless energy and enthusiasm he devoted to it despite his age—almost as if he were desperately trying to make up for lost time.

I valued Cunninghame Graham beyond rubies. We will never see his like again. He was unique and incomparable—a human equivalent of that pure white stag with great branching horns the appearance of which, tradition says, will betoken great good luck for Scotland at long last, and what I have said about his old age and his 'romantic' gestures must not pass for any suggestion that he did not play his part in the donkey-work of the organization of contemporary Scottish nationalism. He did. He did his full share and far more. The trouble was not that he was unpractical in this sense, not that he failed to do the necessary donkey-work—but that donkey-work was almost all that circumstances permitted him to do, and that he was never enabled to serve the movement effectively on his own best plane. It was all right for most of the others, but he and Mackenzie were used by the Nationalist Party, in so far as suspicion and jealousy and sheer incomprehension permitted the Nationalist Party to avail itself of their services at all, only as fine swords might be used to chop wood or like herding cows with a couple of horses that had won the Derby.

The Nationalist Party became involved in a vicious circle in which it revolved impotently. One of the results of such a situation, and it has been particularly conspicuous in the Scottish movement, has been what my friend Ronald Duncan, of *The Townsman*, a shrewd analyst, calls

arsenpardness: the tendency for parties to hatch their theology in the abstract and slowly drift reluctantly to action. This inverted order means that acts are first limited to the original ideas, which are probably inadequate; and later, time is again wasted in fitting the idea to explain the act. Whereas, if action could take its proper place! ... Only one mind in a million can grasp an idea in the abstract ... In this way a revolutionary party becomes a mere running commentary on the acts of the Government—at least a week behind. By spending its energy criticizing it fails to create, and gradually its activity is determined by the Government. In this way an experienced Government can make use of the so-called revolutionary parties to serve its own ends. For if these parties spend their time criticizing the Government's policy they fall into the trap of suggesting an alternative policy—a slightly lesser evil—which the Government then absorbs into its original policy, and then demands that the opposition should support the whole policy as it suggested part of it.

If Cunninghame Graham and Compton Mackenzie had not been so much engaged in other directions but had been able to bend their abilities to make the necessary comprehensive analysis of the whole Scottish question—and if, instead of being bourgeois nationalists and mere reformist socialists they had been thoroughly-instructed Marxists and had gone all out from the beginning for Scottish workers republicanism à la John Maclean, Scotland would be in a very different position today. A great opportunity was lost, and Cunninghame Graham and Mackenzie in council with the officials and branch delegates of the Scottish Nationalist Party were like a pair of golden eagles, with their wings clipped, in a crowded poultry-run, full of poultry far gone with the 'gapes'.

ROBERT FERGUSSON: DIRECT POETRY
AND THE SCOTTISH GENIUS
1952

I have sung in one of my poems:[1]

Ah, happy they who no less lonely
Are companioned by a future—who foresee
The struggle of a nation into consciousness of being,
The significance of that being, and the necessity
Of the forms taken by the struggle towards it
And sing accordingly.
—Subtle, intangible, a distant music
Heard only in the lull of the gusty wind;
They are animated and restrained in the soul
Not by that instinctive love of a native land
To which all can respond but by a mystical sense
Of the high destiny of a nation—swallowed up
Neither in the delights of living nor in the torment
Of the problem of individual existence ...

Where but in Fergusson is this rare Spenserian kind of poetry
to be found in Scots literature? That it has so seldom been dis-
cerned, let alone appreciated at its true worth, gives the measure
of the extent to which Fergusson has gone inadequately studied
or been misprized and belittled. This, it seems to me, at the present
critical juncture of Scots poetry, is the principal angle from which
Fergusson will repay reconsideration—and not Fergusson alone
as the best, if not (having regard to a few passages in our Gaelic
poets) quite the sole exemplar of this high note, but the whole
question of our national poetry. It amply justifies that curious,
and equally justified, tribute of Mr T. S. Eliot to Mr Ezra Pound
in our own day as *il miglior fabbro*, and Burns's tribute 'Inscribed
under Fergusson's portrait':

By far my elder brother in the Muse.

And above all it is of the most crucial consequence today when the renaissance of Scots poetry of the past thirty years shows a tendency to be short-circuited by the fear expressed in many quarters that some of our new makars are tending to fly too high (or, in other words, by a reassertion of that tendency to domesticate the issue which has always been the great curse of Scottish life and letters) — a tendency exemplified in an article by Mr William Montgomerie, the editor of *The Burns Chronicle*, when he writes: 'We must become more clear in our minds whether or not it is possible or desirable to attempt composition in Scots of anything more complicated than song lyrics. Half our lyric poetry, other forms of poetry, and prose may still be the preserve of English which is a much more developed language.'

But the same doubt might well have been expressed of the potentialities of the Italian vernacular of the thirteenth–fourteenth century, before Dante took it in hand. As Lord Kennet has recently remarked, 'Dante's language is molten metal, poured fresh and pure into the common mould of the metre from the fires of a vernacular which was unchilled by previous literary use', and he goes on to point out how the effort to regain a comparable freshness obliges Miss Dorothy L. Sayers in her Penguin Classics translation of the Comedy (the latest of more than fifty translations of it into English) 'to use a variety of styles and of vocabulary, ranging from the archaic to the colloquial, with sometimes an incongruous effect'.

Sir Ronald Storrs, commenting on the same translation, has said:

Dante (as Mr T. S. Eliot has so well shown) achieves his highest and strongest effects entirely without recourse to specifically poetic language. The more surely will the reader, as yet unacquainted with the relative homeliness of the original, begin by missing the romantic English vocabulary, enriched by our compensating wealth of Anglo-Saxon and Latin nuances. Miss Sayers strikes a bold mintage of words: '*Malbowge*' gives a suitably hideous idea of *Malebolge*, and the torture-'*bowges*' are frightening as a Brown House on the wrong side of the Curtain. At what precise points homeliness becomes colloquial, and colloquial 'slang', is a delicate question: suffice it that the more *lungo studio e grand amore* devoted by the reader, the less disposed will he be to cavil at some of Miss Sayers's more challengingly unacademic renderings.

The necessity to which Miss Sayers has been put—and the testimony of a whole sequence of English poets from Meredith, Hardy, Francis Thompson down to Gerard Manley Hopkins and Wystan Auden regarding that 'exhaustion of English for creative purposes' which has forced them to introduce archaic, technical, dialect and foreign elements of all kinds into their vocabulary— throws a revealing light on Mr Montgomerie's conception of English as 'a much more developed language'.

The passages in Fergusson in which I hear this rare music of national destiny include the following (from 'The Ghaists'):

> Black be the day that e'er to England's ground
> Scotland was eikit by the UNION's bond;
> For mony a menzie of destructive ills
> The country now maun brook frae *mortmain bills*,
> That void our test'ments, and can freely gie
> Sic will and scoup to the ordain'd trustee,
> That he may tir our stateliest riggins bare,
> Nor acres, houses, woods, nor fishins spare,
> Till he can lend the stoitering state a lift
> Wi' gowd in gowpins as a grassum gift;
> In lieu o' whilk, we maun be weel content
> To tyne the capital at three *per cent.*

down to the biting lines:

> How maun their weyms wi' sairest hunger slack,
> Their duds in targets flaff upo' their back,
> When they are doom'd to keep a lasting Lent,
> Starving for England's weel at *three per cent.*

Or his gibe in 'A Drink Eclogue' at Scots who

> ... o'er seas for cheaper mailins hunt,
> An' leave their ain as bare's the Cairn-o'-mount.

Or in his 'Elegy on the Death of Scots Music':

O SCOTLAND! that cou'd yence afford
To bang the pith o' Roman sword,
Winna your sons, wi' joint accord,
                    To battle speed,
And fight till MUSIC be restor'd,
                    Which now lies dead?

Or, most remarkable of all, and, though in English, still informed
by the directness of Scots utterance (from 'A Saturday's Expedi-
tion'):

On thy green banks sits Liberty enthroned
But not that shadow which the English youth
So eagerly pursue ...

Mr John Speirs in *The Scots Literary Tradition*[2] made a valuable
point when he stressed the evidence in Fergusson of vigorous local
resistance to Italian and French influences, a matter of no little
relevance at the present time when Edinburgh is the venue of
an International Festival of the Arts in which our native products have little or no place.

Fidlers, your pins in temper fix,
And roset weel your fiddle-sticks,
But banish vile Italian tricks
                    From out your quorum:
Nor *fortes* wi' *pianos* mix,
                    Gie's *Tulloch Gorum*.
                                        'The Daft-Days'

I like, too, the spirit with which he rejects empty flattery:

The rose shall grow like gowan yallow,
Before I turn sae toom and shallow,
                    And void of fusion,
As a' your butter'd words to swallow
                    In vain delusion.
                                        'Answer to Mr J. S.'s Epistle'

Again, Fergusson knows

                    —It aft hads true,
Wi' naething fock make maist ado:
                    'Mutual Complaint of Plainstanes and Causey'

and scorns the

> ... fools, newfangle fain,
> Like ither countries better than their ain.
>
> > 'A Drink Eclogue'

yet recognizes that a prophet has no honour in his own country, and cries,

> Yet I am hameil; there's the sour mischance!
> I'm no frae Turkey, Italy, or France.
>
> > 'A Drink Eclogue'

He seems to have foreseen the continued withering away of Scottish nationality under the English connection:

> Ah, CALEDON! the land I yence held dear,
> Sair mane mak I for thy destruction near.
>
> > 'The Ghaists'

while still stubbornly, if not hopefully, bent on his own course

> Till Scotland's out o' reach o' England's pow'r.

—all of which quotations anticipate elements which are clamorous in Scottish arts and affairs today.

Carlyle said that if Burns had been a better intellectual workman he might have changed the whole course of European literature. Burns did what Mr Montgomerie wishes our makers today would confine themselves to—'If children are taught the tunes and words of our folk-songs so well that Scottish youth can sing them as well as the youth of the more peasant countries of Europe can sing their own folk-songs, there may in time be recreated a tradition in which another Robert Burns could create to music.' Why Mr Montgomerie should wish to bog Scottish poetry in this permanent juvenility I do not understand, but he should not measure what is desirable or possible in Scotland by 'the more peasant countries of Europe', since Scotland is one of the most highly industrialized of countries, and the idea of concentrating on or confining ourselves to the kind of poetry Mr Montgomerie evidently covets is just as stupid and happily impracticable as the idea of undoing all our modern development, repudiating scientific progress and returning to an agrarian

Scotland. Our need and opportunity lie in precisely the opposite direction.

The course suggested by Mr Montgomerie is just that which had led from Burns through the hordes of his mindless imitators to phenomena like the late Sir Harry Lauder before the Scottish renaissance movement called a halt to the degenerative process and restarted the difficult contrary development. What Mr Montgomerie advizes, indeed, is what has led to that deplorable misprizal of Burns himself, which J. Hepburn Millar (in his *Literary History of Scotland*³) describes when he says:

> The inherent force and overpowering spirit of 'The Jolly Beggars' are perhaps sufficient to account for the inferior popularity of that 'cantata' as compared with 'Tam o'Shanter'. Had Burns swerved for one moment from the path of true craftsmanship, had he relaxed the severity of the artist and emitted the least whine of sentiment, had he dowered any one of his marvellous gallery of mendicants and mumpers with those virtues which draw the tear to the eye and the snuffle to the nose, 'The Jolly Beggars' might have stood first in the hearts of its author's countrymen as securely as it does in the estimation of those best qualified to form an opinion. But Burns was loyal to his artistic instincts, and consequently the rank and file of his adorers, while paying the usual quota of lip-service, are puzzled, and do not quite know what to make of a piece which Scott pronounced to be 'for humorous description and nice discrimination of character', 'inferior to no poem of the same length in the whole range of English poetry'.

The true evaluation of Fergusson as against Burns, save at Burns's rare best, as in 'The Jolly Beggars' — since Sir Herbert Grierson has pointed out the need 'to redress the injustice from which both Ramsay and Fergusson have suffered. Their stars paled unduly in the glow of Burns' — must be, first of all, from the angle I have just been indicating, which is that suggested by Hölderlin, when he writes: 'For the rest, love-songs are always a tired business, for, after all, we have got as far as that, in spite of differences in our material; the high and pure jubilation in national songs is a different thing altogether.'

Hölderlin, too, provides an invaluable clue to the most pro-
fitable approach to our subject when he reminds us (in a letter to
Bohlendorf, December 4th, 1801): 'Nothing is so difficult to
learn as the mastery over our natural national gifts.' Again, he
reminds us: 'It sounds paradoxical, but I repeat and leave it to
you to test in theory and practice, natural qualities always
become in the process of learning the lesser merit. On that account
the Greeks are less masters of sacred passions because it was innate
in them; on the other hand they are excellent at *representing* from
Homer onwards, because this extraordinary man was large-
minded enough to appropriate and make use of western Junonian
clearheadedness for his Apolline sphere, and thus truly to assimilate elements foreign to him.' With the Germans the opposite
was the case, and it was for that very reason necessary for them
to study the Greeks, both their nature and their art, in order to
gain knowledge of themselves and what should be the aim of their
art. 'But we have to win knowledge of our own faculties, just as
much as those of others. That is why the Greeks are indispensable
to us. Only we shall not be able to equal them in the qualities
natural to us, because, as was said already, mastery over one's
own nature is the most difficult of all.'

It was thinking along these lines that made me write the
poem, in *Lucky Poet*,[4] from which I quote these lines:

Alas! the thought of ninety-nine per cent of our people
Is still ruled by Plato and Aristotle
Read in an historical vacuum by the few
From whom the masses receive
A minimum of it but also, with that,
A maximum incapacity for anything else.
The Greek (being a Southerner) was (and still is)
By temperament excitable and easily roused
To excessive display of feeling. Greek troops we know—
    unlike Scots—
Were peculiarly liable to sudden panic,
And the keen intelligence of the race
Was no more rapid in its working
Than was their susceptibility to passion.
Wisely, therefore, the Greek moralists preached restraint;

Wisely they gave their impressionable countrymen advice
The very opposite of that
The more steady Northerner requires
And we in modern Scotland most of all!

Mr Montgomerie's argument, on the other hand, is accompanied by characteristic anti-intellectualism (e.g. 'our contemporary Scottish Renaissance is being forced too exclusively along bookish channels') and by the ridiculous plea that 'Scots is a peasant language, with a rural tradition in the main, and if there is going to be a live renaissance of Scots poetry it must be more in accord with the laws of such development', ridiculous because Scots is no more a peasant language than any other and need no more be confined to that level, while the reference to a 'live renaissance' suggests an entirely wrong conception of the necessary or desirable relationship of literature and life. Mr Montgomerie in fact is thinking of the kind of development which would be widely popular—not of the kind of development which would produce better (and therefore inevitably unpopular) poems. Scots poetry in fact needs to develop—and has been developing—in just the opposite directions to those suggested by Mr Montgomerie. It can hardly become too highly intellectual to offset its long restriction to maudlin sentiment, chortling 'wut' and 'matter of Habbie Simson'; it must become urbanized in keeping with Scottish life; and it is more than ever necessary to bring it into keeping with our political and social needs. The crux of the whole matter is, of course, the language question. It was for this reason that I wrote in *Albyn* a quarter of a century ago that 'Burns betrayed the movement Ramsay and Fergusson began' and quoted in *Lucky Poet* in entire agreement a correspondent who, commenting on that statement, wrote (with reference to Edwin Muir's *Scott and Scotland*):[5]

Even in Muir's treatment of Fergusson there is an astounding illogicality; his admissions—true enough—about Fergusson's mastery of language run quite counter to his thesis that Scots is since the Reformation no fit language for literature. But whatever it may be in Burns, who was careless, it is perfectly used by Fergusson. The moral is surely not to abandon Scots, but to study it as Burns did not, and Fergusson did, before using it.

As Robert Chambers wrote in the account of Fergusson in his *Biographical Dictionary of Eminent Scotsmen*: 'The language employed by Fergusson is much more purely Scottish than that of Burns, and he uses it with a readiness and ease in the highest degree pleasing. He has not the firm and vigorous tone of Burns, but more softness and polish, such as might have been expected from his gentler and perhaps more instructed mind.'

Every competent student of Fergusson has come to the same conclusion. J. Hepburn Millar in his *Literary History of Scotland* says of Fergusson: 'Had he lived longer, it seems not extravagant to suppose that he might have accomplished something inferior only to the very best of what Burns has left us, and, short though his career was, we can at least say of him that he helped with Ramsay to furbish up and refashion the instrument with which Burns was to achieve such astonishing effects.' The consensus of literary critics holds that wherever Scottish writers have written both in Scots and in English, by far their best work has invariably been done in the former. Fergusson is no exception, and Millar goes on to say: 'Fergusson's English verse, it need scarce be said, is poor and unimportant.' T. F. Henderson in his *Scottish Vernacular Literature*[6] says: 'Fergusson had a subtler knowledge of vernacular Scots than Burns — or rather his Scots was the Scots not of the rustic but of the educated classes, who made daily use of it in Edinburgh at even a later date.' Mr Edwin Muir goes even further, and rightly. 'Fergusson,' he points out, 'also attempted ambitious poems in dialect Scots, and succeeded better than Burns, for he was a more scrupulous artist and he used a more organic language. Fergusson's use of dialect Scots was infinitely more close and workmanlike than Burns's; one feels, indeed, that had he lived he might have continued, with his genius for words, to turn dialect Scots into a literary language, for it is evident from his poetry, as from no other Scottish dialect poetry, except the Ballads, that he is thinking in terms of the language he uses. But he died when he was twenty-three [sic]; and dialect Scots has never been used with equal solidity and exactitude and deliberate mastery since. "The Farmer's Ingle" is, in any case, a far better poem than "The Cotter's Saturday Night", which is roughly upon the same theme. The two poems, indeed, furnish excellent examples of the genuine and the false use of language.'

John Spiers in *The Scots Literary Tradition* says :[7] 'There seems good ground for the view that the fame of Burns has tended to deprive Fergusson of the attention he deserves and to obscure his peculiar merits ... In so far as Fergusson is different from Burns the difference is expressed by their individual use of the potentialities of the same inexhaustible language.'

Again, in comparing Fergusson and Burns, I find myself in agreement with what Cleanth Brooks in *Modern Poetry and the Tradition*[8] says of Burns, and contrast that with the directness of Fergusson's life and work, and his entire lack of any similar impurity :

Robert Burns will illustrate the extreme to which emphasis on the materials of poetry had been pushed by the end of the century. For Burns's popularity represents, in large measure, an interest in local colour and picturesque primitivism — interests not foreign to our own civilization. And Burns himself was not unwilling to play up to this interest. His frequent apologies for his ignorance and unconventionality fall somewhere between honest naïveté and knowing irony. Burns is never either the simple peasant on the one hand, nor on the other the craftsman who is ironically attacking the reigning conventions. There is a certain self-consciousness about his work that is perhaps not to be completely detached from shrewdness. It is an impurity which injures some of his more serious work. The strongest element in Burns is to be found in his efforts to absorb the conventionally unpoetic into poetry. But the attempt is not made in his more serious poetry; it is limited to the satires and to the lighter verse : for example, 'The Jolly Beggars,' 'To a Louse,' or 'Tam o' Shanter.'

If this praise of Burns as a satirist and writer of light verse seems wilfully perverse in view of Burns's reputation as a simple, artless poet, the poet of the heart, one must simply call for inspection of the poems in question. Ironically, for those who insist on 'nature,' it was not the romantic ploughman who restored liberty to the imagination, but the cockney

Blake. Blake represents, as Burns does not, the return to the daring of Elizabethan metaphor, to the use of serious irony, to a bold willingness to risk obscurity, and even to something very close to metaphysical wit.

In the same way Robert Graves writes about Burns in *The Common Asphodel* :[9]

One of the last surviving rewards of the poet as a privileged member of the community was that, whatever his birth, by writing acceptable poetry he became a gentleman; and this tradition obtained even in the narrowly aristocratic eighteenth century. Burns was, for a while at least, given the freedom of smart Edinburgh society and encouraged to write familiar epistles to members of the aristocracy. Poetical ideas and poetical technique have always been class-institutions, and poets born from the labouring or shop-keeping classes have with very few exceptions tried to elevate themselves by borrowing ideas and techniques to the enjoyment of which they were not born. Even revolutionary ideas are, by a paradox, upper-class ideas, a rebound from excesses of decorum. Burns's romantic sympathy with the French Revolution in its earlier stages could be read as a sign of natural good breeding, the gentlemanly radicalism of the literary *jeunesse*; the social gap between the crofters and the gentry was, moreover, not so wide in Scotland as in England, and he soon learned the trick of drawing-room writing. Keats, not being, like Burns or Clare, an obvious example of peasant genius, or an aristocrat like Shelley, always had difficulty in discovering his temperamental biases. The son of a tradesman, he could not afford to be politically so radical as those inferior or superior to him in class, though he went with Leigh Hunt as far as he dared. Blake, another tradesman's son, was also a radical: one of the few Englishmen who dared walk about London wearing a cap of Liberty. But Blake is the rare instance of a poet who could afford not to learn a class-technique: he was on intimate terms with the angels and wrote like an angel rather than like a gentleman. His radicalism was part of his personal religion, not, like Wordsworth's early radicalism, a philosophical affectation. If a man has complete identity with his convictions, then he is tough about them; if not, his convictions are a sentimental weakness, however strongly he may press them. The Romantic Revivalists were all spoiled as revolutionaries by their gentility. Blake was not one of them; he was a seer and despised the gentry in religion, literature, and painting equally, which is why there is little or nothing of his mature work that could be confused with that of any contemporary or previous writer. He neither forfeited his personality by submitting to any conventional medium, nor complained of the neglect of his poems by the larger reading public.

Fergusson was like Blake in this way, and entirely free of the confusions and contradictions found in Burns. I have said elsewhere: 'A study of Burns from the Marxist angle shows that Burns's poem of which "Such a parcel of rogues in a nation" is the refrain (1794) was, like "Scots Wha Hae" (1793), inspired by Thomas Muir's movement—which Burns himself lived to betray and attack [*vide* "Does haughty Gaul invasion threat?" (1795)]. I also think that Burns betrayed his own keenest realizations of the kind of poetry he should write, lapsing back on too easy models and compromising too much with English standards, since, as J. B. Caird has pointed out, "Burns's remarks on the song 'The Mill, Mill O' show that he had reached conclusions regarding poetic rhythm, without endeavouring to work them out systematically or to put them into practice, which in some respect anticipate those of Gerard Manley Hopkins."'

Fergusson 'regarded the union of his native country with England as a virtual sacrifice of her independence and her glory; even liberty itself he seemed to consider as but a phantom, unless it arose from the achievements of his country's patriots.' If we ask where Fergusson, dying so young, came by his amazing political insight and powers of historical synopsis and prolepsis, we recall that, during the last year of his residence at St Andrews, Fergusson 'had written two acts of a tragedy, founded on the story of Sir William Wallace ...' Burns said the story of Wallace had imbued him with a Scottish sentiment which would boil in his veins as long as life lasted, and a later Scottish genius who also died prematurely, Lewis Grassic Gibbon, had the same subject in mind. As William Power says in *Literature and Oatmeal*:[10]

> Blind Harry's *Wallace* has meant more to Scotland than Barbour's *The Bruce* ever did. By its appeal to the common people of Scotland it made amends for the desertion of the 'ill-requited patriot chief' by the self-seeking Anglo-Norman nobles who figure characteristically in Ragman Roll. It was from Blind Harry that Burns imbibed his Scots patriotism and also his democratic sentiment. Had Lewis Grassic Gibbon lived to write his projected book on Wallace, the world would have realized the magnitude and significance of a selfless hero who gave mankind a new ideal and fought and died for it. It was a blending of the old Celtic humanism of Scotland with the classic conception of freedom that Wallace had derived from his clerical tutors who retained the traditions of the old Celtic Church. Fergusson inherited it and expressed it clearly and 'without variableness or shadow of turning.'

Burns inherited it but in a debased form and his expressions of it suffer from the confused character of his political thought and his lack of integrity in many connections. And the consistency and force of Fergusson's democratic sentiments, his hatred of the rich and championship of the poor, completely outgo Burns's. For example, in 'The Ghaists':

> There's einow on the earth a set o' men,
> Wha, if they get their private pouches lin'd,
> Gie na a winnelstrae for a' mankind;
> They'll sell their country, flae their conscience bare,
> To gar the weigh-bauk turn a single hair.
> The government need only bait the line
> Wi' the prevailing flee, the gowden coin,
> Then our executors, and wise trustees,
> Will sell them fishes in forbidden seas,
> Upo' their dwining country girn in sport,
> Laugh in their sleeve, and get a place at court.

More important to Scots literature, however, is the fact that Fergusson led the way, still all too seldom and unsuccessfully followed, to that *Grosstadtpoesie*, that poetry of city life (of which other Scottish poets like Alexander Smith and John Davidson were among the pioneers, though this Scottish initiative was quickly taken up elsewhere and far more fully developed than it has yet been in Scotland) which is our major literary need today. Fergusson should be thoroughly restudied from this point of view. As Hepburn Millar said in his *Literary History of Scotland*:[11] 'The "Gowdspink" and the "Farmer's Ingle" notwithstanding, Fergusson is essentially the poet of the town, and that town Edinburgh. "Leith Races," "Caller Water," "Hallow-fair," "The Daft-Days," the "Address to the Tron-Kirk Bell," "The Mutual Complaint of the Plainstanes and Causeway,"* and his *Auld Reikie* are fundamentally urban. They waft to our nostrils a whiff from the wynds and closes, a blast from the taverns and merry meetings, of an old, unsavoury, battered but fascinating capital. Its whole life is described with some of Swift's ease and fluency (and some also of Swift's particularity in matters where detail is best avoided) in *Auld Reikie*.' Or, as T. F. Henderson said, 'all this very human, if not highly proper, aspect of the old burghal life is delineated with a sprightly wit and discernment which perhaps have never met with due recognition, especially from the generations of Fergusson's own fellow-citizens.' This urban poetry, and the recovery of a full canon of Scots adequate for all the purposes of modern literary expression, are, however, the growing-points of Scots literature today, and, as they are developed, Fergusson must at last come into his own and secure appreciation in respect of his real significance and seminal quality.

There is one other aspect from which I wish to discuss Fergusson's work—his astonishing power of direct statement in poetry; a quality of the Scots language which he used with mastery and which, of all its qualities, is, it seems to me, that which Scots poets of today, and tomorrow, stand most in need; the quality, in short, all too seldom exemplified in Burns but on occasion magnificently employed as, for example, in what I consider the most powerful line in all Burns's poetry:

Ye are na Mary Morison.

I remember W. B. Yeats and other Irish poets admiring to my astonishment a line in my 'Second Hymn to Lenin' which reads,

* Millar titles, *sic*.

Ye heard what I said!

and coveting the power of making such direct statements in
Scots, which cannot be done at all in modern English (though
Barnes, Doughty and others have achieved it in some of the
English dialects), and while completely removed from the whole
modern English conception of the 'poetic' can have a far greater
poetic power than any of the contrivances of English verbalism.

Before I go on to that, however, there is one other point which
must be made. In calling for a new songwriter, and presuming
to think that Scots poetry should confine itself to lyrics, Mr
Montgomerie has not heeded the wise comments of Edwin Muir
who, in his *Scott and Scotland*, writing of my own work, says on this
very point:

> Even admirers of Hugh MacDiarmid praise him chiefly for
> his first two books of lyrics, whereas easily his most original
> poetry is to be found in the long semi-philosophical poem, *A
> Drunk Man Looks at the Thistle.* They praise his lyrics at the
> expense of his poetry because they think that poetry should be
> simple and spontaneous, because there is an admirable canon
> of Scottish song in the simpler mode by keeping to which one
> cannot go far wrong or indeed far in any direction, and
> finally because their emotions speak one language and their
> minds another. If the English were to judge all their poetry
> by that, say, of Campion, they would be using a standard
> roughly resembling that which is used for Scots poetry indis-
> criminately.

Fergusson's mastery of Scots—which all the best writers on
the subject from Sir George Mackenzie down to Gregory Smith
agree is 'superior to English', albeit its great potentialities have
yet been little realized; his intellectualism and rare proleptic
faculty; and his wonderful pioneer work towards a *Grosstadtpoesie*
are all vitally important at the present juncture of Scots letters,
but most important of all is his power of direct statement, un-
adorned but passionate and penetrative as Hebrew eloquence.
This is one of the great qualities of the Scots (as of the Scots
Gaelic) language, unparalleled in any other European speech,
perhaps, since classical Greek. Scots used by a master can express

in very few words the heart of a matter in a fashion English can never encompass at all with all its verbalizing, and of which English in a greatly weakened form could only convey the 'meaning' in many times the number of words used in the original Scots. While Norman MacCaig has said in a recent essay that the plastic Scots (as it has been derisively termed) of our contemporary makars is a language which 'appears to be trying, with large and woolly gloves on, to pick up pins', *The Times Literary Supplement* tells us that Scots poetry in such recent volumes as *Collected Poems* of William Soutar,[12] *Wind on Loch Fyne* by George Campbell Hay,[13] and *Under the Eildon Tree* by Sidney Goodsir Smith[14] is indeed 'at last beginning to discard its woolly gloves and pick up pins' and achieving work which 'should please not only patriotic Scotsmen but intelligent lovers of poetry, who are not scared by a glossary, everywhere'. So far as the last named are concerned that is, in fact, what has happened—the acceptance and reputation of contemporary Scots poetry is developing extensively throughout the civilized world. Matters at home in Scotland are still much less satisfactory. Patriotic Scotsmen intelligent enough to be interested in poetry—that is to say intelligent enough to be really patriotic—are few and far between.

The Times Literary Supplement review dealt effectively with several arguments levelled recently by Norman MacCaig in one of his essays. Mr MacCaig pointed out that the expressiveness of the Scots vocabulary is limited by the fact that it is perhaps too entirely masculine and vigorous. 'At one extreme,' he wrote, 'when the mood of the writer is permitted to expand, flamboyance is apt to strut about on the stage prepared for power, and poetry gives up its place to rhetoric.' There is also, he suggested, a special technical danger of the Scottish poet, rummaging in the dictionary for roughly expressive words, packing these too closely together, with the result of achieving a comic over-expressiveness, 'bulging all over the place with ridiculous muscles', a danger which Mr MacCaig illustrated by a verse from Maurice Lindsay. It is, however, a canon of criticism that it must be based on a writer's best work, not on an occasional failure, and this solitary instance of grotesque verbal muscle-boundness on Mr Lindsay's part does not, as *The Times Literary Supplement* was careful to

point out, prevent Mr Lindsay's feeling for 'the concrete expressiveness of particular words' leading elsewhere to some of his most
successful poems; while it is also made clear that whatever
element of truth there may be in Mr MacCaig's first point, as
stated above, at least 'in Mr George Campbell Hay's most
expansive moments poetry does not give place to rhetoric'.

Mr R. Crombie Saunders made an effective reply to Mr
MacCaig's arguments in the *Scots Review*, above all when he pointed
out that 'the contemporary, occasionally explicit and nearly
always implicit, idea that poetry can be divided into "eloquence"
and the real Mackay (or "MacCaig," to give the devil his due)
would certainly be regarded as heresy by most of the great critics
of earlier ages', and that 'this singling-out of a specific "poetic"
element in poetry is dangerous in that its progenitors are likely
to prove to be Fashion and Predilection'.

All this is admirable, but there is more — and other — to be said
than Mr Crombie Saunders said in reply to Mr MacCaig's contention that there is a 'comparative poverty of image' throughout
Scots poetry as a whole, and that 'whereas outside of Scotland
modern poets are to an unprecedented degree image-conscious,
within Scotland they display a traditional poverty in this connection.' Mr MacCaig went on to argue that the preoccupation with
the image reflects contemporary sensibility, and that 'what
demands expression now ... insists on finding it in the form of
images'.

This is not the case. It is true that in most modern literatures
there are versifiers afflicted with image-mania, but while their
cult has its supporters and achieves no little publicity, its importance is quite another matter and its 'contemporaneity' still
another except in so far as the existence of Holy Rollers, Jehovah's
Witnesses and other such bodies might equally be held to justify
a contention that in religion what demands expression now
insists on finding it in such forms. There are, in fact, truths which
are best recognized by mediocre minds because they are best
adapted to them; but they do not exclude entirely opposite truths
which can only be recognized by the intellectual and spiritual
elite.

It is a long time now since writers so diverse and as important
as Walt Whitman, Stendhal and Matthew Arnold all insisted

that the poetry of the future must deal with fact, and must be stripped and direct and practically devoid of ornament, and, although Mr MacCaig may insist that image-poetry holds the field today, it can only be with reference to a very limited field in England and a few other countries that he could, if at all, substantiate that claim, and for a corrective to such a partial view Mr MacCaig may well be recommended to read Professor E. M. Butler's *The Direct Method in German Poetry*,[15] in which she asserts that the direct method is gaining ground everywhere in European poetry today—'something is happening to poetry because it is happening to life'—and contrasts with the transcendentalism to which Germany in particular has been so prone and which 'the spirit of this earth rejects' that kind of direct poetry which deals with matters, and in a way, immediately intelligible to most people.

Scotland is not in a like unhappy case to Germany's, however; and the 'widespread human appeal' of the direct method is in keeping with our whole national republican and radical tradition, and it is undoubtedly along that line that significant Scottish genius will continue, as in the past, to find its greatest expression, while, of course, the English distrust of 'over-intellectualism', exemplified in the complaint that Yeats had a 'quite un-English intensity and intellectualism', and in the depreciation of James Joyce on like grounds, should be a pointer to Scots—to proceed as rapidly as possible in the opposite direction to England in this, as in all other respects, and, so far as Ireland is concerned, to remember that, as was said twenty years ago, 'if Scotland is to have a national literary movement, it must begin at that highest point where any literary movement the Irish may have has finished.'

But apart altogether from that great human consideration, Scots poets in regard to all criticism of their comparative poverty in imagery, should hold to the Scots tradition of Fergusson and Burns in this respect (as in certain others), no matter what critics may say—and no matter how justified that criticism may be— just as the great French mathematician, Fourier, fully aware that he had done something of the first magnitude, ignored his critics. They were right, he was wrong, but he had done enough in his own way to entitle him to independence—and when his work was completed and collected in the treatise on heat-conduction in 1822, it was found that the obstinate Fourier had not changed a single word of his original presentations.

Contemporaneity in Mr MacCaig's sense is a poor criterion; there is in all the arts much work of delayed action; and what is completely foreign to the mainstream of practice at any time has been shown again and again to have had a strange power of asserting itself long afterwards as the only thing in its particular field that was of any real consequence, while all that was then generally accepted, and seemed to dominate the field in question beyond a peradventure, has been relegated to comparative and complete unimportance.

In his admirable pamphlet, entitled *The Scottish Renaissance*,[16] Maurice Lindsay has well said:

> Scots literature is made up of essentially popular ingredients — by 'popular' meaning 'of the people.' It still uses rhythms of folk-song origin to a great extent, and it gets its colour and strength from the speech of the working class, the broad mass of the folk from which all vital art must draw its sap. In Scotland, the literary traditions, like so much else, are at present fragmented. When Scotland gets back on to her psychological compass-point again, there should be a general revival of interest in national customs and traditions, including an appreciation of the value of the 'guid Scots tongue.' When this happens it will be found that Scots poetry, having developed the poetic statement rather than concentrated solely on elaborating the Anglo-French image-sequence, is much more likely to close the gap between poet and public than any other literature in Western Europe. There can, of course, be no question of writing down to the people. It is just that in point of fact the ingredients of Scottish literature are not of the more rarefied aesthetic varieties which have gone to make up 18th, 19th and 20th century English poetry.

Fergusson is one of the key-figures in that retention of the essential Scottish genius which has resisted all Anglification, and, while driven underground and for a long time apparently lost, is springing up again now with undiminished force. It may have a great deal to do yet in that 'changing of the whole course of

European literature' which is so obviously and urgently necessary, which Burns was, according to Carlyle, too poor an intellectual workman to accomplish, but which, given better fortune, Fergusson might well have done a great deal more to effect.

Among the final sentences of Ian Finlay's *Art in Scotland*[17] we read as follows:

> The Lallans [i.e. the lowland tongue as distinct from Gaelic] and/or synthetic Scots controversy, by focussing entirely on the medium, obscured the only really important point, that Scotland today possesses, in poets in Scots and in Gaelic, artists whose first aim is neither aesthetic nor obscurely psychological, but directed at the realities by which their country will stand or fall. In fact, there is stirring again something like that 'movement of extended curiosity' which achieved so much around the beginning of the nineteenth century, although this time the movement is not nation-wide. A few poets, and writers and artists, even a composer or two, are at last digging down to something so fundamentally Scottish that they need no longer self-consciously flaunt a thistle or paint the bens and glens to be recognized for what they are. But there is a great work of education to do before the people begin to realize what is happening among them.

And as part of that education it is particularly necessary that the Burns monopoly of Scots poetry should be broken, the whole tradition re-established in the minds of our people, and the fact made clear that Scots poetry no longer 'sleeps with Fergusson' but has reawakened, fully animated with his intrepid spirit, and determined at long last to exercise those great potentialities of the 'auld leid' which he died too young to do much more than adumbrate. It is not true that, as William Power claims,[18] 'Robert Fergusson was able, in the tragically few years that Fate allowed him, to perform the remarkable feat of giving Scots popular poetry a completely artistic form, while heightening its native characteristics.' To do that is the purpose of the Scottish renaissance movement today and of the growing body of younger Lallans makars in our midst. But Fergusson went a long way towards it, and our poets today could hardly have addressed themselves to this great task, or conceived it, but for Fergusson's example. For Mr Power's next sentence *is* true. 'Purely as a poetic artist,' he says, 'Fergusson ranks almost with Villon.'

The best corrective then to speculations like Mr Montgomerie's as to whether ambitious poems and not merely simple lyrics can be written in Scots is, apart from a fair number of successes on high and difficult themes by poets alive today, a competent re-reading and restudy of Fergusson's poems; the best corrective to the all-too-common disparagement of political poems is to reconsider first how large a proportion of the best poems in Scots (as in Gaelic) have always been political; and, finally, to reflect on the fact that it has always been substantially the same kind of politics, rebelling against established institutions and received ideas of all kinds and advocating and ingeminating revolutionary measures, that has informed all the best of these through the more than half a millennium of our poetic history to the present day, and, poetically, if not politically, has always found livelier, more straightforward and far more widely comprehensible and popular expression than is afforded by any comparable elements in English literature, or, so far as these are known to me, with rare exceptions, any other literature; so much so, indeed, as to convey the conviction that it is only in Scots (and Scots of an integrity like Fergusson's own) that such effects can be conceived and achieved; that here in fact the essential genius of the Scots language finds itself most surely and finds for itself a most important function in the contemporary world, the possibility of rendering a major service to poetry at this great turning point in human history.

14

ECONOMIC INDEPENDENCE FOR THE INDIVIDUAL

1952

The death at his home at Fearnan, Perthshire, on September 29th of Mr Clifford Hugh Douglas, originator of the Social Credit Scheme and author of *Economic Democracy, Plan for Scotland*,[1] and numerous other books in which he expounded his economic ideas, has removed from our midst one of the greatest Scotsmen of the past hundred years, and, in relation to his own subject, the greatest of all time. He was seventy-three years of age.

His social credit system (or a partial form of it) was tried out by Alberta, Canada, in the inter-war years and was so successful that social credit governments have not only continued to be returned there ever since but have consistently added to their majorities in the provincial legislature. Major Douglas was appointed chief reconstruction adviser to the social credit government of Alberta in 1935, but he was never in favour of the precise steps taken to apply social credit there, regarding the limited powers of a provincial legislature as unfavourable to a proper 'try out' of his system, and he resigned the following year. Recently British Columbia has also adopted a modified form of Douglas social credit.

There are few men who in their lifetime, acting simply and solely 'off their own bat' and not vested with government power, see their ideas give rise to a world-wide movement. Douglas was one of these few. Although for many years the 'powers that be' kept all mention of his name and discussion of his ideas out of every paper and periodical in the world except a few little-known organs of extremely limited circulation which existed for the specific purpose of promulgating Douglasism, his name won through in the 'thirties and led to the establishment of Social Credit Associations and study circles and active propagandist journals in all the continents.

Douglasism today is a live issue confronting every civilized government; it is pushing its way ahead and numbering its adherents by thousands in the United States, in Australia, and in Canada. Look over history; how many times do you encounter a single man building up a movement against all the strongest vested interests in the world? It is ample proof of Major Douglas's genius that he showed an amazing power of adapting himself to all the complicated circumstances affecting the promulgation of his discovery and stuck to his point, undeflected, 'with cool understatement', despite one of the most vigorous and prolonged press boycotts in the history of journalism, and, without compromising his position one iota, piloted the biggest revolutionary project in the history of humanity into a foremost place in the councils of every civilized country. For, make no mistake, however carefully the issue may be kept 'under the counter', it has been well enough recognized for the past twenty years at least to all the financial and political chiefs throughout the world.

Douglas was disappointed that his own country of Scotland was not the first to give his system a trial. He recognized of course that Scotland could not do so until it re-acquired independence and a parliament of its own. He was therefore one of the early members of the National Party of Scotland and published his *Plan For Scotland* to show how Scotland could adopt social credit as its economic policy. The National Party, however, missed this tremendous opportunity. Douglas himself was well enough aware of the debt he owed to previous Scottish thought on economic matters as well as to Scotland's traditional love of freedom and deep-seated radicalism. His system simply applied all these elements to contemporary purpose and carried them to fresh levels of achievement.

After all, as Ezra Pound has said, an earlier Scotsman had anticipated the realization that lies at the root of Douglas's system. It is expressed in the phrase I italicize in the passage in which Pound says: 'The Bank of England, a felonious combination, or, more precisely, a gang of usurers taking sixty per cent interest, was founded in 1694. Paterson, the founder of the Bank, clearly stated the advantages of his scheme: the bank hath the benefit of the interest on all moneys *which it creates out of nothing.*'

It was on this basis that Major Douglas erected his charge that the issue and withdrawal of credit by the banking system does not reflect the physical realities of production and consumption, and that the theory of money so applied effects a continual and increasing indebtedness of the community to the banks. One debt cannot be liquidated without incurring a greater one. That is the lever of the monopoly of credit. The 'Douglas Theorem' is that, owing to credit being treated as the property of the banks, a loan repayable on demand, instead of being administered as the money of the community held as a right, purchasing power is withdrawn from the public at a faster rate than it ceases to figure in the prices which the public has to meet if all its production is to be sold. That is to say, there enters into the costs of final products a fictitious element due entirely to the property conception of credit, an element which is fictitious in the sense that it does not represent the money equivalent of wealth consumed in making that product. In fact the amount of credit withheld from the community in this way is approximately the money value of the net difference between its total production (capital and ultimate goods) and its consumption (final products bought and depreciation of real capital).

This, it is claimed, is the irreducible cause of the inability to distribute the whole possible volume of consumable production, which increases as the proportion of power equipment to labour increases. Hence the defeat by money monopoly of any benefit which would accrue to humanity by the replacement of human energy by natural power in production. As the products of one set of processes cannot be sold by the purchasing power distributed in respect of those processes, industrialism has only survived at all because the unsaleable product of one period could be partly carried off by credit distributed for inaugurating further production.

But the day of reckoning, in the literalist sense of that word, has now come. And we are confronted with the logical but insane financial advice that the cure for an unsaleable surplus is more production or economy. This is the very crux of the money monopoly. However successful man is, in supplying his wants and saving his limbs, he must enjoy no relaxation of economic activity. In Major Douglas's words, as a mechanism for making work the financial system is as near perfect as possible; but as a means of distributing the products of what is now predominantly a natural-power productive plant, it fails completely. In fact that is not its objective.

Major Douglas was not, however, prepared to accept this 'philosophy' of economic activity as the chief end of man, and consequently made proposals for the return of credit to the people and the issue of national dividends as each citizen's share in the benefit of natural-power production. Major Douglas's proposals were in fact designed to answer the question which with all their talk of freedom this and liberation that, the B.B.C. and all the press and politicians ignore, namely; *And the liberty of not getting into debt — how about that?* A nation that will not get itself into debt drives the usurers to fury.

Mazzini, in his *Duties of Man*, recommended 'the establishment of public storehouses or depots from which, the approximate value of the commodities deposited having been ascertained, the Associations would issue a document or bond, similar to a bank-note, capable of circulating and being discounted; so that the Association would be able to continue its work without being thwarted by the need for quick sales.' Mazzini spoke, too, of a 'fund for the distribution of *credit*', thus anticipating Major Douglas's theories. 'The distribution of this *credit*', Mazzini continues, 'should not be undertaken by the Government, nor by a National Central Bank; but, with a vigilant eye on the National Power, *by local Banks administered by elective Local Councils.*'

Listen to what Douglas himself said in a passage that strikes the very keynote of his philosophy (and incidentally aligns him with all that is best in Scottish thought from the Declaration of Arbroath to the present day) :

There probably never was a time in which disinterested legislation was so rare, just as there probably never was a device which was so effective in silencing criticism of interested legislation as this idea that self-interest on a worldly plane must necessarily be wicked. I would therefore make the suggestion, in order to add to the gaiety of nations by creating a riot at once, that the first requisite of a satisfactory governmental system is that it shall divest itself of the idea that it has a mission to improve the morals or direct the philosophy of any of its constituent citizens. Sir Walter Fletcher said: 'We can find safety and progress only in proportion as we bring our methods of statecraft under the guidance of biological truth.' I think that this is one of those remarks which illuminate a subject much as the sky-line is illuminated upon a dark night by a flash of summer lightning. *We know little about ourselves, and less about our neighbour, and almost nothing at all about the nature of a healthy Society. Nor do we display any particular anxiety to increase our knowledge in these directions.*

Yet there is, nowadays, none so poor that he is not prepared to produce at short notice the plans which will put every human being in his place, within the space of a few short weeks. Preferably with the aid of a few good machine-guns. It is no less than a tragedy that *the inductive method, for which in particular the English temperament is specially suited*, is not in itself a reliable instrument in this emergency. The physical scientist, who wishes to obtain a sure foundation for the formulation of laws, begins by standardizing his re-agents. Temperature would be meaningless if we had not something we call 'zero'. But in regard to biology, we are in a difficulty. We do not even know how unhealthy we are, though we have a strong suspicion that we are very sick indeed. To those, then, who are anxious to make a definite contribution to the salving of a sick world, it may not be impertinent to suggest that the natural creative forces of the universe might plausibly be expected to produce at least as good results if left alone to work themselves out through the agency of the individual, as may be expected from planning which is undertaken without any conception of the relation of the plan to the constitution and temperament of those who are affected. If all history and all observation has not been misread, there is implanted in the individual *a primary desire for freedom and security, which rightly considered are forms of the same thing*. There is no such thing as a freedom and security which is held upon terms, whether these terms are dictated by the State, by a banking system, or by a World Government. Until it can be shown that, with the resources which science has placed at his disposal, the individual is incapable of making freedom and security for himself, this multiplication of organizations whose interference he cannot avoid will only make a world catastrope the more certain.

The values to be safeguarded in the Douglas Commonwealth are liberty, leisure, and culture. The will-to-plenty of the individuals is to be given satisfaction, and the whole business and industrial life of society relegated to a subordinate place, somehow as in the economy of the human body many biological processes proceed automatically or semi-automatically, leaving the psychology of the human being free to develop its interests.

Systems were made for men, not men for systems, declared Major Douglas in the first chapter of his first book, and the interest of man, which is self-development, takes precedence over all systems, economic, political or theological. A ringing statement to come from an economist!

No wonder the newspapers gave him less obituary space than they accord to any film star or Yankee crooner. Douglas himself would not have been surprised at all. His entire propaganda was founded on the centuries-old recognition of the fact that *nescis, mi fili, quantilla prudentia mundus regatur* (you know, my son, with what a small stock of wisdom the world is governed). And he might well have explained at any time during the twenty-odd years of our friendship as another friend of mine did, viz.: 'God knows what gets into all governments at certain stages of their existence. It's easy to understand why Arab princes surround themselves with incompetents, eunuchs, dolts and degenerates, for Arab princes consider themselves infallible: whatever they do must of necessity be right. Consequently they elevate childhood friends or toadying relatives to the most important posts in their kingdoms. But only God knows why such things happen perpetually in countries regarded as politically enlightened, like England, France, America supposedly governed by patriotic men. Yet they always have happened, and with horrifying frequency; the pages of history are sprinkled with dolts, idiots, drunkards maintained in the highest offices—mediocrities whose stubborness has sacrificed armies, whose blindness has destroyed navies, whose bad judgment has ruined their countries' prestige, starved helpless people by the million, wrecked cities, toppled arts, civilization, learning and understanding in the dust—and most of these fools' names hold unsullied place in the lying annals of their respective nations.'

Major Douglas's name belongs to a different and extremely small list, not known at all to the newspapers or the masses of mankind, who are Bing Crosby's fans or Danny Kaye's or the Duke of Edinburgh's. An engineer whose blueprints were all designed to bring about *the economic independence and complete freedom of the individual.*

15

NORMAN DOUGLAS*

1953

George Norman Douglas, a name he never used, preferring to call himself simply Norman Douglas, one of the greatest Scottish writers of the last hundred years, born of old Scottish stock at Tilquihillie by the Dee on December 8th, 1868, died at Capri on February 8th, 1952. In the year since his death, two admirable studies of his personality and writings have been published. They are *Norman Douglas* by H. M. Tomlinson,[1] and *Norman Douglas* by R. M. Dawkins.[2] They have something in common in that both are enlarged and revised editions of studies originally published over twenty years earlier. In other words Douglas's literary stature had been an open secret for all that time. He was known and appreciated only in small exclusive literary circles — and in his own country of Scotland hardly at all.

As matters stand he is not even mentioned in studies of modern Scottish literature, like, for example, Dr Harvey Wood's. This is a distinction of being left out of account he shares with another great Scottish writer who has always been caviare to the general — Mr R. B. Cunninghame Graham. This is no new story, nor is it confined to belles-lettres. It applies equally to an artist like Charles Rennie Mackintosh, to great educationists and thinkers like Sir Patrick Geddes and Thomas Davidson, and to a composer like Francis George Scott. Scottish approval in modern times has been strictly reserved for the tenth-rate. To acquire any considerable reading public in Scotland one must write so as to give readers that mistaken impression which I am sure accounts in great measure for the place accorded to Burns in Scottish affection — the impression, namely, that they could almost, or with a little application, have written the same sort of thing themselves. The majority of Scots seem to want only writers whom they can feel

* A talk broadcast on the Scottish Home Service of the B.B.C. on February 16th' 1953. *Editor*.

are as like themselves as two peas—and the majority of popular
Scottish writers of no literary consequence at all are precisely like
that. 'Propitious for blockheads' as Professor Sainsbury put it.
Alas! I do not think there is any other Western European country
subject in anything like the same degree to the tyranny of mediocrity. We all know the phrase about the 'export of brains' being
our principal industry, and agree that the unparalleled drain of
emigration on our population creams off the most energetic and
enterprising of our stock, but we are not willing to recognize the
mental and moral debility of what is left. Quite a number of
writers like the late Lewis Grassic Gibbon and Mr George Blake
have complained—and rightly—of the tendency in Scotland to
belittle an author because 'I kent his faither'. But it might be
thought that writers, not actually living in Scotland and subject
to its vicious parochialism, but already of high repute in more
civilized countries, would be immune from that sort of disparagement. Not a bit of it. Reputations achieved in Italy and France
count for nothing in Scotland itself.

There are two other reasons for hostility or indifference to
Norman Douglas apart from his being at the opposite pole from
the kailyaird. The first of these is his interest in the physical
sciences and the extent to which he used that knowledge in his
creative writing, and the second is his versatility—always an
offence to mediocre people who know how difficult it is to do
anything of any consequence along one line even and are accordingly affronted when they find a man who can work successfully
along a lot of different lines.

For forty years Norman Douglas wrote no more than an occasional pamphlet mainly on natural history and biology. While his
interests were so remote from those of the average man, and much
of his youth was spent in Austria, and nearly all the rest of his life
was spent on the shores of the Mediterranean, even in these
respects he is a typical enough 'Wandering Scot' and Mr Tomlinson is right when he says that although as a Scot he was remote
from the kailyaird,

at the same time he remained a son of the granite hills and
the heather, and had the national aptitude for a sword in a
lost cause, back to the wall, while provoking his enemies in

cruel humour. In English letters, which he honours, perhaps the best place for Norman Douglas is not in one of the conventional categories, but with that group of aristocratic Scots which has the translator of Rabelais, Sir Thomas Urquhart as its original. He rejected Christianity and Socialism with contumely; and his indications of the springs of several more of our tendernesses and national prejudices were indelicate and painful.

Norman Douglas described himself when he said of Mr Keith in *South Wind*[3], 'Facts were his prey. He threw himself into them with a kind of piratical ardour; took them by the throat, wallowed in them, worried them like a terrier, and finally assimilated them.'

We have a great deal of sentimentality and humanistic rubbish and hangovers from the past of all kinds to get rid of yet in Scotland, but Douglas will rank in many respects as the first Scottish writer to be really modern. Nor is he less Scottish for that than all the Weary Willies who carry all the accepted marks of what is generally regarded as genuine Scottishness. On the contrary he is all the more clearly and indisputably Scottish for his complete lack of these out-of-date characteristics—though one must have an extensive and thorough knowledge of Scottish history and literature to appreciate that fact—and any Scottish writer in the future not obliged or content to confine himself to an audience of idiots will be grateful to him for his lead and glad to follow in his footsteps, away from all the tribal taboos and museum junk and assorted mumbo-jumbo which fill the gulf between the vast majority of our people and any appreciation either of science or art.

If he came late to the writing of his books he came ripe, and turned out in the second half of his life an astonishing variety and wonderful excellence of work. Apart from shorter essays, he published five travel books—*Siren Land*, about the Sorrentine peninsula and the Naples area: *Fountains in the Sand*, a Tunisian book, *Old Calabria*, *Alone*, which describes his solitary travels about Italy, and *Together*, the story of his return to Austria with a young friend. It has been well said of these five books that 'they are all masterpieces and set a new style to that rather hackneyed form, a style which has been extensively imitated but never perhaps equalled'. In each of these five books he takes as his subject the total nature of the area concerning which he writes, its history, its customs, its geology, fauna and flora, its religious beliefs and its pleasures, and, selecting what he will, spins his remarkable erudition about his personal reminiscences of these places, though he never thrusts his own personality into the foreground. He moves with masterly ease, with smooth transition, from subject to subject, writing of each with that urbanity which is the counterpart of his witty and elegant style. Perhaps the secret of the beauty which lies in those books is the obvious love he felt for the peoples and the countrysides of which he wrote. It is a true love, never a patronizing aren't-the-natives-quaint sentimentality, and thus he can write with irony and even with anger on occasion.

Of his best-known book, his first novel, *South Wind*, it has — I think justly — been called 'the most amusing and civilized novel to appear in the English language since *Tristram Shandy*'.

The range of his interests and the wit and learning and beauty of his prose is to be found in all his other books. Let me only recall that he did not like the way of life of the English people — he spoke of the 'industrial eye' that one sees in Oxford Street faces, and even the natural beauties of the English landscape did not appeal to him: 'too green,' he once remarked, 'like living in a salad.'

All his life he preserved a strong antipathy to the messy, the emotional, the mystical. I think he expressed the reason why most Scots are so incapable of appreciating his work when he said, 'Enclosed within the soft imagination of the Mediterranean man lies a kernal of hard reason. We have reached that kernal. Contrariwise the Northerner's hardness is on the surface; his core, his inner being, is apt to quaver in a state of fluid irresponsibility.' And the final word about Norman Douglas himself in this respect, which so utterly differentiates his work from that of nearly every other modern Scottish writer, may be left to Mr Tomlinson, who puts it perfectly when he says,

He had a scientific and not a literary training, though his predilections were for the arts, and that gives his prose a ring of honesty, as though from sound and polished metal, designed for its purpose, its progress ordained, simple and clear if somewhat bleak, and with a glitter in it never seen in what is instinctive and amorphous.

16

ENCOURAGING THE CREATIVE ARTS

1953

I

One of the aims of the Dunedin Society, of which I am president, is to encourage the creative arts in Scotland. The emphasis is on the adjective *creative*. What do we mean by it? As soon as that question is asked we find that almost everybody assumes that *creative* is synonymous with cultural or experimental or simply new and that there is little or no agreement as to what is actually any of these or as to its value. All sorts of societies profess to some extent to have the encouragement of the arts as their aim or one of their aims but all they do is pay a certain amount of lip-service to that object while all they actually succeed in achieving is something quite different. Thus the Scottish Centre of the P.E.N. Club degenerates into a social club, what discussions it has are simply the tittle-tattle of writers of no consequence whatever, and anything in the nature of a thoroughly sustained and searching consideration of any aesthetic problem or in a wider sense any aspect of the national cultural problem is out of the question. The Saltire Society is no better; it is concerned with certain foibles, especially of a backward-looking character (e.g. the preservation of ancient buildings, the provision of cheap new editions of Scottish classics, the encouragement of craft-work and so on). Even our leading newspapers, *The Scotsman* and the *Glasgow Herald*, have not a single critic of any standing writing for them whether on literature, music, drama, or painting, and, with ample space at their disposal, give no encouragement whatever to our contemporary writers. The remarkable developments of a literary movement in the West Indies have owed a great deal to the encouragement given to the new writers by the local newspapers, but nothing similar is available in Scotland. What poetry or descriptive prose is published in these quarters is invariably of a transpontine sort and by writers of no consequence.

Newspapers of a similar standing in the English provinces have encouraged local writers and have frequently had on their staffs critics of one or other of the arts of a national or even international calibre. But in Scotland, to have achieved such an independent reputation is sufficient to debar a man from any employment, staff or free-lance, on any of our papers. The universities and our teaching profession as a whole are just as little to be looked to for any help in this matter. So is the B.B.C. The position in Scotland in regard to all these agencies is further complicated by the fact that whereas English literature is accorded a virtual monopoly a consensus of critics agrees that wherever Scottish writers write in Lallans or Gaelic as well as in English, their best work is invariably done in the former. Not only so, but a succession of leading English critics from Coleridge to Sir Herbert Read have recorded their view that no Scottish writer, writing in English, has made any contribution of an essential and indispensable character to the mainstream of English literature. In these circumstances our university staffs, school teachers etc. are all engaged in an all-pervasive cultural Quislingism which confines the efforts of Scottish literary aspirants to a field in which they can only display a permanent inferiority, while, on the other hand, all these agencies are lined up to prevent any concentration on our real national heritage and on those media of expression in which better work could be achieved.

In regard to the other arts, we find equivalent handicaps. In mere speech there has been much controversy lately about the particular class brand of English favoured by the B.B.C. A great deal of time is accorded, on the Third Programme, to English literature—but none to Scottish. Talks are given on countless aspects of aesthetics from the English standpoint—but none from the very different Scottish standpoint. In Scotland itself the Home Service eschews serious talks on cultural subjects, gives little or no space to new Scottish poetry, imaginative prose, or drama above the 'kitchen farce' level. Why is this? Is it, as the late William Power asserted, because any serious concern with the arts is inimical to the way of life of most Scots? Or is it because of the conflict of genius and talent? What is that conflict? It is simply the fact in relation to the arts that 'the good is the enemy of the best'. Talented people are numerous, genius is rare. Under our peculiar democracy all the former want an innings and resent any concentration on the latter.

It is for this reason that in modern times Scotland has so persistently preferred the inferior. This has been exemplified ad nauseam in all the arts. That is why Charles Rennie Mackintosh, while in the forefront of the artists of his time and exerting a tremendous influence in Europe, got so little encouragement in Scotland itself. In education the same thing happened to Sir Patrick Geddes and to Thomas Davidson—both thinkers and teachers of genius and worth thousands of ordinary university teachers or school teachers. There are always pushful nonentities ready to usurp the place that should be held by the few who really matter. That is why people like the late Sir Hugh Roberton and Mr Herbert Wiseman occupy a far more prominent place in the Scottish musical world than composers of genius like Francis George Scott or Erik Chisholm. That is why, too, on the concert platforms or on the radio, singers achieve reputation by singing the same old songs over and over again. The public suffers from a repetition complex. The cause is commercial at bottom. These singers are simply 'playing to the gallery'. Unless they did so they would get no engagements.

What can be done about this state of affairs? Can a technique for the development of genius be devised, or even a technique for recognizing it when it does appear? Professor Hayek has recently published a book dealing with the need for genius as the outstanding human desideratum—genius, not talent. Biologists, like Professor H. J. Muller, tell us that the majority of people today should be of the stature of the greatest in human history—the calibre, say, of Plato, Shakespeare, Goethe, Leonardo, and so forth. Why, then, are they not? Why, instead of being of that calibre, are they for the most part completely divorced from any share in the arts, let alone any ability themselves to produce work of significance in any of them? The reasons can be set out in a few short paragraphs and in a further paragraph or two it can be shown that this state of affairs not only can be overcome but that it is the prime need of mankind to overcome it. This is not to underestimate the 'powers and principalities of darkness' which are opposed to any such development of the human spirit, but simply to identify these powers and principalities and the reasons for their continued sway over the vast majority of humankind.

But, suffice it to say here that Professor A. N. Whitehead was right when, in *Science and the Modern World*,[1] he emphasized as the greatest human need today that 'organic apprehension' which is the characteristic of the arts, and, again, that Ford Madox Ford was right when he wrote:

> The only human activity that has always been of extreme importance to the world is imaginative literature. It is of supreme importance because it is the only means by which humanity can express at once emotions and ideas. To avoid controversy I am perfectly ready to concede that the other arts are of equal importance. But nothing that is not an art is of any lasting importance at all, the meanest novel being humanly more valuable than the most pompous of factual works, the most formidable of material achievements, or the most carefully thought out of legal codes.

It can be said without hesitation, however, that there is one prerequisite to 'putting' proper emphasis on the creative faculty in our national life and encouraging its increased emergence. When Fourier was in charge of the most advanced educational establishments in France after the revolution, he got a law passed forbidding the appointment to the head of the mathematical department in any of the colleges, with which he was concerned, of anyone who had not made a substantive creative contribution to the science of mathematics. The result of this was a period of France's greatest contributions to mathematics. This example should be followed in all our higher educational establishments. People should not be allowed to hold professorships, lecturerships, or teaching posts, in relation to any of the arts who, prior to appointment, had not themselves contributed original work of a certain high level of value to that subject. That would cut out all the 'dead wood' and have an immensely stimulating effect along the right lines on our students and school-children.

Anything short of that simply hands over these subjects to parasites on our past, artists manqués, and, in general, people with no real understanding since they lack any creative gift themselves and (consciously or unconsciously) hate it in others.

II

In a recent broadcast, Emrys Humphreys said:

> It is not too soon to say that Joyce saved us from being
> smothered in the spurious; without Joyce, Eliot and Pound,
> the atmosphere of English literature today would be that of
> the bar of a suburban golf club. Honest, serious, sensitive
> communication would have become practically impossible ...
> The conditions of our time are fiercely inimical to the practice
> of the arts. Art; the very word invokes derision, contempt,
> suspicion, impatience.

It is not only the subhuman masses—monstrously large,
frighteningly gullible, defenceless as a jelly-fish—who hate the
creative arts. I blame more the so-called educated classes who
pay a little lip-service to the arts but whose objective interests are
bound up with the present set-up, whereas, in Thomas Hardy's
words (true not only of literature but the other arts too), 'Literature is the written expression of revolt against *all accepted things*'.

When, with characteristic English rudeness, Mr Winston
Churchill stigmatizes Scottish Nationalists as Scotland's silliest,
and Lord John Hope terms them 'a lunatic fringe', it is necessary to
remember that not only genius but unpopular purpose of any kind
is apt to be regarded as 'silly' or 'lunatic' by that great mass of
people who exemplify what John Stuart Mill called 'collective
mediocrity' which he considered the great blight of the nineteenth
century. It may be wondered what he would have thought of our
own, which is certainly infinitely worse. In this 'collective mediocrity' and those who truckle to it, who regard Churchill as 'the
greatest man now living' and speak of him as if he had won the two
great world wars single-handed. Churchill may have gone up like
a rocket—but he will certainly come down like the stick.

As to Churchill's tribute to 'the greatness and splendour of
Scotland and the part it has played in history', he may give with
the right hand occasionally but he takes away far more with the left
hand. The general appeal of such remarks as Churchill's and Lord
John Hope's is away from genius in favour of the 'normal citizen',
the 'average man'. Let us look at this creature a great American
scientist, Dr Trigant Burrow, has recently written of as follows:

Let us look into this attitude of normality, so-called, upon which individuals and communities commonly pride themselves. The traditions of normality are preserved in literature, art, religion and philosophy. Its tenets are securely embalmed within the structure of the law. It is the warp and woof of politics, the *raison d'être* of psychiatry, the foundation of our educational systems. It enjoys the solemn endorsement of Church and State. Among all individuals, professional as well as lay, among all groups and all communities, it is 'normality' that regulates and determines the behaviour of family, home, and country.

As a gauge of inter-individual conduct, 'normality' bears no dependable relation to reality, but is supported only by capricious community preconceptions. What is more, normality as now constituted is sustained by a secret and unconscious prerogative that jealously preserves its partisan viewpoint against all inquiry. The shrine of normality at which all of us devoutly worship must on no account be examined into. The old-time religion is good enough for normality, and any investigation into its sacred rites and ordinances is taboo. For, in its hidebound conditioning, normality is always 'right', and the least infringement upon this interrelational mode of feeling and thinking calls forth a reflex defence-reaction in individual and community.

As to the variability and inconsistency of the standards of normality, examples are legion. We are supposedly a democratic country, but we are largely ruled by professional lobbyists. Overtly we support a war for world-unification, but our ulterior intention leans strongly to the side of nationalism. Everywhere codes of morality are juggled beyond recognition. Divorce was formerly anathema, but today no stigma whatever attaches to it.

'Normality' is the great enemy genius must always fight. It is because of this that so many of those who have contributed greatly to the arts and the sciences have always been scorned and opposed by 'ordinary folk' and regarded as freaks. It is because of this that prophets have no honour in their own country. It is this that coins the phrase 'lunatic fringe' to describe what dares to differ from itself, that huge mass of ignorance and stupidity that hangs like a millstone about the neck of mankind.

A correspondent in *The Scotsman* the other day said of that part of the Leaving Certificate paper in higher art, which is termed 'History and Appreciation of Art', that

> the subject can be mugged up and disposed of by any moderately gifted pupil (given, of course, a moderately intelligible paper!) without his ever having seen an original work. There is, indeed, no reason (except administrative ones) why a totally blind pupil should not sit and pass this part of the examination. As for the appreciation aspect, the first requirement is sensibility, which can only be liberated and fostered by direct experience of originals or first-class repro-ductions. The history of art bears the same relation to art as the history of religion to religion. It is quite easy to acquire knowledge from books and to appear learned in art and yet be devoid of sensibility and judgment. This kind of know-ledge is on a par with learning about French poodles; once you know the points to look for it is easy to apply the informa-tion and become passably adept as a dog fancier.

Our schools and universities are doing nothing but turning out thousands of people annually who have 'acquired the patter' in this way and pose as authorities without having any real apprecia-tion of, or live interest in, let alone any creative ability with regards to, literature and the arts at all. As Mr T. Elder Dickson has said: 'A turgid and baseless intellectualism is no tribute to a "sacred virtue" from which have sprung the greatest and most enduring monuments of mankind long before education became a State responsibility and (as in these days) the badge of the clever.'

That is why I condemned our educational system and advised that our schools should be scrapped when I addressed the Annual Conference of the Saltire Society. My own special interest is in literature, and what is true of the other arts is still more generally true of literature that the whole mass of so-called educated people think they are ipso facto qualified to pontificate about it, and do so continually.

But the sad fact is (as Mr John Raymond has said on the B.B.C. Third Programme):

> Our attitude to the literature of the past is almost invariably a kind of genteel idolatry. Instead of asking questions of our great writers we approach them with a pious irrelevancy that makes our reading of their works resemble a tourist's pilgrimage to Stratford-on-Avon. Their books lie on our shelves to be respectfully neglected as so many cultural 'household gods,' or invoked as totems to ward off the onslaughts of history. We retire into the cosy warmth of Trollope's England or throw ourselves on the flat bosom of Aunt Betsey Trotwood to get away from the horrors of our day and age. At its best this kind of literary appreciation results in the sort of critical biography at which English men-of-letters excel. At its worst it leads to the arch parlour-game that we all know so well — the analysis of Branwell Brontë's influence on Charlotte, the discussion of the comparative merits of Jane Austen's heroines ... There is something almost indecent about the way in which we rediscover our great writers, remembering them in their centenary years, recalling their eccentricity and charm, their picture in the National Portrait Gallery, their niche in the Columbarium of genius. The French rediscover their great writers all the time, but with them such rediscovery is a living intellectual process, a continual restatement of the moral 'Great Debate' which has to be fought out in each generation.
>
> Since I first read it, I have been haunted by a kind of parable in M. Sartre's *What Is Literature*, which I think expresses the peculiar danger facing English literary criticism today. 'It must be borne in mind that most critics are men who have not had much luck and who, just about the time they were growing desperate, found a quiet little job as cemetery watchmen ...'

Cemetery watchmen! That goes for at least ninety-nine per cent of all our university professors and lecturers, our teachers, our newspaper book reviewers and art and music 'critics', our B.B.C. men, and all those so-called educated people who in our midst express themselves on the subject of literature and the arts.

The result is that if they told the truth any of that ninety-nine per cent would need to say: 'I conveyed the impression that I had brains and was a sharp character. I don't know how I did that; but I did it. It was all false, phoney as the gold brick you buy on a train. I have no brains and I'm not sharp. I'm a pretty average sort of clunk — and that's giving myself the best of it. I have no more idea of what the score is than the next man. I never learnt anything, never read anything. I never had time. All I ever did was to run round, keeping up the false impression of being smart. I had a few successes. But do you know how I earned them? Not through being smart, not through making things add up or reasoning anything out. I was successful simply because I could listen. Few people can listen. But I could and did listen. Listen and you learn all. But even that was phoney. I didn't listen because I wanted to. It was just because I was so goddamned bored with myself that I'd rather listen to others than talk about myself. That's all. A trick, a fake! I float along in a blissful cloud of illiterate fumbling. I know nothing, get no ideas. And people think I'm clever. A lot of intelligent people. Funny, isn't it?'

17

TOWARDS A CELTIC FRONT

1953

While still insisting on remaining 'non-political' the Celtic Congress during its recent sessions in Scotland showed that a new determination is manifesting itself among the delegates to establish a more dynamic common policy throughout the Celtic nations. This is only common sense. The whole range of social, cultural, and practical issues in all the countries involved has much in common, and while there need be no party-political development, it is clear that the future of the Celtic languages and the Celtic way of life can only be guaranteed by a substantial measure of autonomy in each of these countries, together with a common policy and thorough-going co-operation by all of them.

It is too frequently assumed that the Celtic languages are doomed. While it is true that the number of native Gaelic speakers in Scotland is small and steadily shrinking and that only a very small percentage of these are monoglot, the fact remains that there were never so many people learning Gaelic, and enthusiastic about its preservation, in Scotland as there are today. Mr Oliver Brown's article, in a recent issue of this *Scottish Journal*, on the diversion of funds from the Gaelic department in Edinburgh University and the unsuitable character of recent occupants of the Gaelic chair there—themselves unable to speak Gaelic—showed clearly enough that the changes in our national economy, and even the constant pressure of Anglicizing influences, does not entirely account for the parlous position of our ancient language today. Despite provisions on paper for Gaelic teaching, there is systematic sabotage in official quarters which make these provisions virtually a dead letter.

The root of the trouble in the educational field is the practice of teaching Gaelic through the medium of English. This is a fatal policy. Oil and water do not mix. The situation cannot be divorced either from the social context. An Comunn Gaidhealach draws too big a proportion of its leadership from the upper class who spend too much of their time in London 'society' and who, while paying lip-service to Gaelic, are inclined to keep it as a private hobby rather than work sincerely and systematically for the extension of its use. Above all these people are mostly far too backward-looking. Again, while there has been during the past few decades a succession of Gaelic poets of a quality unequalled since the glorious period round about 1745, these people have done little or nothing to encourage such true poets as Donald Sinclair, William Livingston, Sorley Maclean, George Campbell Hay, and Derick Thomson, but have preferred to stick in the muddy rut of moralistic *bardach*—which means that they have done just what our Lallans writers would have done if they had been content to wallow in the kailyaird and sedulous not to rise above the standards of verse of the *People's Friend*.

What applies to poetry applies also to drama. As the Hon. Ruaraidh Erskine of Marr observed:

> There has come down to us no example of Gaelic literary talent in true dramatic form, and such modern plays as have been written do not support the notion that the authors of them are conversant with any stage, save perhaps the English, or are well-grounded in ancient Gaelic literature. We must, therefore, set aside these modern Gaelic essays at playwriting, and, firm in the conviction that, for a variety of reasons into which it is not necessary here to penetrate, these are not those that should come, we must look for others ... I mean, of course, such a choice as a true Gaelic craftsman would make, who knows the history of his race and literature, is conversant with the psychology of his people, and has a sound knowledge of the European stage, especially with the dramatic writings of these countries the genius of whose inhabitants is near to our own, such, for example, as France; Spain; or Italy.

And in all the departments of literature the first concern must surely be to get above the kailyaird or pulpit level and re-acquire hauteur, an absence of rustic coarseness—what, dealing with the same rare quality in Aodhagán O Rathaille, Séumas O h-Aodha happily calls 'literary pride' *uabhar na litriochta*.

Look again at one of the phrases in the quotation given above from Mr Erskine of Marr—'who knows the history of his race and literature'. Professor Daniel Corkery in *Hidden Ireland*[1] stressed the need to 'get back behind the Renaissance' and to undo that deplorable whitewashing whereby Greek and Latin culture has prevented other European nations realizing their national genius in the way Greece and Rome themselves did. There are many signs that this long overdue return to our real roots—and our truest and most important potentialities—is taking place now. The Celtic Twilight has largely disappeared. There is a wide recognition that the values it promulgated were largely phoney and based on misunderstanding and falsification. Nevertheless, since 'by indirections we find directions out', the Celtic Twilight was probably the only way at first to get even a modicum of Gaelic culture across in an overwhelmingly hostile environment. It succeeded in doing so and led on to the genuine article. To see what happened it is only necessary to compare the translations of Irish Gaelic poetry by Sir Samuel Ferguson and other early workers in this field with the later renderings by Professor Bergin, Mr Robin Flower, and others who got rid of the decadent fin-de-siècle elements and achieved a much closer approach to the true spirit of the poems. This has been happening in Scotland and Wales too. We have got a long way from the false mystique of 'Fiona Macleod' and his colleagues at the end of last century. But in regard to our true historical foundations and spiritual ideology and symbolism—'the myths we live by'—it is still a tremendous handicap that the whole body of Celtic myth is still so little known in comparison with the myths of Greece, Rome and Judaea. Fortunately even in this connection, where the systematic falsification of history is at its worst and the determined belittlement and exclusion of the Celtic elements most difficult to penetrate, steady progress is at last being made. We can comfort ourselves with the clear and certain knowledge that, once started, the wine would inevitably work, irresistibly and without pause, towards clarifying themselves. This tendency has already been brilliantly displayed in the work of Cier Rige (Roger O'Connor) and his editor, Dr Albert; in the Scotsman Laurence Austine Waddell; in the poets Charles Doughty and David Jones; and in many other miscellaneous writers of whom the greatest is perhaps John Cowper Powys. And even as we write this article there comes to hand a sheaf of new writings by a brilliant Scotswoman who has made herself mistress of the folklore of all the Celtic nations and of many other peoples and succeeded in 'splitting the atom' of some of the most intractable secrets of Celtic spirituality in poems whose lines remind us of the splendid 'barbaric' rhythms of the Welsh *penillion* singers and many of which will assuredly get across to no inconsiderable company of Scots today despite the incomprehensibility of many of the allusions and terms employed — 'get across', since 'deep calls to deep', and these poems thrill the very roots of our nature and 'reawaken forgotten kinships' in no uncertain manner. The reference is to Miss Ada Nelson, of whom more will be heard in these columns shortly. It must suffice here to end with one brief quotation from one of her recent poems which show the depth and beauty of her seizure of the innermost essence of the Scottish soul:

> This dree night!
> And the tread be the gainest. To the Brig of Urdh, the Way!
> And the Gabriel Hounds and Charon and the mad gusts wail
>   and shrill
> And the fading leaves — and fewer are they than the Souls where
>   the Red Wind's blasting spray sweeps above Wendel's Hill —
> Murmur and whisper on in the black night's forest gloom, with
>   their thousands' dying breath.
> To the Brig of the unstepped crossing, path of the birds
> Where never a wing flits through and the Holy Oaks and the
>   Eller tree's and the Ash's Fruits of Death!
> A dree night. A dree night! For a Soul must go this way!
> A dree night! A dree night! Nor faring Soul may stay![2]

All this may seem very far away from the urgent practical concerns of today. But is it? A reviewer of S. Maccoby's *English Radicalism, 1886–1914*[3] puts the matter in a nutshell — and it is just as applicable to the Celtic spirit in Scotland and Wales as in Ireland (which was why John Maclean urged that the Scots should make common cause with the Irish in 1916) — when he says:

> Why, then, did Victorian Radicalism accomplish so little and why did almost the whole programme have to wait for a

quarter of a century before it began to reach the Statute Book? The answer, of course, is to be found in a single word — Ireland. When the Liberal Party, under Gladstone's inspiration, embarked upon the greatest constitutional struggle in its history, every domestic issue inevitably receded into the background. The Radicals themselves saw quite clearly what was happening. On July 5th, 1886, Labouchere wrote to Chamberlain: 'A General Election, without you on our side, may lead to a Whig-Tory or Tory-Whig Government, which would relegate to the dim and distant future all these measures which you and we so ardently desire may become law. Under these circumstances is it too much to ask you to make an effort to avert all these contingencies.' If Chamberlain had been able to respond to that appeal the history of British politics would have been vastly different. The social reforms of 1908–14 would have been enacted twenty years earlier. The struggle with the House of Lords might well have been concluded by the end of the century. The streams of Left Wing opinion might never have been diverted from Radical to Socialist channels, and the fateful division between Liberalism and Labour might never have happened. In that event there would have been no prolonged period of Conservative ascendancy between the wars. The Irish have certainly had their revenge!

The lesson here for Scotland and Wales is certainly clear enough.

Even more applicable to Scots Gaelic and to Welsh writing in the past two centuries is what Stephen McKenna, the Irishman who translated Plotinus, said about modern Irish Gaelic literature in one of his letters, viz.:

Get a blue pencil and make two re-writings per page on Patrick O'Conaire's stuff, and you have the only thing of modern Ireland that could be written by a French, a German, a Russian, a Swedish novelist or playwright or essayist … Patrick is often grammatically careless and inconsistent, sometimes confused, a hundred faults: but he belongs to the European kind; compared with any other Munster writer he stands about as a rather crackedly crotchety university don to a schoolgirl: he is mature though faulty, he has range: the

Munsterites are bright limited childishness. I don't know one Munsterite that has any notion of literature whatever ... no notion of literary congruity, no sense of literary architecture or carpentry, no sense of dignity, no sense of depth or range, no notion of true observation or of significant selection; no spiritual emotion, no nothing that makes literature ... I maintain that with all Patrick O'Conaire's little flaws he's such that an imaginary non-English-speaking Irishman steeped in him would be prepared for all European conversation and literature: no Munster writer prepares the mind for anything but a Munster cabin or old Irish story life.

He adds that O'Conaire, speaking not of his mental value but of his range and language, goes very close to Maupassant, whereas 'Munster keeps to the *aonach* and to *cro na muc*' (i.e. to 'the fair' and 'the pigsty!'). Even so Munster Gaelic writing is richer and livelier than modern Scots Gaelic writing which keeps for the most part to far duller things than the fair or the pigsty, namely the kirk vestry and the choir.

McKenna raged against those who thought of Irish as a patois for peasants, 'who in grotesque ignorance or lying malice assert that the Irish of so much poetry is fit only for discussing the feeding of pigs and the promise of cows.' 'A man could do anything in Irish,' he wrote to a friend in 1914, 'say and express anything and do it with an exquisite beauty of sound ... I consider it the flaw and sin of my life that I didn't twenty years ago give myself body and soul to the Gaelic to become a writer in it as some — God forgive me! — some Conrad in English or some Flem flammanding in French, and help to make the literature that would re-root the language.'

How he hated the contemporary fiction and poetry that was beginning to be written in Irish as 'narrow in range, tenuous in substance, and too often childishly sentimental'. This is the curse that has fallen even more heavily on modern Scottish Gaelic letters. And the cause of it all? McKenna puts it splendidly, and for the Scots and the Welsh as much as for the Irish, when he says: 'We never did fry our own fish, but did always be jumping into the fire to yank out the herrings for the other man — and small leavings to ourselves when that one had them gozzled!'

18

ROBERT BURNS: HIS INFLUENCE

1959

There can be no question at all about the tremendous influence Burns has had—and, since the number of Burns clubs throughout the world continues to increase and celebrations of his birthday multiply everywhere—is increasingly having.

But the question is, in what connections is this influence operative? Here I am principally concerned with literary influence (influence on subsequent poets up to, and including, the poets of today, and on the development of poetry)—and on Scotland. So far as the latter is concerned, going up and down Scotland continually and addressing all sorts of audiences for the past thirty to forty years, I have found that there has been a great decline in knowledge of Burns's works and of the Scots language. It is sometimes forgotten that another Scottish poet once occupied a similar position in popular esteem to that so long occupied by Burns. I mean Sir David Lindsay. In cottages and castles all over the country Lindsay's poems were to be found cheek-by-jowl with the family Bible, and this immense popularity endured (as Burns's has done) for over a couple of centuries. But (not forgetting the tremendously successful production of his *Satire of the Three Estates* at the Edinburgh Festival) how many Scottish houses today hold a volume of his work, how many Scots have read any of it? Is it possible that Burns's great vogue may similarly disappear?

Lindsay owed his popularity to much the same basic qualities as account for Burns's. I agree with the historian who wrote:

It is not Lindsay's imagery or music that rivets us; it is the strength of his moral convictions, the vigour of his political sketches, the audacity of his satire, the broad light that he throws on the age in which he lived, and the assurance we thus derive that, beneath the turbid surface of feudal life, there

177

were still some men in Scotland who loved justice and mercy
and peace; whom the outrages of the great fired with indig-
nation, and the miseries of the poor melted with compassion.
The arguments have no great originality. That indeed is not
a conspicuous quality of our poet. His sincerity makes his
thought simple; his earnestness makes his language plain;
yet there is at all times in his serious flights a sermonic vigour
that must have struck home to the popular heart.

This could all be said of Burns's work too. But Lindsay had something Burns lacked. Writing of the second part of the *Satire* the
same historian continues: 'In it Lindsay has put forth all his force
as a practical reformer. Every mischief, every abuse, every
enormity in the national life is pictured, discussed and condemned.
But even this is not enough. He demands reform and describes
the means by which it may be attained.' This is just what Burns
failed to do. Even his great declaration—that 'Man to man the
warld owre shall brithers be for a' that'—vouchsafes no clue as to
how that consummation is to be secured.

   Yet Burns owes his vast reputation to the fact that, albeit
imprecise and contradictory, he was on the same side—the side
of the poor and oppressed, the side of justice and mercy and
peace. But by the time Burns wrote, the poetic currency, and the
Scots language itself, had been sadly debased. It cannot be con-
tended that he ranks as a poet with Dunbar or Henryson. He owes
his unique appeal to the fact that he was a song-writer rather than
a poet, and composers invariably prefer poor to good poetry. It is
true that Burns pleased—and still pleases—a vast public with his
love songs, the horse-sense of his homespun philosophy, and his passionate love of Scotland. But these are all matters of the content of
his poems and songs and not of the quality of the poetry as such.
   It is the latter alone that finally matters. I agree with the late
Ford Madox Ford when he says:

   The only human activity that has always been of supreme
   importance to the world is imaginative literature. It is of
   supreme importance because it is the only means by which
   humanity can express at once emotions and ideas. To avoid
   controversy I am perfectly willing to concede that the other
   arts are of equal importance. But nothing that is not an art is

of any lasting importance at all, the meanest novel being humanly more valuable than the most pompous of factual works, the most formidable of material achievements, or the most carefully thought out of legal codes.

It has been said truly of Sir Walter Scott that he turned men's eyes to what Stevenson called the background and stamped on the minds of his disciples a hopelessly false and anachronistic image of Scotland, for, at a crucial moment of history, Scotland's greatest genius was a backward-looking sentimentalist, writing about alchemists and astrologers, as Professor Knott complained, in the Edinburgh of the anatomist Knox and of Burke and Hare, reviving Scottish baronial in his absurd Abbotsford, seeing in the highlands what Karl Marx called 'the promised land' of romantic literature at a time when 'areas as large as German principalities were being "cleared".' Burns too wrote of a rural Scotland that was about to undergo an inconceivable transformation under the impetus of the industrial revolution. Everything in Scotland has changed out of all recognition since his time. Like many great geniuses he came at the end of a historic period and summed it up and crowned it. But he introduced no new initiative into Scottish poetry and new initiatives were never more necessary to cope with the stupendous changes taking place or soon to take place. Poetry must always renew itself.

If Scottish poetry has been singularly lacking in innovations, so much the worse for Scottish poetry. Scotland of all countries, one would think, should never have forgotten that the injunction is always to 'sing a *new* song to the Lord'. Consequently contemporary poets have little or nothing to learn from Burns. The horde of Burns imitators in the past hundred years and more reduced Scots poetry to an abyss of worthless rubbish unparalleled in any other European literature. It should not be forgotten that the efforts of first Allan Ramsay and then of Burns to revive Scots literature, bring it into accord with the changed times, and carry it to fresh levels of achievement, failed. As Dr David Daiches says in his recent book, *The Present Age from 1920*,[1] in the 'Introductions to English Literature' series:

It was the fate of Scots to be forced after the seventeenth century from a literary language into a series of regional dialects, in which rustic poets wrote sentimental local verse. Even the achievements of Robert Fergusson and Robert Burns could not really arrest this movement; indeed, Burns's magnificent exploitation of the rustic folk tradition, while a great achievement in itself, proved to have a harmful effect on Scots poetry, for it encouraged an affected rusticity and discouraged poets writing in Scots dialect from coming to grips with the realities of Scottish life after the Industrial Revolution. Scots verse in the nineteenth century, drawing on an escapist caricature of Burns, became consistently vernacular, exploiting into pathos, whimsicality, sentimentality, nostalgia or dialect humour selected aspects of an idealized Scottish rustic life. The 'kailyaird' school of Scottish poetry, as of Scottish fiction, dealt in facile emotional stereotypes with a monstrously sentimentalized rural Scotland. As J. H. Millar expressed it over fifty years ago, 'the land was plangent with the sobs of grown men, vainly endeavouring to stifle their emotion by an elaborate affection of "peching" and "hoasting".'

It has taken us all this time to get rid of that—and we have done it in the teeth of the vast majority of Burns lovers who regard the bard's work as the be-all and end-all of Scots poetry and resent and resist by every means in their power any attempt to depart from the Burns models. Nevertheless poetry in Scots *has* been carried to new levels of achievement in the past thirty years, the Scots language *has* once again been made a medium for the expression not merely of the domestic and parochial but of the whole range of literary expression and leading critics are agreed that whereas the revivals attempted by Ramsay and Burns failed, the third time is proverbially lucky and the present movement may succeed. An American critic has observed that as a result of the contemporary effort, an 'altogether different prestige is enjoyed by the vernacular' making it 'possible, indeed natural, for Scots poets both to write in Scots and be judged by fully European standards, a rather large accomplishment when one glances at the history of Scots verse since Burns. By, as it were, bodily throwing poetry in Lallans into the main stream of European letters, the new movement has fulfilled its original intention "to keep Scotland in the main march of the world's interests".'[2]

That this has been possible at all, however, is due to Burns, no matter how he himself in his actual practice 'betrayed the movement begun by Fergusson'. Lord David Cecil has said : 'Abstracted from that soil of common life which alone could generate the sap necessary to keep it alive, it was inevitable that the flower of creative inspiration in English poetry should wither, and it has withered. There is no living tradition of major poetry in English today.' That Scots poetry has not been divorced from the common people in this way is due almost wholly to Burns. That he also was largely responsible for its reduction to parochialism and made incapable of dealing with the realities of modern life are remediable faults. It is not Burns's fault that Scots language and literature are not taught in our schools and our young people not put in anything like full possession of our national heritage, but signs are not lacking of a change on the part of the Department of Education and much has already been done by the School of Scottish Studies at Edinburgh University, the Saltire Society, and other bodies, and it is to be hoped that the bicentenary celebrations in January [1959] will give a fresh and decisive impetus to these developments.

The demand everywhere is for higher levels of consciousness and we ought not to forget what the great French scientist, Louis Pasteur, said at the tercentenary of Edinburgh University: 'Centuries ago the fortunes of Scotland were joined with those of the human mind. She was one of the earliest nations to realize that intellect rules the world.' Burns was anti-intellectual and apt also to jeer at foreign things and express a sort of xenophobia. In both of these connections he was going counter to two of the strongest drives in our whole national history—our internationalism and our intellectualism; the two characteristics also in which we are most strongly differentiated from our southern neighbours.

Writing an obituary notice of the late Walter Elliot, Mr Ivor Brown quoted Burns's remark, 'Gi'e me ae spark of native fire, that's a' the learning I desire,' and commented that while he possessed the spark of native fire all right, Walter Elliot could never have echoed the second phrase. That is the element in Burns which has most limited his influence. The consequence has been that the Burns movement has, as I put it thirty years ago, denied his spirit to honour his name, denied his poetry to laud his amours, preserved his furniture and repelled his message. It has built itself up on the progressive refusal of his lead in regard to Scottish politics, Scottish literature, and the Scottish tongue. It knows nothing about him or his work—or the work that should be done in continuance of his—except the stupid and stereotyped sentiments it belches out annually. It is an organization designed to prevent any further renaissance of the Scottish spirit such as he himself encompassed, and in his name it treats all who would attempt to renew his spirit and carry on his work as he himself was treated in his own day.

But there are welcome signs today of a stirring of new life in the Burns movement and it may yet reorient itself in a way that will bring to bear on Scottish life and literature in a dynamic way the worthier influence Burns should have had and may (rightly understood at last) yet have.

Whether or not that comes to pass—and no matter what faults and failings are to be set against his great qualities and incomparable service to Scotland—it will remain true, as Walt Whitman said, that for a vast public all over the world Burns will always be 'deemed the tenderest, manliest, and (even if contradictory) dearest flesh-and-blood figure in all the streams and clusters of bygone poets'.

19

TO A YOUNG POET

1959

Dear Iain,

As you know, I think you are a poet of real promise. I look forward eagerly to whatever you send me. But it is very difficult, if not impossible, for me to give you advice as you ask me to do. You must decide for yourself where your duty to yourself—in the way of achieving the highest possible expression of which you are, or may become, capable, I mean—lies, in choice of subject-matter, form, language, sense of responsibility to the whole course and present most pressing requirements of Scottish poetry, and so forth. I cannot help you there, save by counselling you to study all such matters as thoroughly as possible. Do not leave any of them to chance, do not depend on 'inspiration'. Man, know thyself, is the old injunction with which European civilization is familiar. I prefer the oriental form: 'Man, know thyself by thyself', and that is vitally necessary for any creative artist.

But perhaps I can be most helpful by putting into parables what I think is the necessary attitude of the poet to everything outside himself, poorly called 'Wonder', and certainly essential if his work is to have that element of mystery which is essential to poetry. That, and also precisely wherein lies the secret of the true artist which gives his work the uniqueness that stamps it as his and none other's.

First of all, however, let me remind you in this bicentenary year of what Burns said (Burns whom fools imagined to have relied on sheer spontaneity!). In a letter of February 22nd, 1789, probably to Henry Erskine, he wrote: 'I have no great faith in the boastful pretensions to intuitive propriety and unlaboured elegance. The rough material of Fine Writing is certainly the gift of Genius; but I as firmly believe that the workmanship is the united effort of Pains, Attention, and repeated Trial.'

It is well to remember, too, what Burns said of his creative
technique in a letter to Thomson (September 1793):

> Until I am complete master of a tune, in my own singing
> (such as it is) I never can compose for it. My way is: I consider
> the poetic sentiment, correspondent to my idea of the musical
> expression; then choose my theme; begin one stanza; when
> that is composed, which is generally the most difficult part of
> the business, I walk out, sit down now and then, look out for
> objects in Nature around me that are in unison or harmony
> with the cogitations of my fancy and workings of my bosom;
> humming every now and then the air with the verses I have
> framed; when I feel my Muse beginning to jade, I retire to
> the solitary fireside of my study, and there commit my effu-
> sions to paper; swinging, at intervals, on the hind legs of my
> elbow-chair, by way of calling forth my own critical strictures,
> as my pen goes on. Seriously, this, at home, is almost in-
> variably my way ...

In modern life one of our greatest difficulties lies in the ever-
increasing multiplicity of choices. How in the midst of such a
nimiety can we choose? It is ever more and more difficult to see
the wood for the trees. This little story may possibly help.

Once I had a dream—all this queer junk on my desk and in
my room reminds me of it—a dream that I was at a fair. All
around were all sorts of things like these, which people think
they need. One would think a man would take hundreds of years
to get used to this surprising world into which he is born. But no—
quite the contrary! He gets used to it so incredibly fast that it is
almost as though he had expected everything to be the way it is.
Who knows? People are so quick at taking in what they see and
coming to terms with it, it's as though the idea of it existed in their
heads already. Well, there I was in that fair, with booths and
candy stalls, roundabouts, mirrors, raffles ... I got quite giddy in
my dream, for all I knew was that I was seeing those things for
the first time. I had just been called up out of the void to see this
nonsense. And what frightened me was that nothing of it could
surprise me in the slightest. Somehow I knew it all so well. And I
felt there was an unseemly arrogance in this familiarity. For how

could I have known what a motor-car was, or an aeroplane, or, say, a camera?

And then suddenly it all turned to stone. Every tiniest bit had become eternal. Until that moment all that transient rubbish hadn't mattered much, but now it had become different, almost sublime. I felt that human beings had never reckoned with this possibility, and now here was all this hocus-pocus of theirs, petrified, preserved to all eternity! Everything superfluous, everything that had gone sour, or run to seed, had been turned into a memorial. Only think of that! Archangels passed this way and that in the midst of the masquerade, and patriarchs with long beards, and God Himself ... Then an angel came and comforted me in my horror and led me out of that place.

What angel was this? The angel above all you must pay heed to, my friend. I don't know if you've read Heidegger. Here's what Heidegger says of that angel, the angel he calls conscience.

The essential character of conscience is found in its call. Whereas Dasein primarily and mostly 'listens' to others, gaining its restricted and unauthentic potentiality of Being and its kind of understanding in the world of its care and in the publicity of the 'one like many', the 'call' of conscience breaks into such 'listening' of the Dasein to the anonymous 'one like many' and appeals to the 'self' in man to fetch it back out of this anonymity. Heidegger considers the 'call of conscience' to be a mode of 'speech' in the strict sense, emphasizing again that the voicing of a sound is not essential for 'speech' or for a 'call' like this one. 'Speech' in any of its modes articulates what is 'understood', and so does, in its own way, the 'call' of conscience. Heidegger refuses to accept the common interpretation which tries to trace conscience back to one of the presumed 'faculties of the soul', intellect, will, or feeling, or to explain it as the complex product of all of them.

The 'call of conscience' is characterized as a mode of speech in the following way: (a) What is spoken of is Dasein itself, not in a vague and indifferent way, but in the way in which it understands itself concretely in its everyday and average kinds of care. (b) What is appealed to is one's own 'self', not what the Dasein is reputed to be able to do, has achieved or stood up for in the publicity of community life, which, in its 'worldly' aspects is passed by by the call of conscience, but the 'self' which is thereby aroused, while the 'one like many' collapses. This 'self' is not the 'object' of introspection and of self-criticism, not something which is separate from the 'outer world', which likewise is passed by, but the 'self' as one mode of 'being-in-the-world'. (c) What is said in this 'call' of conscience is in one sense nothing; it offers no information about any events nor does it open up a soliloquy or an inner negotiation. But the 'call' appeals to the self's own potentiality of being. (d) There is no sounding of a voice in this call. Conscience speaks constantly in the mode of silence and in it alone. Yet it does not lose in audibility thereby, but, on the contrary, forces upon the Dasein which is appealed to and aroused a silence which is to be of great relevance. (e) The call disclosed something which is unambiguous, despite the apparent vagueness of its content, namely a sure direction or drive in which the Dasein of the 'self' is to move.

Conscience calls the self of Dasein out of the state in which it is lost in the 'one like many'. The 'self' is unambiguously and un-exchangeably meant, but beyond this there remains an astonishing vagueness regarding the 'what' of the call as well as its source: the caller. The one main thing is that the call is to be 'listened' to.

According to Heidegger, Dasein calls in conscience for itself. This call is not planned nor prepared nor voluntarily carried out by ourselves. 'It' calls against one's own explanations and even one's own wishes. Yet the call comes not from anyone else, but from myself and upon myself.

The 'that' is disclosed to Dasein, the 'why' is concealed. It is suggested that Dasein, being placed in the ground of its uncanni-ness, is the caller of the call of conscience.

A number of phenomena are adduced in its favour, e.g. that the caller is unfamiliar to the 'oneself' in its everydayness, that the call speaks in the uncanny mode of silence to call the self back into the silence of the 'existent' potentiality of being, that uncanniness is a fundamental mode of 'being-in-the-world', though concealed in everyday Dasein, and that in the call of conscience, tuned by dread, which enables Dasein to 'project' being, the 'uncanniness' follows Dasein closely and threatens its state of being lost in self-forgetfulness. The final proposition is that 'conscience reveals itself as the call of care'. The caller is Dasein which dreads in its

thrownness (already-being-in-the-world) on behalf of its potentiality of being. What is called upon is this same Dasein appealed
to in its own potentiality of being (being-in-advance-of-itself).
And Dasein is appealed to by the call out of the *Verfallen* in the
'one like many'.

That Dasein is guilty does not result from one special fault or
wrong done, but, reversely, such fault is possible only on the basis
of an original being-guilty of Dasein.

Only when man projects himself also into the potentiality of
being and becoming guilty (which is entirely different from making
oneself actually guilty by way of a fault or neglect) can he be open
for his own potentiality of existence and can he 'choose himself' in
the existential sense.

The will to have conscience is 'chosen' by the self when it
understands the call of conscience in the right way. Thereby it
becomes free for its own 'guilt' as well as for its own potentiality
of being. Understanding the call, Dasein lets its own self 'act' in the
way of 'inner action' and of its 'chosen' potentiality of being. Only
in this way can Dasein be 'responsible'.

The will to have conscience is self-understanding in one's own
potentiality of being, and in this respect a mode of Dasein as being
'disclosed' (*Erschlossenheit*). To understand oneself existentially
means to project oneself into an actual potentiality of being-in-
the-world which is essentially one's own. Only when one actually
'exists' in the mode of such a potentiality can it be 'understood'.

The mood that corresponds to such an 'understanding' is that
not of dread as such, but of a readiness for dread, in view of the
uncanniness of the individualization.

The projecting of oneself, in silence and in readiness for dread,
into one's own being-guilty—an outstanding mode of the disclosed state of Dasein, testified by conscience—is termed 'resolve'.
The 'resolve' is characterized as 'authentic self-being', which
means not a Dasein isolated from the world, but 'being-authenti-
cally-in-the-world'.

With best wishes,
Yours sincerely,
HUGH MACDIARMID

20

LEWIS GRASSIC GIBBON
1960*

It is a well-known fact that men who share the same faith but disagree on details are apt to be far more bitter enemies than men whose faiths are diametrically opposed. Consequently, James Leslie Mitchell ['Lewis Grassic Gibbon'] and I, when we met in London in the early 'thirties and later at his house in Welwyn Garden City, might well have found it difficult, if not impossible, to come to terms of friendship. For we both had a vision of Scotland—as it had been and as we might help it to become—but our visions had little or nothing in common. I was the older man and had lived all over Scotland and for years had been trying systematically to make good the deficiences of my education and possess myself fully of our Scottish national heritage. Leslie, on the other hand, knew intimately only Aberdeenshire and the Mearns, was not well read in Scottish literature, and instead of exact knowledge, hard facts and, where possible, first-hand personal experience, had a conception of history that seemed to me a pipe-dream not only unsupported by the actual facts and figures but controverted by these when they were available. We did become good friends, however, collaborated shortly after in the miscellany of poems, essays and short stories entitled *Scottish Scene*,[1] planned the series of little books called 'The Voice of Scotland'[2] series, designed to survey the whole range of Scottish arts and affairs, and had no difficulty in agreeing on the writers we invited to write books for that series. They included Eric Linklater, Neil Gunn, William Power, Victor McClure, Compton Mackenzie, A. S. Neill, Willa Muir and Edwin Muir, and Morton Shand. An amusing fact is that although Leslie and I promoted this series and secured the publishers, neither he nor I had books published in it.†

* Originally broadcast as 'A Vision of Scotland' on the Scottish Home Service of the B.B.C. on Monday, February 29th, 1960. *Editor.*
† Grieve wrote the unpublished *Red Scotland* for it. *Editor.*

It has been said that 'genius and a Scotsman' spell tragedy. It has far too often done so. Few literatures have sustained throughout the centuries such a succession of disabling losses. Of our early literature only a small fraction has come down to us—sometimes only in a single manuscript. When we are considering the corpus of work by the great makars of the fifteenth and sixteenth centuries we must remember that only a little of it has survived. In our later literary history Scotland has had consistently bad luck. Fergusson, Michael Bruce and David Gray were poor men and died in their twenties. Hogg was a bankrupt farmer. The last years of Burns and Scott were clouded with ruin, suffering and despair. 'The City of Dreadful Night' was the habitation of James Thomson's soul during nearly the whole of his brief existence, which belonged to London. In Scotland there were no fallen stars of magnitude between the death of Scott and the advent of Stevenson; because in the northern firmament there were no bright stars—only the glow of the great star of Carlyle, shining in the south, and for the rest, the fulginous glare of industrial prosperity. Genius and tragedy began again with Stevenson and John Davidson, Francis Adams, author of *Songs of the Army of the Night* committed suicide in Cairo. Evelyn Douglas, or John Barlas as he was christened, was confined in an asylum. William Soutar was bedridden for over twenty years. So the terrible tale goes on. And the premature death of Lewis Grassic Gibbon was unquestionably one of the heaviest of these losses.

I am sure he and I would have done a great deal together if he had lived even a few years longer. We were both full of plans and ideas. While we were of opposed opinions in most matters—and even in matters pertaining to Scottish politics and to the possibility of a Scottish literary revival and the shape and substance it should have—we could complement each other most effectively and there was nobody else on the Scottish literary horizon at that time with whom either of us could have collaborated so well, if at all. Underlying all our differences of matter and method, we had the same objective in regard to Scotland—a regionalism seen under the conditions of universal poetry.

When I met Leslie I had immediately the thrill of recognizing one of my own kind—a born writer, a desperately hard worker, one destined to go places. Despite our initial differences of background, equipment and vision, it soon became clear that our main aims and interests would converge. We approached the Scottish question from entirely different angles at first. Leslie's main familiarity and interest was with the landscape and rural people—mine with urban life and the development of the machine age. We had both a very wide range of interests as is shown by the diversity of our books. Leslie's deal with archaeology, exploration, anthropology, biography, the novel and the short story. Mine, with poetry, literary criticism, politics, economics and topography. But essentially he was a novelist whereas I was a poet, with practically no interest in fiction at all or any belief in its future as a literary form. It was already apparent to me that the novel had lost focus. I agreed with another critic that the novel is only the youngest of artistic forms and foresaw that even its commercial varieties might well decay in the next fifty years, destroyed by the competition of television and the televized film. Poetry, however, which demands repeated reading and a recollected state of mind before it can deliver its message, must, like music, and like painting, survive in its present forms if it is to survive at all. In poetry, therefore, remains the hope for literature's survival. Leslie would in the end have agreed with me about all this—and did so with regard to his own earlier novels and with regard to the whole vast production of conventional fiction. But the trilogy, *A Scots Quair*,[3] comprising the three novels, *Sunset Song*, *Cloud Howe* and *Grey Granite*, did not fall into that category. They were in their different way as great a departure from the run of Scottish novels as James Joyce's *Ulysses* from the run of Irish novels; and I am sure it will be with *Scots Quair* as it is with *Ulysses*—any student of literature already or in the future will have great difficulty in remembering even the names of any other contemporary Scottish or Irish novel. In the whole range of modern Scottish fiction only four other books seem to me fit to put beside it—George Douglas Brown's *House with the Green Shutters*;[4] J. MacDougall Hay's *Gillespie*;[5] R. L. Stevenson's *Weir of Hermiston*, and Sydney Goodsir Smith's *Carotid Cornucopius*. This may seem hard on the industrious writers of so many well-plotted, well-written novels, but though these still command a great body of readers—far more readers indeed than *Scots Quair* or even *Ulysses*—the fact is that they mean nothing but a way of passing the time; they have no literary significance. Leslie himself was as clear as I was about this. He declared in *Scottish Scene*:

Modern Scotland, the Gaels included, is a nation almost entirely lacking a Scottish literature output. There are innumerable versifiers, ranging from Dr Charles Murray downwards to Mr W. H. Hamilton (he of the eldritch glamour); there are hardly more than two poets; and there is no novelist at all. To be oneself a provincial or an alien and to write a book in which the characters infect one's literary medium with a tincture of dialect is not to assist in the creation or continuation of a separate national literature—else Eden Philpotts proves the great, un-English soul of Dartmoor and Tennyson in 'The Northern Farmer' was advocating Home Rule for Yorkshire. The chief Literary Lights which modern Scotland claims to light up the scene of her night are in reality no more than the commendable writers of the interesting English county of Scotshire.

More in Neil Gunn than in any other contemporary Anglo-Scot (with the exception, perhaps, of George Blake, in a very different category from Gunn, and the finest of the Anglo-Scots realists) the reader seems to sense the haunting foreignness in an orthodox English; he is the greatest loss to itself Scottish literature has suffered in this century.

In that essay Leslie goes on to pass in review Naomi Mitchison, Willa Muir, John Buchan, Catherine Carswell, A. J. Cronin, Eric Linklater, and others, and insists that none of them are contributors to a distinctive Scottish literature as opposed to English literature, and decides with the late James Barke, with respect to Gaelic literature: 'In the realms of imaginative literature—in fiction and drama—there is little or no original work in evidence, and what does exist is of poor quality and vitiated by a spineless sentimentality.'

These words were written twenty-six years ago. I think they still hold good. As the B.B.C. pamphlet, *Annals of Scotland*, issued in connection with that series broadcast three or four years ago said, Scottish literature lacks innovators. And innovators any live literature must have. It cannot subsist on writers just taking in each other's washing. The trouble is that reviewers and fellow-authors seldom recognize — or admit to recognizing — the phenomenon of a genuine innovator when confronted by one; and in *Scots Quair* Gibbon was one most emphatically, as he was not in his earlier novels published under his own name of J. Leslie Mitchell. He differed from all the other Scottish fictionists of his time in that he managed to break away from the stock type of writing altogether, and in so doing did by far his best work. Compton Mackenzie wrote in his book, *Literature in my Time*:[6]

It seems indeed that unless some catastrophe of war or pestilence on a scale immensely greater than anything the world has yet known by exacerbating the struggle for existence intervenes to prolong the way of human thought since Genesis, the second millennium of the Christian era will see humanity launched upon a way of thought a thousand times more different from our present ways of thought than ours from the thought of neolithic man. While it seems fairly certain to me that except *Ulysses* no major work of art has yet been produced by those who, aware of the transition from one kind of man to another, are trying to achieve that transition within their own lives, I am perfectly certain that no major work of art will ever be produced again by those who fail to achieve that transition.

Gibbon saw that, too, and attempted that great transition in part at least — paradoxically enough with a vanishing and irrecoverable way of life in the knuckle-end of Scotland as his subject matter — but that realization, which no other Scottish novelist seems to have shared in any degree at all, led to his greatest work. Did he find a way out of the impasse of conventional fiction by which other writers can escape too? I am afraid not. *Scots Quair* stands alone and has had no successors nor is it likely to have any. But it anticipated in some ways what writers since in France, Germany, and some other countries have done in escaping from the conventional novel form.

The only subsequent Scottish work that can be named in the same breath is Sydney Goodsir Smith's *Carotid Cornucopius*, an immense work of which only the first four chapters have so far been published.[7] This carries its experiment with immense verve far beyond the point Leslie would have regarded as dangerous in his own case, for Leslie in one of his essays expressed the fear that the peculiar style he had used in *Scots Quair* 'may become either intolerably mannered or degenerate, in the fashion of Joyce, into the unfortunate unintelligibility of a literary second childhood'. I am confident Leslie would have come to a very different view of Joyce's achievement if he had lived a few years longer. As it was, Dr David Daiches is right when he says of *Scots Quair*

> In some respects it represents the same kind of blow against the kailyaird school of sentimental rural fiction as George Douglas Brown's *House with the Green Shutters* had struck in 1901, but it is more ambitious and more original. The work has many flaws, but it remains a lonely attempt to achieve something really new in the modern Scottish novel.

We must remember how young he was and how much he had done in his brief life—various, uneven, hustled (to use Mr Ivor Brown's adjectives) as that had been. In a period of seven years he had written seventeen books, ranging from novels, short stories and essays, to biography and archaeology. And, as his widow has told us, at the end he was planning a future programme — he has left synopses of *A History of Mankind*, *The Story of Religion*, and *Memoirs of a Materialist*. But no matter how disparate his subject-matter, no matter how vain his belief in a past Golden Age of Innocence without war or class distinctions or dire want and the notion that that might come again, he was always at his best when he came back to Scotland in his writing—to Scotland and his memories and hopes for his own people. His *Scots Quair* magnificently illustrates the truth of my own declaration that, 'the subterranean persistence of unchanged Scottishness under official Anglification and apparent acquiescence in assimilation to English standards occasionally rises to the surface in more significant forms than 'legislation by appendix' makes inevitable every now and again in every practical connection.' In this sense the whole Scottish movement today might define its purpose in the lines of Matthew Arnold (himself half a Celt—his mother was a Cornishwoman):

13

To see if we will poise our life at last,
To see if we will now at last be true
To our own only true deep-buried selves,
Being one with which we are one with the
whole world.

Scots Quair was essentially a tremendous feat of memory rather than of imagination. It is a wonderful instance of total recall. The way Leslie's memory of the Mearns worked can hardly be better expressed than it is in that other Aberdeenshire Doric classic, *Johnny Gibb o' Gushetneuk*, when Johnny says to his wife:

The Apostle speaks o' the life o' man as a vawpour that appeareth for a little and then vanisheth awa', an' seerly there couldna be a mair nait'ral resemblance. Fan we begood the pilget here thegither, wi' three stirks an' a bran 'it coo't cam wi' your providin', tae the side o' the place was ta'en up wi' breem busses an' heather knaps half-doon tae faul'ies and the tither was feckly a quaakin' bog, growin' little but sprots and rashes. It luiks like yesterday fan we had the new hooses biggit, an' the grun' a' oon'er the pleuch, though that's a gweed therty year syne. I min' as bricht's a pentit picter fat like ilka knablich an' ilka sheugh an' enrig was!

That was exactly how Leslie remembered every detail of the Mearns. He himself said that in writing *Scots Quair* the whole thing came flooding in on him. It was less like something he was composing than something that was being dictated to him, and it took him all his time to keep up with the dictation.

What manner of man was Leslie? When I met him first of all he impressed me as gaunt from overwork, yet with a steely determination in his eyes that showed no relenting. He was tall and lean, and looked—as indeed he was—like one stripped for battle.

I do not think I have ever met any writer who was so completely devoid of affectations of any kind. He talked shop with immense enthusiasm and a clear purpose. Where Leslie and I really came closest together was on the question of the future of Scottish literature and in particular the language question. For he saw clearly that what he wanted—what he believed the novel, and literature generally, urgently needed—could not be expected from the English or from Anglo-Scots. Thus he wrote: 'To expect contemporary experimentation from the Anglo-Scots themselves appears equivalent to expecting a central African savage in possession of a Birmingham kite to prove capable of inventing a helicopter.' And on the language issue Leslie said,

> Braid Scots: 'is still in most Scottish communities (in one or other Anglicized modification) the speech of emotional ecstasy and emotional stress. But it is not genteel. It is to the bourgeoisie of Scotland coarse and low and common and loutish, a matter for laughter, well enough for hinds and the like, but, for the genteel, to be quoted in vocal inverted commas ... But for the truly Scots writer it remains a real and haunting thing, even while he tries his best to write as a good Englishman. [8]

Leslie made a magnificent thing of it. No wonder Ivor Brown wrote in the first one-volume edition of the trilogy:

> Even more than any other of his qualities did I admire his superb mastery of words and rhythms, his spate of images, his prose of the earth which continually dissolved into air to become the poetry of sky and cloud. Has anybody ever written better about the mist of Scotland and the 'far-off mountains turned into clouds', the steam of the land?*

A Scots Quair has received due recognition by many critics furth of Scotland, but in Scotland itself it got for the most part a grudging reception and even yet is far from adequately esteemed. I remember a story which gives a parallel to that mean-spirited and deprecatory and cavilling response of our philistine Scotland to a unique writer, inspired by a great vision. The story I have in mind is about Old Tom, the rigger in a works who spliced all the wire slings and ropes. He was an old shell-back who had spent most of his days in sailing-ships. We loved to listen to Old Tom's yarns. One day he was telling about a day in the tropics. The sailors stripped and plunged over the side to cool off. While enjoying his swim Tom espied a shark coming. He knew he had no time to make the ship's side, so he waited. Just as the shark

---

* In the original broadcast there followed several quotations from Gibbon's work with connecting phrases or sentences by MacDiarmid. *Editor.*

turned over to bite him Tom whipped his knife from his belt and ripped up its belly with one long swipe. At this point one clever youngster chimed in, 'But I thought you were bare scuddy when you jumped over the side? Where did your belt and knife come from?' Old Tom fixed the culprit with a withering stare: 'It's not a yarn you want,' he said, 'it's an inquest.'

An inquest! That indeed is all our doubters and denigrators and defeatists may have got from Leslie Mitchell. For from the arts you only get in proportion to what you bring to them. And Leslie Mitchell when he went over the side into the cold waters of public indifference and philistinism was never without the sharp knife of a superb wit, and the tongues will turn to dust in the mouths of his retractors while his high place in the succession of the chroniclers of the authentic Scottish spirit becomes ever more and more clearly established in the minds of all who have ears to hear and eyes to see.

For Leslie's work is consubstantial with the things that endure — that do not change with the changing but have been accomplished once and for all and constitute the true glories of Scotland. That his detractors may survive is not a fear we should indulge, for Leslie's own work must have done a great deal to rid Scotland now of the provincial attitude of those who regard Scots literature as a mere branch and feeder of English literature, restricted to 'matter of Habbie Simson', third-rate thinking, and the kind of cosy sentiment, stereotyped romanticism, and facile funniosity that appeals to people who are wrapped up in the cotton-wool of bourgeois respectability. He rendered a great service to Scotland.

21

JOHN DAVIDSON:
INFLUENCES AND INFLUENCE
1961

Mr Maurice Lindsay and others have commented on the fact that I have been greatly influenced by John Davidson in my poetic development. That is true and I have gladly admitted it, and in this connection said in a broadcast talk on the occasion of Davidson's centenary that Davidson is 'the only Scottish poet to whom I owe anything at all, or to whom I would be pleased to admit any debt'. He is certainly the one who interests me most between the great makars of the fifteenth and sixteenth centuries and one or two of my own contemporaries, save for Fergusson and Burns, some Gaelic poets like Alasdair MacMhaighstir Alasdair, and Duncan Ban MacIntyre, and two Latin ones, George Buchanan and Arthur Johnstone. With these exceptions, there is scarcely any Scottish poet in these three or four centuries of any technical or intellectual interest whatever. Davidson stood out head and shoulders above all the Scottish poets of his own time. He alone had anything to say that is, or should be, of interest to any adult mind.

I did not know him personally, but I remember as if it were yesterday how the news of his suicide by walking into the sea off Penzance in March 1909, when I was a lad of seventeen, affected me. I felt as if the bottom had fallen out of my world.

Later I wrote of this:

> I remember one death in my boyhood
> That, next to my father's, and darker, endures;
> Not Queen Victoria's but, Davidson, yours,
> And something in me has always stood
> Since then looking down the sandslope
> On your small black shape by the edge of the sea
> A bullet-hole through a great scene's beauty,
> God through the wrong end of a telescope.[1]

Young as I was, it had already become obvious that I was destined to become a poet, and my parents were alarmed at the thought that I was about to devote my life to so unprofitable a business — a business in which there was no money and no security. They, and other friends, were already representing to me that versifying should be kept, if at all, merely as a spare-time affair. In Davidson's death, coming on top of such anxieties as to the course my life was to take, I probably had a premonition of what Muriel Stuart, a subsequent Scottish poet friend of mine, wrote in this connection:

> Thou knowest at what cost
> Thy sleep was taken on those awful hills —
> What thou has gained, and lost;
> Thou knowest, too, if what thou art fulfils
> The pledge of what thou wast,
> And if all compensates the poet's wreath
> That wounds the brow beneath.

Why did Davidson influence me so greatly? There were a number of reasons. I have always been a minority man. Andrew Lang, reviewing Davidson's *Fleet Street Eclogues*,[2] said, 'Sometimes, after a "torrent of applause" you hear one lonely belated pair of hands clapping. Such a demonstration is this of mine.' But in several cases, Davidson's, Charles Doughty's, Francis Adams's, I have been one of the 'few but fit' whose isolated hand-clapping has preceded, and still precedes, any torrent of applause.

Readers of my *Scottish Eccentrics*[3] and other books will know that I have shown that in so far from being 'kindly brither Scots', 'canny' or anything of that sort, the majority of distinguished Scots have always conformed to the character of the world long before ascribed to the Scot in the epithets '*fier comme un Écossais*' and '*piper in naso*', and also to the even earlier conclusions that the Scots were men of curious and restless learning, versatile, with little or no use for 'water-tight compartments', and likely to be found bestraddling several disciplines at once. Davidson was of this type. As Israel Zangwill said of him:

Fancy and imagination, wit and humour, fun and epigram, characterization and creation and observation, insight and philosophy, passion and emotion and sincerity—all are his. Nothing is lacking from that long catalogue by which Imlac convinced Rasselas that it was impossible to be a poet ... and all these glorious gifts have found vent in the most diverse artistic or inartistic shapes—novels, dramas, eclogues, ballads, Reisebilder—some written for the market, but the bulk in defiance of it ... and it is significant that all Mr Davidson's chief successes are won when he surrenders himself to the inspiration of the modern. This is the work we need. Let all who wish to see how the poet's eye may body forth, not the shapes of things unknown, but what is much more taxing, the shapes of things known and disesteemed, betake themselves in haste to *Fleet Street Eclogues, In a Music-Hall, A Random Itinerary,* and the rest of Mr Davidson's books.

Mr James Douglas emphasized another element in Davidson which, even in 1909, had begun to prompt my own mind in the direction in which it was most fully to find itself two or three decades later. 'He states fact in terms of poetry,' wrote Mr Douglas, 'and the statement scars one's consciousness. He is the first poet to digest the new wonders of science which have subtly changed the old cosmogony, and made the very foundations of existence crumble away.' It was this element which made me write my own second poem to Davidson—it is in Scots, but, Englished, it says: 'The relation of John Davidson's thought to Nietzsche's is more important than all the drivel about "Home, Sweet Home" four million cretins iterate. And if we can't throw off the world, let us hear of no "Old Grey Mother" at all, but of Middle Torridonian Arkose with local breccias, or the pillow lavas at Loch Awe.'

Another Scot, the poet-scientist Ronald Campbell Macfie, also wrote poems on Davidson, but he was—as also was Alfred Noyes, another poet who handled scientific subject-matter—far less modern, far less truly scientific in his thinking, than was Davidson.

Davidson was a true prophet: 'The insane past is the incubus: the world is really a virgin world awaking from a bad dream. These are some of the seeds of the new thing I bring, of the new poetry which the world will make. Poetry is the flower of what all men are maturing in thought and fancy; I reap a harvest unsown; I come a hundred years before the time—that time foreseen by Wordsworth—"when what is now called science, familiarized to men, shall be ready to put on a form of flesh and blood".'

Albeit it is perhaps more difficult than ever just at this moment to indulge the stupendous and typically Scottish humour that could hazard 'the poetical suggestion' that it is the presence of the incommunicable elements—dead gases, ghosts of elements herding with the vapour of dissolution nitrogen—'that maintains the mechanical mixture of the oxygen and the nitrogen of the air: were their ghostly frontier eliminated, the two main members of the atmosphere would unite chemically, forming protoxide of nitrogen, which is laughing gas. Great Pan! How close we are to that rare old fantasy, that the crack of doom will be a universal shout of laughter!'

What Davidson, alone of Scottish poets, did was to enlarge the subject-matter of poetry, assimilate and utilize a great deal of new scientific and other contemporary material, pioneer in poetic drama and other forms, and recognize thus early the exhaustion of English, writing as he did:

> Our language is too worn, too much abused,
> Jaded and overspurred, wind-broken, lame—
> The hackneyed roadster every bagman mounts,

and, above all, to write urban poetry (a development Scots like Alexander Smith and Thomas Hood had heralded, but which subsequent Scots poets failed to carry on, although already the rural Scotland of the bulk of Scottish poetry had been succeeded by the depopulation and dereliction of vast areas and the crowding into a narrow industrial belt of over two-thirds of our population). Yet most of our versifiers continued to write nostalgic, pseudo-pastoral rubbish about an Arcadian life which had no relation to the facts at all. For the matter of that, they are still doing so.

The most powerful influences on Davidson himself were Ibsen and Nietzsche—both first translated into English by Scots—Nietzsche by Thomas Common and Ibsen by William Archer. Davidson was very well read in English literature, and also in French and German literatures, but like most modern Scots seems to have known little or nothing about Scottish literature nor suspected for a moment that he was posing himself against a hopelessly wrong background in English literature. When Dr Gertrud von Petzold in her *John Davidson und sein geistiges Werden unter dem Einfluss Nietzsches*,[4] referring to one of Davidson's stories, expresses regret that he did not give us 'more Jenny Macintoshes and fewer Earl Lavenders, more Scottish heart-notes of so full and deep a resonance, and fewer super-clever London extravagances', she was expressing what most discerning critics have felt about practically all modern Scottish writers (e.g. Lady Cynthia Asquith's remarks on Sir J. M. Barrie, as 'defeated by the English', and her regret that he did not stay in Scotland and become the great Scottish dramatist he might have been), but the pity was that, like most educated Scots of the time (and still) he was never put at school in possession of more than a few discrete fragments of his proper national heritage, and, above all, that he was unable to realize the far greater suitability of Scots for the expression of his ideas than English could ever afford. Social protest, espousal of the cause of the underdog, anti-religion, materialism, Rabelaisan wit, invective—all these find a place much more easily and prominently in the Scottish than in the English tradition. All these are salient features of Davidson's work. In short, like Byron, he was a Scottish, not an English, poet, although he used an alien language, and had apparently no knowledge of the independent Scottish tradition. Nor did he express much in the way of Scottish nationalist sentiment. However, as Professor B. Evans says, 'the sympathy is with the Scots throughout'.

In other directions, however, Davidson's work was a valuable corrective to two of the greatest curses that have affected, and still affect, modern Scottish literature—namely, the superfluity of minor versifiers and absence of poetic ambition, and, associated with that, the horrible humility of mediocrity which is willing enough, as Kierkegaard said, to admit anyone who dares to lift his head above the ruck.

Statements of Davidson's with regard to these last two matters have stuck in my mind, and influenced me profoundly, for over forty years. For example, from *A Rosary*:[5] 'A poet is always a man of inordinate ambition and of inordinate vanity. In his heart he says, "I want my poetry to be remembered when Homer and Dante and Shakespeare are forgotten".' Again, specially applicable to the Scottish scene, from *Sentences and Paragraphs* :[6] 'The want of poetical power is the impelling force in the case of most versifiers. They would fain be poets, and imagine that the best way is to try to write poetry and to publish what they write. They will never see their mistake. *Equus asinus* still believes that the possession of an organ of noise is sufficient, with a little practice, to enable him to sing like a nightingale.' In another paragraph in the same book, Davidson hopes of those who were reconstructing Provençal poetry, that 'the head, as of yore, and not the heart, will be the source of the poetical passion'—a view I share, and have frequently propounded, in a far wider context. I have always agreed with him, too, that 'if one has a healthy mind it is wholesome to go from extreme to extreme, just as a hardy Russian plunges out of a boiling bath into the snow'.

But the most important element in Davidson—and one to which attention should be directed most strongly if justice is to be done to him at last and his influence brought to bear effectively where it is most needed—is expressed in the following passage from *A Rosary*. It re-echoes for today what has been a main theme of Scottish poetry back through Burns to Henryson and Sir David Lyndsay:

Poetry is not always an army on parade: sometimes it is an army coming back from the wars, epaulettes and pipeclay all gone, shoeless, ragged, wounded, starved, but with victory on its brows; for Poetry has been democratized. Nothing could prevent that. The songs are of the highways and the byways. The city slums and the deserted villages are haunted by sorrowful figures, men of power and endurance, feeding their melancholy not with heroic fable, the beauty of the moon, and the studious cloisters, but with the actual sight of the misery in which so many millions live. To this mood the vaunted sweetness and light of the ineffective apostle of culture are, like a faded rose in a charnel-house, a flash of moonshine on the Dead Sea. It is not now to the light that 'the passionate heart of the poet' will turn, The poet is in the street, the hospital. He intends the world to know it is out of joint. He will not let it alone. Democracy is here; and we have to go through with it. The newspaper is one of the most potent forces in moulding the character of contemporary poetry. Burns's eyes were open; Blake's, perhaps, for a time; and Wordsworth had profound insight into the true character of man and the world; but all the rest saw men as trees walking; Tennyson and Browning are Shakespearian. The prismatic cloud that Shakespeare hung out between poets and the world! It was the newspapers that brought about what may be called an order of pre-Shakespearianism. It was in the newspapers that Thomas Hood found the 'Song of the Shirt' —in its place the most important English poem of the nineteenth century; the 'woman in unwomanly rags plying her needle and thread' is the type of the world's misery. The 'Song of the Shirt' is the most terrible poem in the English language. Only a high heart and strong brain broken on the wheel of life, but master of its own pain and anguish, able to jest in the jaws of death, could have sung this song, of which every single stanza wrings the heart. Poetry passed by on the other side. It could not endure the woman in unwomanly rags. It hid its head like the fabled ostrich in some sand-bed of Arthurian legend, or took shelter in the paradoxical optimism of 'The Ring and the Book'. It is true William Morris stood by her when the priest and the Levite passed by. He stood by her side, he helped her; but he hardly saw her, nor could he show her as she is. 'Mother and Son', his greatest poem, and a very great poem, is a vision not of a woman, but of a deserted Titaness in London streets; there was a veil between him also and the world, although in another sense, with his elemental Sigurds, he is the truest of all pre-Shakespearians. But the woman in unwomanly rags, and all the insanity and iniquity of which she is the type, will now be sung. Poetry will concern itself with her and hers for some time to come. Not much of the harlot: she is at ease in Zion compared with actual woe. The offal of the world is being said in statistics, in prose fiction; it is besides going to be sung. There it is in the streets, the hospitals, the poorhouses, the prisons; it is a flood that surges about our feet, it rises breast-high, and it will be sung in all keys and voices.

Poetry has other functions, other aims; but this also has become its province.

As J. Russell Lowell said, 'Not failure, but low aim is crime.' Davidson almost alone of the poets of his time cannot be convicted of this crime. This is his great significance. It is time that was fully realized.

22

CONTEMPORARY SCOTTISH LITERATURE AND THE NATIONAL QUESTION

1965*

I have travelled a great deal in recent years in the Soviet Union, the German Democratic Republic, People's China, Czechoslovakia, Hungary, Rumania, Bulgaria and elsewhere, discussing literary matters with university audiences and conversing with groups of writers. But I have never met anyone in these countries who knew anything about contemporary Scottish literature or was aware that there was any such thing. In this respect the peoples of these countries were not unlike the Scottish people themselves, since they too know little or nothing about their native literature, least of all of its contemporary manifestations. What accounts for this extraordinary state of affairs? It is not difficult to find the cause.

In Scotland itself in our schools and universities little or no place is accorded to Scottish literature or to our two native languages, Scots and Gaelic. A virtual monopoly is given to English language, English literature, and English history — and the corresponding indigenous Scottish subjects, when any attention is given to them at all, are treated as unimportant sub-divisions of their English counterparts. Yet Robert Louis Stevenson was right when he said that no two neighbour peoples were so utterly — and unalterably — different as the Scots and the English. Despite surface assimilation of Scottish standards of all kinds to English standards that difference remains profound and unbridgeable, especially among the working class. Most of our Scottish newspapers, however, are centralized in London, as are our radio and T.V. and other mass-media and all the principal publishers, and these naturally, appeal to the big undifferentiated public and treat British literature, history, politics and culture generally as if it were unified and any local differences of no consequence whatever.

* Lecture given at Humboldt University, German Democratic Republic. *Editor.*

This state of affairs has increasingly based itself on this assumption of English superiority ever since the Union of Scotland and England in 1707, and though the Treaty of Union contained safeguarding clauses preserving the independence of the Scottish church, legal system, education etc., all these clauses have been completely abrogated and the English have persistently encroached on the remaining vestiges of difference in these matters and sought complete assimilation of Scotland to England.

Although the Scots have acquiesced in this denationalizing process, it is significant that a deep political difference has remained. That is why Scotland has provided the spear-head for the labour, trade union, and co-operative movements in Great Britain. The Scottish element in these movements has always been far more radical than the English elements, but the latter are numerically enormously greater and with a parliament in which the Scottish representation is in a permanent minority, the Scottish members have been unable to give effect to that difference.

Yet the fact that, by and large, the Scottish electorate voting Labour has been, and still is, revolutionary and republican, whereas the English electorate is monarchical and constitutionalist, is of great potential significance. It must also be remembered that unemployment in Scotland is always fifty per cent higher than in the worst areas of England, and that Scotland's slum and housing problem is one of the worst in Europe [1965]. Hundreds of thousands of acres of Scottish land are depopulated and reserved by aristocratic and plutocratic landlords as rich men's sporting grounds, while two-thirds of the entire population are crowded into a narrow industrial belt. The rate of emigration from Scotland is without parallel in any other advanced industrialized nation. Scotland is losing over thirty thousand of its people annually and has lost more than half a million in the last ten years.

In the early days of the labour and socialist movement, all the pioneers were Scottish nationalists, but a few years ago the Labour Party eliminated Scottish Home Rule from its platform.

This was simply for vote-catching reasons, since the amalgamation of Scottish trade unions with their English counterparts — consequently putting them in the control of their vastly more

numerous English membership—rendered it impossible to un-
scramble the state of affairs thus created and revert to any
independent Scottish position. The objective facts of Scotland's
very serious problems, largely due to English mismanagement and
the systematic sacrifice of Scottish interests to English (leading
to the present position in which Scotland's contribution to the
exchequer exceeds the amount Scotland receives in any services
by at least £150 million per annum—a forced subsidization of
England by Scotland, by a sum which, retained in Scotland and
under Scottish control, could go a very long way to solving Scotland's most crucial problems) are beginning to register, however.

During the past half-century there has been a steady development of Scottish nationalism. While Scottish Nationalist candidates have not succeeded in getting themselves returned to
Westminster,* the total vote for them is increasing, and there is
without doubt an overwhelming mass of Scottish opinion in favour
of some degree of devolution. The disadvantages Scotland labours
under in its present relationship to England have been pressed
home and are now widely appreciated. That this revival of Scottish
consciousness has not yet registered definite political gains is not
difficult to understand.

How could it when for so many generations the Scottish people
have been denied access through the educational system to their
national heritage? That disadvantage is only slowly being made
good—slowly, but I think, very surely. One unmistakable sign of
this is the fact that at the general election last year [1964] the
Scottish committee of the Communist Party of Great Britain
issued a manifesto entitled *Communist Policy for Scotland*, boldly declaring: 'Present economic and social conditions in Scotland make

* The recent triumph of the Scottish National Party candidate (Mrs Winifred
Ewing) at Hamilton has transformed the political situation in Scotland, Mrs Ewing,
polling 18,397 votes, won by a majority of 11,799 and overturned a Labour majority
of 16,576; the defeated Conservative candidate came third with a poll of only
4,986 thus losing his deposit. After her victory Mrs Ewing said, 'every Tory and
Labour M.P. in Scotland should feel uncomfortable now—their seats have become
pretty draughty. This is no flash in-the-pan result. It's just the start of an irresistible movement towards a truly free Scotland. Hamilton has set the ball rolling—
others will follow.' And events are now moving so rapidly that it is difficult to keep pace
with them. The Nationalist successes in the municipal elections in May 1968 showed
that the S.N.P. candidates had won over 100 seats and polled altogether over 300,000
votes.

the demand for more Scottish control, steps towards the setting-up of a Scottish Parliament and Self-Government, more urgent than ever before.'

I have no doubt that the Labour Party's betrayal of the Scottish cause is on the point now of being effectively countered by the development under communist leadership of a Scottish National Liberation Movement. Certainly Scottish writers in the last forty years have blazed a trail in that direction. When a great mass rally was held in Glasgow a few years ago to commemorate John Maclean, Scotland's greatest proletarian leader, who died in 1923 as a result of a savage prison sentence for so-called sedition, the platform was occupied by leading Scottish poets, writing in Scots and in Gaelic. And it must be remembered that the broad difference between Scottish and English literature has always lain in the far greater democratic character of the former. The very word 'democracy' means something quite different in Scotland than in England, since Scotland is almost entirely lacking in the social stratification of England, and while Frank Harris is not a critic to whose judgments on literary matters one must necessarily subscribe he was quite right when he stressed the difference between one English and one Scottish poet in the following passage:

> Whenever I recall Tennyson's death and the unmeasured glorification of him in the English press, I am compelled to think of poor James Thomson and his end. The poet of 'The City of Dreadful Night' died ten years before Tennyson, died in miserable poverty and almost unappreciated; yet, in my opinion, he was as gifted a poet as Tennyson and far wiser; intellectually indeed one of the greatest, a master of prose as well as verse. His life and fate throw a sinister light on English conditions. In every respect he comes nearer to ideal wisdom than any other modern English poet. While Tennyson lauds the Crimean War, Thomson condemns it as a 'mere selfish haggle, badly begun and meanly finished.' ... He showed sympathy for all the struggling nationalisms of his time, for Italy and Poland, and even for the Basques, who had supported the Carlist cause in 1873. Here are his words: 'Such was the loyalty of these people, far more noble than ours;

for they were giving freely of their substance and their lives, whereas we give chiefly snobbish cringing and insincere adulation, and our rich give the money of the nation in large part wrung from the poor.' Unlike Tennyson he was devoted to the cause of the people, and fought against every form of privilege and capitalism. Every Englishman should read his satirical essay on Bumbledom. He points out that though there is more liberty in England than on the Continent, in matters affecting political discussion 'the reverse is true as regards questions of morals and sociology, for here the power of Bumble's purse rules our so-called free press and free institutions with a hand heavier than that of any Continental despot.'

Thomson is really the only Englishman who stands with Heine and Leopardi as a great modern master, and his translations of their poems are the best in English. And Thomson was kindlier and sweeter in all his personal relations than either of them. Even Heine at times distresses one by the contempt he shows for the greatest, such as Goethe. We have no such apology to make for Thomson ... Thomson's essays, especially on the poets, are far and away the best in English. His view of Tennyson shows the sureness of his judgement, the width of his impartiality: 'Scarcely any other artist in verse of the same rank has ever lived on such scanty revenues of thought (both pure and applied) as Tennyson' ... 'He is continually petty ... A great school of poets is dying out; it will die decently, elegantly, in the full odour of respectability with our laureate [Tennyson].'

And Mr Harris concluded:

Tennyson and Thomson—between these poles you can find England: the one man, supremely endowed with genius for words, but with the mind of a sentimental schoolboy, was ruined by too great adulation and too many rewards; the other, of far higher mental endowment, bred as a charity orphan, was gradually disheartened by neglect and finally broken by the universal indifference that kept him a pauper.

What Mr Harris does in these passages I have quoted is to
14

bring out the differences between Scottish poetry and English poetry. The Union with England, and the abandonment of Scottish subjects in Scottish schools and colleges, threw the independent Scottish literary tradition into the discard. No poet in literary history has had such world-wide acclaim as Robert Burns, but Burns wanted to preserve the tradition of poetry in the Scots language and his followers have on the contrary allowed it to all but disappear from literary, and even spoken, use. It is a class question, because Scots, though eschewed by the so-called upper classes, is still widely spoken (albeit in impoverished form) by the working class and is popular in song, in the variety theatre, and in the dialogue elements in fiction.

But Burns has had a deplorable influence on subsequent Scots poetry. There has been a vast outpouring of imitative verse, full of maudlin sentimentality and cheap jocosity. T. S. Eliot was right when he said that Burns was 'the decadent representative of a great alien tradition' — alien, that is, to the English tradition.

It is that tradition in all its fullness that recent Scottish poets have sought to revive, to apply to modern needs, and to carry forward to new levels of achievement. And they have succeeded in doing so, or, in other words, where Scottish poetry after Burns took the wrong turning and became a matter of mindless doggerel, Scottish poetry has now gone back to the great Scots poets of the fifteenth and sixteenth centuries and resumed their high traditions — traditions which included a social realism, and scorn of religiosity, quite foreign to English poetry. Most Scottish poetry, old and new, has been a poetry of song — and song 'is nearer the hearts of the people' — whereas English poetry has always been, comparatively, very deficient in the element of song.

James Thomson was not a solitary figure among the Scottish poets after Burns who should have been followed instead of the drivellers who in fact monopolized attention and distorted the whole tradition to which Burns devoted his life.

In addition to Thomson, there was John Davidson, Tom Hood (author of 'The Song of the Shirt' which has been well called the 'most terrible poem in the English language'), Francis Adams, author of *Songs of the Army of the Night*, a great series of anti-imperialist, anti-militarist poems, inspired by a burning sense of social justice, and several others, all socialists, all atheists, all swept aside by the mainstream of English influence—but all now at long last coming into their own, and serving to inspire the Scottish poets of today who have broken free of English apolitical poetry and reverted to the authentic Scottish native tradition.

These young poets have created a new Scots folk-poetry in their ballads against the siting of the Polaris base in Scotland and in their songs against other manifestations of English reaction and injustice. Some of these make magnificent marching songs, and have a dynamic force in their hatred of American war-making that is having powerful effects on public opinion when sung at big open-air demonstrations. As in song, so in drama and in fiction, Scottish radicalism is steadily reasserting itself and recapturing the force it had in the best of Burns and in our tradi-tional songs and ballads.

Demobilization around about 1920 brought back to Scotland many young men whose minds had been sharpened by experiences abroad and who consequently were able to take a more objective view of their native country. Above all, they asked themselves what they had been fighting for.

If it was for 'little Belgium', why not for little Scotland? The result was that a new movement was started to recover Scottish independence culturally and politically.

These young men found to their surprise that they knew little or nothing about Scotland. This was not surprising since Scottish schools and colleges taught little or nothing about Scottish litera-ture, history or the two Scottish languages but gave a virtual monopoly to the very different literature of England, and to English language and history.

Asking why this should be, and if it was a good thing, or, if not, if it was irreversible, these young men had cause to reflect that other nations had taken a very different view of the importance of their native languages and literatures.

At first they were told they were trying to 'put back the hands of the clock' but as time went on it became apparent that they were, on the contrary, simply seeking to do for Scotland what was being done successfully in many other countries.

So far from being out of step with world tendencies, the opposite was the case, and in due course the fact became clear that far from the world moving towards unity—towards one world state—

the number of independent nations in the world had more than doubled within half a century; and many of these nations had been able to reconnect with long-lost national roots and revive and carry forward to new levels of achievement languages which had become too impoverished for any significant literary use or had lapsed more or less completely from the speech of their peoples.

In Scotland, this was of greater importance than in most of these newly independent countries, because in the fifteenth and sixteenth centuries Scotland had ranked as having one of the finest outputs of poetry in Europe, and that almost wholly in Scots, which is not a dialect of English but a separate language with a very different genius of expression from English.

Burns used a mixture of Scots and Augustan English, and the late T. S. Eliot was right when he said: 'I suspect Arnold of helping to fix the wholly mistaken notion of Burns as a singular untutored English dialect poet instead of a decadent representative of a great alien tradition.'

To recover that great alien tradition in all its fullness and carry it forward and apply it to modern purpose became the aim of the new Scottish literary movement. But to do that required first of all to rediscover the bases of the tradition.

A great deal of scholarly work was required. A tremendous leeway had been incurred and required to be made good.

The young writers of the 'twenties set themselves to this task. It has now been almost completed. The chief Scottish writers of the past have been effectively revalued. The whole range of Scottish literary history has been mapped.

There have been splendid anthologies—like John Buchan's *Northern Muse*[1] and Moray Maclaren's *The Wisdom of the Scots*.[2]

Alongside this has gone a thorough study of Scotland's demographic, economic and political history, an inquiry into its untapped mineral and other resources, and a succession of first-class studies of Scotland's educational system (e.g. *The Scots Constitution* and *The Scottish Realm*,[3] both by Duncan H. McNeill) and Scottish law (e.g. *British Justice*[4] by Professor T. B. Smith.)

How great has been this process of recovery and reorientation can only be appreciated by looking at a bibliography of such works published in the past forty years. There are scores of such books, all absolutely essential to an understanding of the position and potentialities of Scotland today.

At the beginning of the movement, the aim was to revive the use of Scots as the literary medium, to encourage creative literature in Gaelic, and alongside these to improve the literary standard of writings in English by Scottish authors.

There has been a considerable measure of success achieved in all three of these. Dr Edwin Muir pointed out that 'since English became the literary language of Scotland, there has been no Scottish imaginative writer who has attained greatness in the first or even second rank through the medium of English.'

Muir himself is widely regarded today as the great modern Scottish poet writing in English, but it is questionable if he did not pay too great a price for this, since, as a recent English critic has pointed out, Muir's poetry lacks 'that linguistic vigour without which fine poetry cannot exist. His want of verbal alertness offers a tentative explanation for his failure to bring to bear those rhythmic overtones and linguistic resonances whereby the poetic intuition is primarily kindled.'

That does not apply however to three younger (and still living) Scottish poets writing in English, each of whom has a substantial volume of new poems appearing this year.

They are Norman MacCaig, George Mackay Brown, and Iain Crichton Smith. MacCaig and Smith have the advantage of having, and been largely concerned with, their Gaelic background, and Brown is an Orkneyman, largely influenced in manner and theme by the Norse and Icelandic sagas.

But it is generally agreed that it is the poets who have written in Scots (or Lallans) who have done the most important work.

The most important of them are, probably, Sydney Goodsir Smith, Alexander Scott, Robert Garioch, Albert Mackie and Tom Law, but it is certainly safe to say that the output of verse in Scots since 1920 makes the period the richest in our literary history since the Middle Ages.

Alongside this has gone a redevelopment of folk-song, of political balladry, and of poems in Scots dealing with urban and highly industrialized life.

While Scots is little spoken today it ought to be remembered that it is still widely understood and its continuing popularity is shown by the fact that it is the medium used by variety artists with great success, and is also employed in drama and in the conversational passages of novels and short stories.

Above all, the best work done in it in recent years has completely refuted the defeatism generally entertained at the end of last century, when it was believed that Burns was the be-all and end-all of Scots poetry.

The poets I have named and others owe practically nothing to Burns; they have approached the Scots language and Scottish life from a different angle altogether, and amply justified T. S. Eliot's statement that:

> I am convinced that many things can be said, in poetry, in Lallans that cannot be expressed at all in English. I think that Scots poetry is, like that of other Western European languages, a potentially fertilizing influence upon English poetry, and that it is to the interest of English poetry that Scots poetry should flourish.

There is word now that at least one of our five Scottish universities is about to establish a course in Scottish literature for the ordinary M.A. class. This will give a great fillip to Scots writing. Already many classes in it are run by the extra-mural departments of the universities and by the Workers' Educational Association.

In Gaelic too there have been great developments since 1920, and despite the general decline of the language and the fact that native Gaelic speakers now number only a few thousand, there has been in Gaelic poetry the emergence of several of the greatest Gaelic poets we have ever had.

Certainly they are head and shoulders above any between the present time and the great efflorescence of Scottish Gaelic poetry about the time of the Jacobite Rising in 1745.

The two principal Gaelic poets today are Sorley Maclean and George Campbell Hay, but Professor Derick Thomson and Donald Macaulay must also be named among those showing that Scottish Gaelic letters today are displaying an unwonted and most promising virility.

In drama, too, as Professor Thomson says, 'the work of the Glasgow Gaelic Drama Association has now, indirectly at any rate, encouraged some highly original, contemporary, and disturbing drama to appear, in the work of Finlay Macleod.'

In Scots drama there has been no successor to the greatest, and really the only great, dramatist Scotland has yet had, 'James Bridie' (pseudonym of Dr O. H. Mavor), but excellent plays in Scots have been written by Robert Maclellan, Alexander Reid, Robert Kemp and others.

While in the novel, the brilliant Scots writing of Lewis Grassic Gibbon has had no successor of equal power, Sydney Goodsir Smith in *Carotid Cornucopius*,[5] has connected up over the centuries with Rabelais, and with Dunbar and other great Scottish mediaeval poets, just as Eric Linklater did in his earlier novels.

But in English there are today many brilliant Scottish novelists, whose work is quite different from, but not less accomplished than, that of their English contemporaries.

I need not mention in this connection the veteran Sir Compton Mackenzie but in novels with a Gaelic background there are Neil Gunn, and Fionn McColla, in English, Robin Jenkins, and in Scots (or using Scots for dialogue), at least half a dozen able writers.

More recently there have been significant Scottish developments in science-fiction. I have only space here to name Mrs Naomi Mitchison's *Memoirs of a Space Woman*[6] and J. P. McIntosh's *One in Three Hundred*.[7]

Chief of them all perhaps is the late David Lindsay, whose *A Voyage to Arcturus*[8] is a very remarkable piece of imaginative writing. Lindsay's work virtually fell without recognition. It is good to see it is at last receiving something like its due meed of recognition.

23

THE SCOTTISH RENAISSANCE MOVEMENT
AFTER FORTY YEARS
1966

Sydney Goodsir Smith had a long and fully documented essay,
'Trahison des Clercs or the Anti-Scottish Lobby in Scottish
Letters', in *Studies in Scottish Literature*, vol. II, no. 2 (October 1964),
in the course of which he wrote:

> At the start of Hugh MacDiarmid's career in the 1920s the
> idea of a Scottish Renaissance, political and cultural, was
> merely funny to his enemies, the old and the middle-aged. In
> the 'thirties just about every considerable Scottish writer of
> the time was an adherent of the cultural programme (which
> was largely concerned with the revival and intellectualisa-
> tion of the Scots and Gaelic languages for poetry) and most of
> them also supported the political programme, which desired
> separation from England, the exploiter of Scotland ... The
> war and the early postwar years saw the second wave of
> MacDiarmid's Renaissance and a great outburst of publish-
> ing, both book and periodical, mostly poetry, good, bad and
> indifferent, as one might expect, and gets, in any period
> anywhere. The battle, the young poets then thought, was
> won, or at least winning ... they even got into the school
> books and examination papers; they were not just laughable
> any more.
> But in the 'fifties the Beats began exerting their attraction
> and the young poets coming up sheered away from the
> Renaissance banner; it was becoming what they called an
> Establishment ... By the 'sixties this had hardened into posi-
> tive literary antipathy to the Renaissance or Scottish or
> National idea. There were even desertions by some of the
> chief figures of the 'forties and 'fifties ... and new champions
> of the anti-Scottish lobby appeared ... The position was now

that all three generations were allied in opposition to what might be called the Scottish Movement: the old (who have never liked it), the middle-aged (who never like anything), and the young (who generally like the latest thing—and the Scottish thing was definitely old hat). It is a matter of curious fact that this three-headed opposition, though extremely vocal in critical opposition, is not ... very productive of original, imaginative work ...

This anti-Scottish lobby is such a recurring phenomenon in the history of Scottish literature that it is really a wonder that the literature has survived its continual bashing since the eighteenth century. What is even more curious is that its enemies consider it worth bashing.

Mr Smith went on to refer to, and quote, instances of this opposition to Scottish literature, and in particular to the literary use of Scots, from Dr James Beattie in 1771, Henry Mackenzie (the Man of Feeling—who advised Burns to write in English) in 1786, Dr John Moore in 1787 advising poor Burns to the same effect, and on to T. F. Henderson in 1898, holding that 'as regards vernacular poetry, Burns's death was really the setting of the sun; the twilight deepened very quickly; and such twinkling lights as from time to time appear only serve to disclose the darkness of the all-encompassing night', then Professor Gregory Smith, advising Scottish writers to drop the 'masquing gear of Braid Scots', and suggesting 'a way for the freer expression of nationality in style. It may be described as the delicate colouring of standard English with northern tints'. And finally the anti-Scots cry was taken up once more notably by Edwin Muir in his *Scott and Scotland*.[1] 'But now,' as Mr Smith says, 'a new dimension opened up; the lobby extended its field of denigration to include the whole of Scottish literature.' Mr Smith goes on to cite astonishing examples of anti-Scottish defeatism from Professor R. L. Mackie in 1934, Dr H. Harvey Wood in 1947, Dr John Speirs in 1940, and many others up to the present day. 'Can any country', he asks, 'match such a continued belittling of its own literature by its own literary pundits?'

I know of no such instance. It would be a mistake, however, to think that Mr Smith's article is up-to-date. All that he says is certainly true enough, but there is another side to the matter. Since 1962 there have been scores of articles by well-known writers all over the world appreciative of what has been actually achieved by the Scottish renaissance movement. It is true there seems to have been a cessation of the outpouring of original work which characterized the 'twenties and 'thirties, and, in sum, established that period as one of the richest in the whole of our literary history. But there has been a steady work of consolidation, and the last few years have seen a succession of splendid books which have put the whole matter on a much more secure footing than was previously available. Not only so, but the strident denials of the case for a separate Scottish literature made by Dr David Craig and others have not prevented remarkable developments in our universities and elsewhere.

> The new Department of Drama at Glasgow University has been much publicised—and I applaud the decision to create it (wrote a Glasgow journalist the other day), but possibly of much greater significance is that a new Higher Class in nineteenth and twentieth century Scottish literature is also to start in October at Glasgow. Curiously little has been said about it. But this breakthrough is vital to the full understanding and continuance of Scottish literature, whether it takes the form of plays, novels, or poetry ... Other Scottish universities should stop lagging behind. All Scots should have the opportunity of studying their own literature.

I have no doubt the other Scottish universities will soon follow Glasgow's example.* Quite a number of Scottish schools have already developed to some extent along the same direction, and my *Golden Treasury of Scottish Poetry*[2] and other books of

---

* They have not lagged behind. I have just had a letter, for example, from a Professor at Aberdeen University pointing out that in some recent published remarks on this subject I have, he says, 'greatly underestimated my influence on Scottish universities' and giving me facts and figures about the development of the courses in Scottish literature there—and the increasing number of students taking either the Ordinary or Honours classes. I have recently been in the United States and Canada, and know the extent to which interest in Scottish literature has developed in the past few years in the universities there, while in several of them plans are now afoot for the establishment of Schools of Scottish Studies, not based on folklore and balladry like that attached to Edinburgh University, but on modern literature and linguistics.

contemporary Scottish literature are being used in the class-
rooms. Even more significant is the fact that the subject has now
secured a remarkable body of scholarly expositors in American
and Canadian universities. Thanks to the enterprise of Professor
G. Ross Roy, of the University of South Carolina, in establishing
his quarterly *Studies in Scottish Literature* (now completing its third
volume), an impressive number of scholars have been found
devoting themselves to Scottish studies.

So once again, in so far from the demise or futility of expecting
any development in Scottish literature being established, it is
obvious that a far greater rescue operation is mounted now than
those previous efforts, of Fergusson, Burns, Allan Ramsay, and
others which appeared to save it again and again at what seemed
literally 'the eleventh hour'.

Nor is a counter-attack lacking. In an essay on poetry today in
The Modern Age,[3] Charles Tomlinson, of the University of Bristol,
says:

In the English poetry of the 'fifties, one has, to use the words
of a recent reviewer, an arbitrary attempt 'to criticize the
values of subtopia by those of suburbia' ... Instead of the
conscious formulation of a position, one has a provincial
laziness of mind adopted as a public attitude and as the framework for an equally provincial verse. Against such a background poetic culture in Britain would seem to be living on
an overdraft, the overdraft being the work of the writers of
the older generation who are still with us.

I think this is true—true, also, of all the Scottish poets writing
in English today; and it is not surprising in these circumstances to
find the essayist turning away from such writers and, stressing
'the need for the poet's consciousness of what he is doing, of his
need actively to resist the provincializing effects of our suburban
culture', finding what he seeks in a Scottish poet and an Irish one
—in the former case, one who has 'retained in his best verse the
presence of "the mind of Europe" and "worked in the full knowledge of what he was about" and has thus been able to "forge a
Scots verse, neither antiquarian nor provincial, but one in which
a modern awareness can nourish itself on the Scottish past, and
that can absorb into itself Chaucer, Dunbar, Villon".' As to the

other poet, 'a sense of not only what Ireland is, but what it was, enables Austin Clarke ... to speak with a national voice, that ... represents not the inertia of chauvinism, but a labour of recovery. Clarke's skill in using traditional Irish rhyming patterns is similarly not merely a technical recovery, but the measure of a worked-for relation with the past'.

In his book *The Modern Poets* Professor M. L. Rosenthal of New York University observes of a whole sequence of leading English poets of this century (and he cites the Sitwells, Walter de la Mare, Robert Graves, Housman, Kipling, A. E., Monro, Sassoon, Stephens, Aldington) 'the great surge of "modern" poetry in the English language in the second and third decades of this century was, except for Yeats, and Eliot since his transference of citizenship to England, and Lawrence largely American in its most forceful and influential aspects'. Then, naming the poets listed above, he says: 'These names have loomed large at one time and have their places; a few have a distinguished place indeed. But the main drift has passed these writers by.' And again, as against that state of affairs in English poetry today, Professor Rosenthal finds hope and achievement in some of the poetry of the Scottish renaissance movement.

In my prefatory note to Ian S. Munro's biography of James Leslie Mitchell (Lewis Grassic Gibbon),[4] I said:

The *Scots Quair*[5] was his major achievement ... There are only a handful of such non-English novels but they constitute at least the foundation for a tradition of Scottish novel-writing that is quite separate and owes nothing whatever to the English novel. This quality of sheer Scottishness in literature has naturally had a chequered course. It reflects a great part of Scottish life which underlies superficial assimilation to English standards, and only occasionally forces its way to the surface ... They all in some measure link up with the best of the Makars and of Fergusson and Burns and with Sir Thomas Urquhart's translation of Rabelais. Edwin Muir pointed out that Sir Walter Scott was 'the first writer of really great powers to bow his knee unquestionably to gentility and abrogate his responsibility ... There were not many genteel writers before Scott; there have not been many ungenteel ones since.' There is nothing genteel about *A Scots Quair.* It is a major contribution to the line of succession I have indicated and, as Dr Kurt Wittig points out in *The Scottish Tradition in Literature,* 'by far the most promising attempt that has yet been made towards the creation of a modern Scots prose'.

The new one-volume edition of Gibbon's trilogy and Munro's biography of Gibbon evoked in *The Times Literary Supplement* the significant contention that

> literary critics today find it hard to do justice to work which does not fit the standard that has grown up out of educated taste in, say, Metaphysical poetry, fiction in the line from Jane Austen and George Eliot to Henry James and E. M. Forster, and the modernist work of Joyce and Eliot. In these cases the cultural advantages of a middle class born to enjoy, as of right, easy access to cosmopolitan resources of education and taste, and the long leisure to develop their individual talents by making these resources their own, issued in intensely worked-over and considered works of art, which are the peaks of their kind. Another tradition, sometimes dipping into and overlapping with the above but sometimes springing straight from the soil of our own farm, village, and back-street cultures, has also been fertile and fairly continuous. Flowing from the well-heads of folk-song and folk-tale (and stage and platform) it takes on greater scope and complexity, but also a horrible uncertainty of aim and self-knowledge, in writers such as Burns, Dickens, in Russia Gorky, and in our own time Brendan Behan and Alan Sillitoe.

After that extraordinary collocation of utterly unequal names, the reviewer went on to note that

> in the Pelican Guide to English Literature, *The Modern Age ...* Robert Tressell, author of *The Ragged Trousered Philanthropist* ... and Lewis Grassic Gibbon ... are ignored. Yet these books *are* literature — the familiar property and source of images and phrases — to the great majority of people to whom 'quality' literature is a closed book.

Quality literature indeed! That passage alone would have made a Scots renaissance urgently desirable, if there had not been other vitally important reasons. No wonder Cecil Gray, the only music critic of any consequence Scotland has produced, said in his volume of brilliant essays, *Predicaments*[6] in 1936:

> Present circumstances and conditions are uniformly propitious to creative activity in this country [Great Britain] save only one which unfortunately also happens to be a very important one; namely, the attitude of mind and code of aesthetic values which largely dominate English life today, and are mainly responsible for all its worst features, and for our complete inability to induce other nations to take us seriously in literature and the arts — *the cult of the English gentleman!* It permeates every aspect of our national life. It may well be true that our military triumphs have all been won on the playing fields of Eton; but it is very certain that most of our artistic failures have been sustained there. This spirit stunts or oppresses or forces into a pusillanimous compromise every potential native talent and is the absolute antithesis of everything that we call art, and *must be fought as one fights the devil, without rest and without quarter.*

One of the reasons for the general scepticism in Scotland itself with regard to the fact or even the possibility of a Scottish renaissance is the many-sidedness of the effort required. And not only required, but actually at work for the past forty years. Professor David Daiches was right when he wrote in *Library Review* that the effort towards a Scottish renaissance was

> not simply a literary endeavour: it was bound up with questions of Scottish identity which had for the most part been slumbering for nearly two centuries ... And not only with questions of Scottish identity, for the question of the quality of modern industrial democratic society, which prevails over the whole western world, is also involved. The Anglicanization of Scotland is part of the general *Gleichschaltung* of all western culture, and an investigation of its nature and causes is therefore bound up with social and political — and economic — ideas. Arguments about the use of Lallans or the relative

merits of Burns and Dunbar or the place of Gaelic in Scottish culture could not therefore, in the context of any adequately conceived Scottish Renaissance movement, be merely arguments about a literary trend or skirmishes preliminary to the emergence of something parallel to the Pre-Raphaelite movement or the publishing of the *Yellow Book*. They were in the last resort not only about the meaning of culture, of nationality, or history: they were, to put it quite simply, about the meaning of life.

It is impossible to appreciate what has been achieved without reading such books as Dr George Davie's *The Democratic Intellect*,[7] Professor T. B. Smith's *British Justice*,[8] Moray MacLaren's *The Wisdom of the Scots*,[9] Tom Scott's splendid book on Dunbar, and the books that have appeared in the past year or two on John Davidson and James Thomson, author of 'The City of Dreadful Night'. These two, along with other socialist and atheistic poets like Tom Hood, and Francis Adams, were swept aside by the torrent of populist doggerel that runs (and is still running) in the wake of Burns. Nevertheless Burns himself is being properly revalued and the Burns cult purged of its mindless and hypocritical excesses, in which connection I am delighted to have received the other day a letter from a brilliant young historian researching into the history of the Friends of the People, in which he says:

I have also been able to prove quite conclusively that Burns did not (as Meikle states) join the Volunteers 'in order to reinstate himself in the good graces of his employers', but as part of a plan which was being carried out on a national level by the radicals, to infiltrate the ranks of the Volunteers, who were after all being raised for the sole purpose of suppressing the Friends of the People. The first society to adopt this policy was that of Perth, and another society quickly followed it up by offering their services to the Duke of Buccleuch. The news of these exploits was carried by John Fairley, the courier of the Committee of Ways and Means, to the societies in the west, and was in turn passed on by Hastie, the Paisley leader, to Kilmarnock, Dumfries, etc. As for the loyal ballad, 'Does Haughty Gaul Invasion Threat?' a brief glance at the message contained in the last four lines in the light of this new information, quickly reveals it to be of a very different breed entirely.

Not the least of the proofs that we are at last making headway in setting our house in order is the bibliographical work which has appeared in *The Bibliotheck* and in the long-overdue but extremely useful (if still requiring much amplification) interim bibliography of the Scottish working class movement edited by Ian MacDougall, secretary of the Scottish Committee of the Society for the Study of Labour History. These represent two of the numerous channels along which the renaissance movement has developed.

> Far back through creeks and inlets making
> Comes silent, flooding in, the main.

Many such discoveries are being made and Scottish history and biography purged of innumerable distortions and deliberate falsifications. I have been unable to find space here to mention among the many positive achievements of the renaissance movement the Gaelic poetry of Sorley Maclean, George Campbell Hay, and Derick Thomson, the plays of James Bridie and Robert Maclellan, the political balladry of Morris Blythman (infinitely more important than the resuscitation of the 'corn-kisters' and other culturally negligible folk-song developments, though the genuine work in this connection of men like Norman Buchan and Jack Stuart should be noted); the songs of Francis George Scott and, more recently Ronald Stevenson; and the musical researches of Helena Shire, Harry Willsher and Ian Whyte; but all these, and other, tributaries have gone to swell the developing current of our movement, and there is no question but that important fresh accessions are in the offing. I know of many important books pending publication, and if many of the general public believe that the poetic impetus of the 'twenties and 'thirties has spent itself, they have only to read the current issue of Duncan Glen's Scottish poetry magazine *Akros* (August 1966).

I could add several names to the new poets Mr Glen lists, most importantly that of T. S. Law, who has a lot of so far unpublished Scots poems which I have read in typescript and regard as a most important contribution to the Lallans output.

But for me the crux of the whole matter and the essential pointer to the development of the Scottish renaissance movement from now on lies in the realization of just where the difference lies between the English literary tradition and the Scottish, and it is brought out splendidly in the following passage in which Frank Harris compared Tennyson and James Thomson:

Whenever I recall Tennyson's death, and the unmeasured glorification of him in the English press, I am compelled to think of poor James Thomson and his end. The poet of *The City of Dreadful Night* died ten years before Tennyson, died in miserable poverty and almost unappreciated; yet, in my opinion, he was as gifted a poet as Tennyson and far wiser; intellectually indeed one of the greatest, a master of prose as well as verse. His life and fate throw a sinister light on English conditions. In every respect he comes nearer to ideal wisdom than any other modern English poet. While Tennyson lauds the Crimean War, Thomson condemns it as a 'mere selfish haggle, badly begun and meanly finished' ... He showed sympathy for all the struggling nationalisms of his time, for Italy and Poland and even for the Basques, who had supported the Carlist cause in 1873. Here are his words: 'Such was the loyalty of these people, far more noble than ours; for they were giving freely of their substance and their lives, whereas we give chiefly snobbish cringing and insincere adulation, and our rich give the money of the nation in large part wrung from the poor.' Unlike Tennyson he was devoted to the cause of the people, and fought against every form of privilege and capitalism. Every Englishman should read his satirical essay on Bumbledom. He points out that though there is more liberty in England than on the Continent, in matters affecting political discussion 'the reverse is true as regards questions of morals and sociology, for here the power of Bumble's purse rules our so-called free press and free institutions with a hand heavier than that of any Continental despot'.

Thomson is really the only Englishman who stands with Heine and Leopardi as a great modern master, and his translations of their poems are the best in English. And Thomson

15

was kindlier and sweeter in all his personal relations than either of them. Even Heine at times distresses one by the contempt he shows for the greatest, such as Goethe. We have no such apology to make for Thomson ... Thomson's essays, especially on the poets, are far and away the best in English. His view of Tennyson shows the sureness of his judgment, the width of his impartiality: 'Scarcely any other artist in verse of the same rank has ever lived on such scanty revenues of thought (both pure and applied) as Tennyson ... He is continually petty ... A great school of poets is dying out; it will die decently, elegantly, in the full odour of respectability with our Laureate [Tennyson].'

Think of Thomson's final word which I would put in the forefront of every English Bible if I could: 'England and France are so proudly in the van of civilization that it is impossible for a great poet to live to old age in either of them.'

Tennyson and Thomson — between these poles you can find England: the one man, supremely endowed with genius for words, but with the mind of a sentimental schoolboy, was ruined by too great adulation and too many rewards; the other, of far higher mental endowment, bred as a charity orphan, was gradually disheartened by neglect and finally broken by the universal indifference that kept him a pauper. I know that this judgment will not be accepted readily; the English would much rather blame a great man than take any shame to themselves for maltreating him. But one proof occurs to me: in the 'nineties, more than fifteen years after Thomson's death, H. D. Traill, one of the first journalists and men of letters of the time, wrote an article in *The Nineteenth Century* on English poets of the Victorian era. He gave a list of sixty-six who were able to speak 'the veritable and authentic language of the poet'. He puts Tennyson as the first, mentions even a Mrs Graham Tomson; but omits James Thomson altogether. Yet of the two, Tennyson and Thomson — the lord and the outcast — it was the outcast orphan alone that reached the heights.

There can be no question as to which of these two roads the

effort to re-establish the independent Scottish literary tradition must take.

Fifty years is not a long enough time to reverse entirely the centuries-long belittlement and repudiation of the national tradition and get rid of the consequences of the relentless indoctrination and encroachment of an alien literature and language. But a great deal has certainly been achieved. It was foreseen at the outset that the objectives of the renaissance movement could not be secured unless there were also political changes which would put the Scottish people in full control of their own affairs and resources. The recent remarkable upswing in membership and influence of the Scottish National Party indicates that this essential condition will be forthcoming. What can be done in the meantime in all the departments of Scottish arts and affairs has at least a far greater chance of success than seemed at all likely in 1920.

24

THE UPSURGE OF SCOTTISH
NATIONALISM

1967

I am not a member of the Scottish National Party or any of the other nationalist organizations. But I have been an active Scottish nationalist for nearly fifty years. My opposition to, or lack of sympathy with, almost all the leading Scottish nationalists I know is due to my having an entirely different set of priorities.

I am not a shopkeeper or a businessman. I do not believe that a nation can be regenerated by arguments based on statistics or improved business techniques. The true saying is that without a vision the people perish. I underline the word vision. It is by no means synonymous with the P.R.O.s' and advertising agents' favourite cant term today—namely, image.

In all the other countries I know of where independence has been gained or regained the necessary impulse came from poets and other artists. So it was in Scotland, too, over forty years ago.

The bulk of the Scottish population then (I refuse to call them Scots) were in precisely the same position as Mr Alexander Maclehose, who, in his *The Scotland of Our Sons*,[1] arraigned England's studied neglect of Scotland's economic welfare—the dwindling population of the glens, the vicious concentration of over fifty per cent of the inhabitants of Scotland in a handful of large towns, an infant mortality rate half as high again as that of England, a proportion of houses unfit for human habitation six times as great as that south of the Border, and so on.

Yet, after marshalling all these damning facts, after thanking the Scottish nationalists too for having 'stirred up Scotland', he was not prepared to advocate the establishment of even limited Home Rule for Scotland, on the grounds that (1) good government might come from Whitehall yet, and (2) a parliament in Edinburgh would very likely have a majority of socialists (where else, one asked in these far-off days before the Labour

Party's abandonment of socialism, could the impulse towards reconstruction spring in Scotland save from socialists?).

Finally, he had nothing practical to propose at all except an ambition to see 'more craftsmen from Sutherland to Galloway engaged in the manufacture of small wooden replicas of Dunstaffnage and Dunolly Castles'. And I wrote:

> No one has ever had any capacity for saying anything worth a docken about Scotland who has not felt about almost all that has been, and is being, said of it and about all the glib sayers, as Burns felt when, on one occasion, a self-elected guide was pointing out the capabilities of a scene for practical treatment.
>
> Burns listened and looked on stolidly. A lady of the party ventured to ask him if he had nothing to say about the scene. 'How can I, madam,' he exploded, 'while that ass is braying over it?'

There is precious little in all the propaganda written and spoken in relation to the great upsurge of Scottish nationalism in the past year or two which does not affect me in the same way.

There are still among those who call themselves Scottish nationalists far too big a proportion of Mr Maclehoses, as witness, to give only one example, a recent contention that if her majesty the Queen would only take up residence for a month or two annually in Holyroodhouse that would go a long way to solve Scotland's crucial problems.

Burns wrote in one of his letters, 'Alas, I have often said to myself, what are all the boasted advantages which my country reaps from the Union that can counterbalance the annihilation of her independence and even of her very name?'

Like him, I have no use for any Scottish Nationalist movement that is not above all concerned with the position of Scottish culture and determined to do everything possible to restore it to the proud eminence it had before increasing Anglification obliterated our old traditions and assimilated us more and more to the very different traditions of England.

I have never been able to see that any good could come from the establishment in Edinburgh of a miniature replica of Westminster, with the same conception of politics, subscribing to the same economic system, and filled with M.P.s ignorant of and indifferent to our past achievements and present potentialities in a literature, and other arts, utterly different from their English counterparts, and making a contribution to world culture that only Scotland could make, and could make only in her own languages, Scots and Gaelic.

I have travelled a great deal in European countries in recent years and found in most of the university student audiences and writers' and other cultural groups I addressed an inability to recognize that Scotland was a separate country and that the use of 'English' or 'England' as synonymous with 'British' or 'Britain' was quite wrong.

Most of the countries I visited had fought hard, but successfully, for the retention and modern development of their own native languages and liberties. When I made my point to them they took it readily and sympathetically enough.

The fact of the matter is that, as R. L. Stevenson pointed out long ago, 'despite their proximity, there are no other two peoples in the world so different from each other as the Scots and the English.'

And English poetry and Scottish are quite incomparable and have little or nothing to do with each other; indeed, their especial qualities are almost mutually exclusive.

In the early days of the Scottish literary revival it was at once apparent to myself and others that any hope for the re-establishment of a distinctive independent Scottish literature would be impossible of full development unless there was a parallel political development that would give the Scottish people once again real power and control over all their institutions and resources.

The world-wide growth of Burns clubs was no remedy for a state of affairs which gave English language and literature, and even English history, a virtual monopoly in our schools and colleges to the almost complete exclusion of any attention to Scottish literature, our Scottish languages (Scots and Gaelic), and Scottish history.

In passing, I cannot forbear to point out as a typical error, caused by the sad state of Scottish historical studies under the over-influence of England, that in his introductory article to this series* Mr Robert Kemp was seriously wrong when he said Burns's

---

* This is one of a series of articles in the *Glasgow Herald. Editor.*

nationalist mood was 'perceptibly changed by the threat of war with France'.

The late Dr Henry Meikle, Historiographer Royal for Scotland, was under the same mistaken impression. It is often said that 'nothing new remains to be said about Burns'. Nonsense.

A brilliant young historian, researching into the history of the Friends of the People, wrote to me recently: 'I have also been able to prove quite conclusively that Burns did not (as Meikle states) join the Volunteers "in order to reinstate himself in the good graces of his employers", but as part of a plan which was being carried out on a national level by the radicals, to infiltrate the ranks of the Volunteers, who were after all being raised for the sole purpose of suppressing the Friends of the People.'

The late Mr T. S. Eliot was right when he said: 'I suspect Arnold of helping to fix the wholly mistaken notion of Burns as a singular untutored English dialect poet instead of a decadent representative of a great alien tradition.'

There can be no Scottish nationalism worth the name that has not as its central purpose the recovery of that 'alien tradition' in all its fullness, and the aim of carrying it on to great achievements in accordance with contemporary requirements.

A great deal has been achieved in the past forty years. At long last classes in Scottish literature have been established in some Scottish universities, and the subject is now being taught in many Scottish schools.

The Edinburgh poet Mr Sydney Goodsir Smith recently demonstrated in a fully documented essay that an anti-Scottish lobby had been such a recurring phenomenon in the history of Scottish literature that it was really a wonder that the literature survived its continual bashing since the eighteenth century.

What is even more serious is that its enemies considered it worth bashing. That is belatedly being changed. It is worth bashing now — and perfectly able to defend itself and bash its enemies in return. Even more significant than what I have said about our Scottish universities and schools is that the subject has now secured a remarkable body of scholarly expositors in American and Canadian universities.

What, then, is the deep difference between Scottish and English poetry? An Edinburgh professor last century put it thus.

There is a connection between the Scottish tradition of poetry as natural and the democratic basis of Scottish society.

The English devotion to artificial poetry is due to the stratifications and segregations of English society. There is nothing national in either Spenser or Milton or Pope or Dryden or Wordsworth or many more.

They are great poets no doubt, but the people don't sympathize with them, though portions of the educated classes may do so, and taking them altogether what kind of congruity either of sentiment or form do you find in their work?

But take Burns and Scott and Hogg and Motherwell and Allan Cunninghame with their predecessors David Lyndsay and Allan Ramsay and Robert Fergusson—they are adored by the people (or were until the Anglicization of the Scottish people).

And why were they so much adored? Because they are minstrels and because they embody in vivid strains the emotions, thoughts—nay, prejudices if you will—which are most rife in the national bosom.

I realize, of course, that most people will fail to recognize in what I have written any case for Scottish nationalism. That they alone of European peoples should have been reduced to such a contemptible state of mind is precisely the most urgent reason for a psychological revolution in Scotland.

I am not denying the importance of practical affairs. But all the Scottish issues one can think of—emigration, rural depopulation, housing, and all the rest—cannot add up to Scottish nationalism.

25

POETRY AND SCIENCE*
1967

Asked if he did not sense that the public resistance to the sort of most basic ideas in science is changing at all, Jacques Monod, the molecular biologist, who is Professor of the Faculty of Science in the University of Paris and head of the Department of Metabolic Chemistry in the Pasteur Institute—also 1965 joint winner of the Nobel Prize for Medicine—replied in a recent interview: 'I don't think so and I think it is a great danger and a tragedy. Science has moulded our whole society, by technology, but even more by the creation of new ideas and new outlooks at the universe; and the fact that this is not fully understood and recognized by the general public and governments and the Church and the universities and the philosophers is one of the causes of what we might call the neurosis of modern societies.'

One effort to solve this problem, in a particular direction at least, may be seen in the new methods of teaching mathematics. Mathematics is the structure of human ideas and hypotheses concerning abstract concepts based on the 'real' world. Its processes and concepts are particularly amenable to analysis, description, and recording by concise symbols and patterns of symbols and this fact, coupled with the extreme practical importance of some parts of the subject, accounts for the rapid expansion of mathematics over the centuries, and its present unfortunate position—the position or fact that it is quite possible to get good results in maths examinations at any level up to and including Honours degree by sheer facility and practice with techniques and procedures yet with almost negligible appreciation of the ideas and concepts involved. Maths is not about symbols on a blackboard or piece of paper, which is the impression most people are hard put to avoid from the time they enter infant school onwards.

* From a lecture given in the University of Lund, Sweden, and later in the University of Massachusetts at Amherst, May 1967. *Editor*.

The object of the present attempted change in the teaching of mathematics is to try to get across to people the ideas and concepts first before bothering about how to write them down—just as children are taught to write a language only after they have become thoroughly familiar with its use.

There is a passage in Chekhov's story, *The Wife*, which runs:

> I listened to her doctor, and, according to my habit, applied my usual measures to him—materialist, idealist, and so forth, but not a single one of my measures would fit even approximately, and, curiously, while I only listened to him, and looked at him, he was a man perfectly clear to me, but the moment I began applying my measures to him, he became, despite all his sincerity and simplicity, an extraordinarily complex, confused, and inexplicable nature.

Is not this what the great majority of critics do to literature—applying their formulae of this kind or that, until the wood cannot be seen for the trees? Even with the best of them we feel as the Portuguese poet, Eugenio de Castro, describes himself as feeling on awaking to catch a glimpse of himself in the antique looking-glass of a Toledo hotel—he could not see himself, as he thought he really looked, but only as he might have been painted perhaps by an imitator of Greco.

Susan Glaspell in her play *Bernice*[1] deals with the problem very well in the following dialogue between her two characters Margaret and Craig.

MARGARET: We give ourselves in fighting for a thing that seems important, and in that fight we get out of the flow of life. We had meant it to deepen that flow—but we get caught. I know people like that. People who get at home in their fight and stay there and are left there when the fight's over. You write so well, Craig—but what of it? What is it is the matter with you—with all you American writers—most all of you? A well-put-up light, but it doesn't penetrate anything. It never makes the fog part. Just shows itself off—a well-put-up light! (*Growing angry*) It would be better if we didn't have you at all. Can't you see that it would? Lights which only light themselves keep us from having light—from knowing what the darkness is. (*After thinking*) Craig, as you write these things, are there

never times when you sit *dumb*, and know that you are glib
and empty?

CRAIG : Did you ever try to write, Margaret?

MARGARET : No.

CRAIG : I suppose you think it's very simple to be real. I suppose
you think we could do it—if we wanted to. Try it. *You* try.

MARGARET : So you do this just to cover the fact that you *can't*
do anything? Your skill—a mask for your lack of power?

That's it. That's what we want—Chekhov's clearness before
the application of 'measures'.

We are all, more or less consciously, troubled as we read, as
Katherine Mansfield was when writing her stories. 'I feel', she
said, 'that this kind of knowledge is too easy for me, it's even a
kind of trickery. I know so much more. I know exactly where I
fail, and yet when I have finished a story, and before I have
begun another, I catch myself actually *preening* my feathers. It is
disheartening. This interferes very much with work. I look at the
mountains—and I think of something *clever*.'

Most writers—certainly all but a few poets—never look at the
mountains at all, of course, and are to be condemned because as
J. Russell Lowell said, 'not failure but low aim is crime.' As the
Scottish poet John Davidson said:[2] 'The want of poetical power
is the impelling force in the case of most versifiers. They would
fain be poets, and imagine that the best way is to try to write
poetry and to publish what they write. They will never see their
mistake. *Equus asinus* still believes that the possession of an organ
of noise is sufficient, with a little practice, to enable him to sing
like a nightingale.'

It was said of Davidson—and so truly that it largely accounts
for the way he has been neglected ever since neglect made him
commit suicide in 1909—'He states fact in terms of poetry, and
the statement sears one's consciousness. He is the first poet to digest
the new wonders of science which have subtly changed the old
cosmogony, and made the very foundations of existence crumble
away.' That is why I myself wrote: 'The relation of John Davidson's thought to Nietzsche's is more important than all the drivel
about "Home, Sweet Home" four million cretins iterate. And if
we can't throw off the world, let us hear of no "Old Grey Mother"

at all, but of Middle Torridonian Arkose with local breccias, or the pillow lavas at Loch Awe.' Davidson knew what he was about all right. 'The insane past is the incubus:' he said, 'the world is really a virgin world awaking from a bad dream. These are some of the seeds of the new thing I bring, of the new poetry which the world will make. Poetry is the flower of what all men are maturing in thought and fancy; I reap a harvest unsown; I come a hundred years before the time — that time foreseen by Wordsworth "when what is now called science, familiarized to men, shall be ready to put on a form of flesh and blood".'

There has recently been a great debate between the critic F.R. Leavis and C.P. Snow, now Lord Snow, the novelist, about the two cultures — the gap of mutual unintelligibility and antipathy between science and the arts, a local application of that increasingly divisive force which springs from the fact that the sciences are becoming so greatly a matter of specialization that it is becoming virtually impossible for the specialist in one to communicate at all with the specialist in another, and general understanding — the ability to think or understand not in bits and pieces, but all round the circle — seems out of the question altogether.

To get these considerations into perspective, we should consider in conjunction with them what James Harvey Robinson says in his *The Mind In The Making*[3] on 'the general show-up of man's thought throughout the ages'. 'The astonishing and perturbing fact that almost all that has passed for social science, political economy, politics, ethics in the past may be brushed aside by future generations as mainly "rationalizing" — the opposite of thinking' — and, in particular, the paragraph in which he says, 'When we are offered a penny for our thoughts, we always find that we have recently had so many things in mind that we can easily make a selection which will not compromise us too nakedly. On inspection we shall find that even if we are not downright ashamed of a great part of our spontaneous thinking it is far too intimate, personal, ignoble or trivial to permit us to reveal more than a small part of it. We find it hard to believe that other people's thoughts are as silly as ours, but they probably are.'

It has been truly said then that

the inventions and organizations that have produced the

peculiar opportunities and dangers of the modern world have been the work so far of a few hundred thousand exceptionally clever and enterprising people — a very small percentage of mankind, which has been a constant throughout the whole of human history, and if that small percentage could be eliminated all the vast remaining mass of mankind could do nothing whatever to reconstitute the arts and sciences, or, in other words, even such measure of civilization as we have so far achieved. The rest of mankind has just been carried along by that tiny minority, and has remained practically what it was a thousand years ago. Upon an understanding and competent minority, which may not exceed a million or so in all the world, depends the whole progress and stability of the collective human enterprise at the present time. They are in perpetual conflict with hampering tradition and the obduracy of nature ... For a number of generations at any rate a deadweight of the dull, silly, under-developed, weak and aimless will have to be carried by the guiding wills and intelligences of mankind. There seems to be no way of getting rid of them. The panics and preferences of these relatively uneducable minds, their flat and foolish tastes, their perversities and compensatory loyalties, their dull gregarious resistances to comprehensive efforts, their outbreaks of resentment at any too lucid revelation of their inferiority, will be a drag, and perhaps a very heavy drag, on the adaptation of institutions to modern needs and to the development of a common knowledge and a common conception of purpose throughout mankind ... The struggle of intelligent and energetic minds throughout the world to clear out their own lumber and get together for the conscious control of the affairs of the strangely mingled multitude of our kind to develop the still largely unrealized possibilities of science and to organize a directive collective will is the essential drama of human life.

What is the relation to all this of poets today — are poets still 'the unacknowledged legislators of mankind', 'the movers and shapers of the world for ever it seems'? I have said in one of my poems:[4]

Once again we seek to heal the breach
Between genius and scholarship, literature and learning,
(These two which share the knowledge
Of a broken unity of the human spirit,
Which to genius appears
Mainly a moral and personal disaster
To be mended by intuition, by divination,
But to the second, equally conscious
Of the discontinuity of tradition,
Of the accidents of time, language, place and race
That hinder sympathy and understanding,
Presents itself as an intellectual trouble
To be solved by piecing together
Minute particulars of evidence)
Which, since consummate learning is far more rare
Than genius, has led to the ridiculous condition
That the world, which holds out both hands to genius,
Is unhappy in the presence of scholarship,
Often contemptuous, sometimes even resentful of it,
Siding naturally with the spiritual valour
Which dashes itself to pieces
On the unbreachable walls which fence Truth
But having little sympathy
With the slow and cautious movement of learning,
Yet we all know now the world might get on better
If it ceased to produce great men of action;
Speculative genius is a mixed boon too.

In the same very long poem I quote Paul Valéry's statement:
'We have the privilege — or the great misfortune — to be present
at a profound, rapid, irresistible and total transformation of all
the conditions of human activity and of life itself.' And I comment:
'In this connection it is true of Joyce, as was said by and of another
poet: "I will not leave a corner of my consciousness covered up,
but saturate myself with the strange and extraordinary new
conditions of this life".' This willingness and ability to let himself
be 'new born into the new situation, not subduing his experience
to his established personality, is a large part if not the whole
secret of the character of Joyce's best work. It was his exposure

of his whole personality that gave his work its quality of imper-
sonality.' And I wrote that it is said in the twelfth chapter and
second verse of Luke: 'For there is nothing covered that shall not
be revealed, neither hid that shall not be known.'

The general predicament I have been describing leads me in
the same poem, which is an enormous In Memoriam poem to
James Joyce, to say:

> The ancestors of oysters and barnacles had heads,
> Snakes have lost their limbs,
> And ostriches and penguins their power of flight.
> Man may just as easily lose his intelligence.
> Most of our people already have.
> It is unlikely that man will develop into anything higher
> Unless he desires to and is prepared to pay the cost.
> Otherwise we shall go the way of the dodo and kiwi.
> Already the process seems far advanced,
> Genius is becoming rarer,
> Our bodies a little weaker, with each generation.
> Culture is slowly declining.
> Mankind is returning to barbarism
> And will finally become extinct.

What then is the use of the incredible strategems of words in
which Joyce describes *Finnegans Wake* or Ezra Pound devises his
Cantos? I answer as follows:

All but an infinitesimal percentage of mankind
Have no use whatever for versatility and myriad-mindedness.
Erudition means less than nothing to them
(Larvae, hallucinated automata, bobbins,
Savage robots, appropriate dummies,
The fascinating imbecility of the creaking men-machines,
Set in a pattern as circumscribed and complete
As a theory of Euclid—essays in a new human mathematic)
Yet, as Gaudapada says, even as a bed
Which is an assembly of frame, mattress, bedding and pillows,
Is for another's use, not for its own,
And its several component parts render no mutual service,
Thence it is concluded that there is a man who sleeps upon this bed
And for whose sake it was made; so this world

Of words, thoughts, memories, scientific facts, literary arts,
Is for another's use. Ah, Joyce, enough said, enough said.
Mum's the word now! Mum's the word!
Responsibility for the present state of the world
And for its development for better or worse
Lies with every single individual;
Freedom is only really possible
In proportion as all are free.
Knowledge, and, indeed, adoption (*Aneignung*)
Of the rich Western tradition,
And all the wisdom of the East as well
Is the indispensable condition of any progress.
World-history and world-philosophy
Are only now beginning to dawn;
Whatever tribulation may yet be in store for men
Pessimism is false. Let us make ourselves at home
In das Umgreifende, the super-objective,
The final reality to which human life can attain.
Short of that every man is guilty,
Living only the immediate life,
Without memory, without plan, without mastery,
The very definition of vulgarity;
Guilty of a dereliction of duty,
The 'distraction' of Pascal,
The 'aesthetic stage' of Kierkegaard,
The 'inauthentic life' of Heidegger,
The 'alienation' of Marx,
The self-deception (*mauvaise foi*) of Sartre.

I believe it will be in every connection soon
As already in the field of colour
Where the imitative stage
Has long been passed
And coal-tar dyes are synthesized no more
To imitate the colours of nature,
Whether of Autumn or Spring.
The pattern cards of dye-stuff firms today
Display multitudes of syntheses
That transcend Nature to reach

Almost a philosophic satisfaction
Of the aesthetic sense of colour.
Apart from a handful of scientists and poets
Hardly anybody is aware of it yet
(A society of people without a voice for the consciousness
That is slowly growing within them.)
Nevertheless everywhere among the great masses of mankind
With every line it is growing and emerging
Like a mango tree under a cloth
Stirring the dull cloth,
Sending out tentacles,
—It's not something that can be stopped
By sticking it away in a zinc-lined box
Like a tube of radium
As most people have,
Calling all who approve of it mad,
The term they always apply
To anyone who tries to make them think.

For Schoenberg was right, the problem involved
In mental vocalization
Is not that the evolution of music
Must wait on the human ear,
But that the human ear must catch up
With the evolution of music.
As with Schoenberg's so, Joyce, with your work
And scant though the endeavour be
Of progress here we have ample proof
(While yet the vast majority of mankind
Are but inching to close the infinite gap
And may succeed in a few billion years perhaps)
That the complicated is Nature's climax of rightness,
And the simple at a discount. The Apocrypha is right.
Of our Muse, 'She needs no simple man!'
We have learned the lesson of the Caddoan saying:
'When a woman grinds the corn with one hand
Don't let it into your belly!'
As in the clash between Red Indian and White Man
Sophistication was with simplicity everywhere

With only one possible conclusion. There can be no doubt
That the bed of which I have spoken will be filled,
All life's million conflicting interests and relationships,
Even as nerves before ever they function
Grow where they *will* be wanted; levers laid down in gristle
Become bone when wanted for the heavier pull
Of muscles which *will* clothe them; lungs, solid glands,
Yet arranged to hollow out at a few minutes' notice
When the necessary air shall enter; limb buds
Futile at their appearing, yet deliberately appearing
In order to become limbs in readiness
For an existence where they *will* be all-important;
A pseudo-aquatic parasite, voiceless as a fish,
Yet containing within itself an instrument of voice
Against the time when it *will* talk;
Organs of skin, ear, eye, nose, tongue
Superfluous all of them in the watery dark
Where formed—yet each unhaltingly preparing
To enter a daylit, airy, objectfull, manifold world
They *will* be wanted to report on. Everywhere we find
Prospective knowledge of the needs of life
Which are not yet, but are foreknown.
All is provided. As Aristotle says,
'To know the end of a thing is to know the why of it!'
So with your work, vastly outrunning present needs
With its immense complication, its erudition,
(The intricacy of the connections defies description.
Before it the mind halts, abased, *In tenuis labor*)
But providing for the developments to come.
Even so long before the foetus
Can have either sensation or motion,
When, in fact, its cellular elements
First begin to differentiate themselves,
The various nerves which are to govern
The perceptions and reactions essential in life
Develop, as they shape themselves, a faculty
For discovering and joining with their 'opposite numbers',
Sensory cell 'calling' to motor cell
By a force we may call Cytoclesis.

Nor is this mysterious call
A phenomenon of the nervous system only.
Throughout the body cell calls to cell
That the elaborate and intricate development
Of tissues may proceed aright.
Thus in the case of the kidney tubules
The myriad secreting tubules are formed
In one portion of the primordial embryonic tissue
Budded out from the ureter.
Nevertheless although these two entities
Are involved in the completion of all the kidney tubules
There is the marvel that results in each secreting tubule
Meeting a collecting tubule
Accurately end to end.
Each complete duct is composed of two sections
Preformed from different embryological elements
But guided to meet each other by a 'call',
A 'call' so wonderful that each kidney tubule
Meets each ureteric tubule end to end
And so completes the canal.

The programme for poetry I advocate is in Walt Whitman's words: to conform with and build on the concrete realities and theories of the universe furnished by science, and henceforth the only irrefragable basis for anything, verse included: and like Whitman I cry: 'Think of the absence and ignorance hitherto of the multitudinousness, vitality, and the unprecedented stimulants of today. It almost seems as if a poetry with cosmic and dynamic features of magnitude and limitlessness suitable to the human soul were never possible before. It is certain that a poetry of absolute faith and equality for the use of the democratic masses never was.'

More attention should have been—and should be—paid to Sir Compton Mackenzie's declaration that

A new kind of man is beginning to reveal himself. Speed is the basic foundation of this new man. The mind has already begun to change its processes to take advantage of the speed with which every day the body is being more and more richly endowed. It seems indeed, that unless some catastrophe of war or pestilence on a scale immensely greater than anything the world has yet known by exacerbating the struggle for existence intervenes to prolong the way of human thought since Genesis, the second millennium of the Christian era will see humanity launched upon a way of thought a thousand times more different from our present ways of thought than ours from the thought of neolithic man.

It is impossible to agree with Edwin Muir that when some postulation of a transcendental reality—the belief in eternity—fails, 'imagination suffers an eclipse, and if that belief were to fail completely and for good it is possible that it would mean the final end of all imaginative literature and art.'

I believe that all such beliefs will speedily fail and for ever, and that that will be the beginning of imaginative literature and art for everybody—not, as hitherto, only for a favoured few. The effective alternative to Mr Muir's 'belief in eternity which is natural to man' is Mr Santayana's 'primal and universal religion, the religion of will, the faith which life has in itself because it is life and in its aims, because it is pursuing them'—'the heart and mystery of matter lies in the seeds of things, *semina rerum*, and in the customary cycles of their transformation.'

Discussing Professor Morris Cohen's *Reason and Nature*[5] an American critic observed:

Professor Cohen states that his greatest debt is to Bertrand Russell's *Principles of Mathematics*, and a comparison of the chief traits of the two men may perhaps be fruitful. Russell and Cohen have in common two valuable characteristics. Both possess minds of immense logical acuteness and neither has confined himself to a single field of endeavour, but has ventured with great success into many domains of thought. Their range of interests is practically co-extensive, but each exhibits the same surprising limitations. In fields where the aesthetic content predominates over the intellectual, neither displays any special knowledge or aptitude. In *Reason and Nature* the literary allusions are almost non-existent. A few names of the first magnitude, such as Sophocles, Shelley, and Dante are invoked to illustrate a point. There is an unfortunate reference

to Sainte-Beuve—wrongly spelt and with the Sainte abbre-
viated into the contraction for a street—and there is (for
philosophical scientists) the inevitable quotation in the original German from *Faust*. It is perhaps a biological peculiarity
that intellectual and aesthetic mastery unite so seldom in a
single individual.

A still more significant case is that of Professor A. N. Whitehead
in his *Science and the Modern World*.[6] He stresses the need to draw
out habits of aesthetic apprehension—to foster the creative
initiative towards the maintenance of objective values. He devotes
a whole chapter to showing that the literature of the nineteenth
century, especially English poetic literature, is a witness to the
discord between the aesthetic intuitions of mankind and the
mechanism of science. 'The romantic reaction was' he contends
'a protest on behalf of value'—and an invaluable corrective to
current scientific misconceptions and precursor of the better
scientific understanding since attained. But in propounding his
own new doctrines he does not take advantage of that important
discovery and stop to ask what the relations between poetry and
science today may disclose of a like sort. He deals with Wordsworth and Shelley, but subsequent poetry is apparently completely
out of his ken, while the importance of his thesis in the chapter in
question should surely have compelled him to widen his inquiries
into the poetry of the period and not confine himself to two or
three English poets and exclude the poets of other countries. And
his conclusion that the passage in Shelley's 'Prometheus Unbound'
beginning 'I spin beneath my pyramid of night' could only have
been written by someone with a definite geometrical design
before his inward eye—a diagram it has often been my business to
demonstrate to mathematical classes—is of course thoroughly
unscientific. Shelley may have come at the conception in question
quite independently: science itself abounds in instances of unrelated researchers arriving independently—and from different
angles of approach—at identical discoveries. G. B. Dibblee's
really epoch-making book *Instinct and Intuition*,[7] with all its
abundant knowledge and extreme dialectical ability, illustrates
to a lamentable extent how the growth of civilization can yet
leave the spiritual stature of man not increased by one iota, and

Mr Dibblee's inept illustrations, jejune personal recollections, and lack of recourse to the very people who embody the 'refined spiritual faculties' with which he is concerned, is just another sorry instance of the failure of most scientists and philosophers to avail themselves of the aid they could have derived from a really thorough and up-to-date knowledge of poetry. To give only one illustration, Paul Valéry for example made a present of his speculations in *L'Idée fixe* to the medical profession. What has the medical profession made of this important gift from a man of an intellectual stature to which few of its own members can ever aspire?

We have got a long way in this discussion from one of my own simple perceptions which at the outset of my career as a poet I expressed as follows:

The rarity and value of scientific knowledge
Is little understood—even as people
Who are not botanists find it hard to believe
Special knowledge of the subject can add
Enormously to the aesthetic appreciation of flowers!
Partly because in order to identify a plant
You must study it very much more closely
Than you would otherwise have done, and in the process
Exquisite colours, proportions, and minute shapes spring to light
Too small to be ordinarily noted,
And more than this—it seems the botanist's knowledge
Of the complete structure of the plant
(Like a sculptor's of bone and muscle)
—Of the configuration of its roots stretching under the earth,
The branching of stems,
Enfolding of buds by bracts,
Spreading of veins on a leaf
Encircles and snakes three dimensional
His awareness of its complex beauty.

So I conclude that it is supremely desirable that every writer should be able to lay his hand on his heart and say with Anton Chekhov

Familiarity with the natural sciences and with scientific

methods has always kept me on my guard, and I have always tried, where it was possible, to be consistent with the facts of science ... I may observe in passing that the conditions of artistic creation do not always admit of complete harmony with the facts of science. It is impossible to represent on the stage a death from poisoning exactly as it takes place in reality. But harmony with the facts of science must be felt even under these conditions—that is, it must be clear to the reader or spectator that this is only due to the conditions of art and that he has to do with a writer who understands. I do not belong to the class of literary men who take up a sceptical attitude towards science: and to the class of those who rush into anything with only their own imagination to go upon, I should not like to belong.

REFERENCE NOTES

INTRODUCTION

1 Methuen, London, 1943.
2 Leonard Parsons, London, 1926.
3 Nott, London, 1934.
4 Jarrolds, London, 1934.

1 THE POLITICS AND POETRY OF HUGH MACDIARMID 1952

1 Methuen, London, 1943.
2 Constable, London, 1913.
3 Blackwood, London, 1926.
4 Maclellan, Glasgow, 1947.
5 *A Hope for Poetry* (Blackwell, Oxford, 1934).
6 *This Modern Poetry* (Faber & Faber, London, 1936).
7 Oxford University Press, 1936.
8 Printed in *The Voice of Scotland*, vol. 6, no. 1, (April 1955), and in *Three Hymns to Lenin* (Castle Wynd Printers, Edinburgh, 1957).
9 *Collected Poems* (Macmillan, New York, revised edition, 1967).
10 Maclellan, Glasgow, 1943 f.
11 *Collected Poems*, op. cit., entitled 'Edinburgh'.
12 Civic Press, Glasgow, 1942.
13 Maclellan, Glasgow, 1941.
14 Blackwell, Oxford, 1940.

2 A RUSSO-SCOTTISH PARALLELISM 1923

1 Hodder and Stoughton, London, 1923.

4 PAUL VALÉRY 1927

1 H. A. L. Fisher, *Paul Valéry* (Clarendon Press, Oxford, 1927).

5 MY NATIVE PLACE 1931

1 Blackwood, Edinburgh, 1926.
2 Blackwood, Edinburgh, 1930.

6 THE CALEDONIAN ANTISYZYGY AND THE GAELIC IDEA
   1931-2

1 *Scottish Literature* (Macmillan, London, 1919).
2 Secker, London, 1935.
3 Reprinted in *At the Sign of the Thistle* (Nott, London, 1934).
4 Lindsey Press, London, 1915.
5 'In the Outer Hebrides', *The End of Fiammetta* (Grant Richards, London, 1923).
6 Faber and Faber, London, 1927.
7 Daniel Corkery, *Hidden Ireland* (M. H. Gill, Dublin, 1925).

7 CHARLES DOUGHTY AND THE NEED FOR HEROIC POETRY 1936

1 Duckworth, London, 1906, 6 vols.
2 Nott, London, 1934.
3 Gollancz, London, 1934.

8 JOHN SINGER 1942

1 *The Fury of the Living* (Maclellan, Glasgow, 1942).
2 Watkins, London, 1921.
3 Blackwell, Oxford, 1940.
4 Pelican Books, Harmondsworth, 1940.
5 Routledge, London, 1942.
6 International Non-Aristotelian Library Publishing Co., Lancaster, Pennsylvania, 1933.
7 C. A. Watts, London, 1934.

9 WILLIAM SOUTAR 1944

1 Dakers, London, 1948.
2 Macmillan, London, 1936.
3 Penguin Books, Harmondsworth, 1948.
4 Dakers, London, 1944.
5 Dakers, London, 1944.
6 Moray Press, Edinburgh, 1935.
7 Privately printed, Perth, 1939.
8 Macmillan, London, 1919.

10 THE SCOTTISH RENAISSANCE: THE NEXT STEP 1950

1 Cresset Press, London, 1939.
2 Oliver and Boyd, Edinburgh, 1938.

11 THE QUALITY OF SCOTS INTERNATIONALISM 1950

1 Kegan Paul, London, 1936.
2 Cape, London, 1936.
3 Faber and Faber, London, 1942.
4 Penguin Books, Harmondsworth, 1936.
5 Newnes, London, 1936.
6 Smith, Elder, London, 1913.

12 THE SIGNIFICANCE OF CUNNINGHAME GRAHAM 1952

1 *Cunninghame Graham*, Caledonian Press, Glasgow, 1952.
2 *Contemporary Scottish Studies* (Leonard Parsons, London, 1926).

13 ROBERT FERGUSSON: DIRECT POETRY AND THE SCOTTISH GENIUS 1952

1 'Lament for the Great Music', *Stony Limits and Scots Unbound* (Castle Wynd Printers, Edinburgh, 1956).
2 Chatto and Windus, London, 1940; revised edition, Faber and Faber, London, 1962.
3 T. F. Unwin, London, 1903.

4 Methuen, London, 1943; 'The Gaelic Muse', *Collected Poems* (Macmillan, New York, revised edition, 1967).
5 Routledge, London, 1936.
6 Nutt, London, 1898.
7 Chatto and Windus, London, 1940.
8 Oxford University Press, 1939.
9 Hamish Hamilton, London, 1949.
10 G. Routledge and Sons, London, 1935.
11 Op. cit.
12 Dakers, London, 1948.
13 Oliver and Boyd, Edinburgh, 1948.
14 Serif Books, Edinburgh, 1948.
15 Cambridge University Press, 1946.
16 Serif Books, London, 1948.
17 Oxford University Press, 1948.
18 *Literature and Oatmeal* (Routledge, London, 1935).

14 ECONOMIC INDEPENDENCE FOR THE INDIVIDUAL 1952

1 Nott, London, revised and enlarged edition, 1934.

15 NORMAN DOUGLAS 1953

1 Hutchinson, London, 1952.
2 Hart Davis, London, 1952.
3 Secker and Warburg, London, 1946.

16 ENCOURAGING THE CREATIVE ARTS 1953

1 Cambridge University Press, 1936.

17 TOWARDS A CELTIC FRONT 1953

1 M. H. Gill, Dublin, 1925.
2 'Glory of Elmet.' *Choose You This Day* (Maclellan, Glasgow, 1954).
3 Allen and Unwin, London, 1953.

18 ROBERT BURNS: HIS INFLUENCE 1959

1 Cresset Press, London, 1958.
2 Geoffrey Wagner, 'The Scottish Renaissance', *The Adelphi*, vol. 30, no. 1 (November 1953).

20 LEWIS GRASSIC GIBBON 1960

1 Jarrolds, London, 1934.
2 Published by Routledge and Kegan Paul, London.
3 Hutchinson, London, new edition, 1966.
4 Macqueen, London, 1901.
5 Constable, London, 1914.
6 Rich and Cowan, London, 1933.
7 Revised and extended edition, Macdonald, Edinburgh, 1964.
8 'Literary Lights', *Scottish Scene* (Jarrolds, London, 1934).

21 JOHN DAVIDSON: INFLUENCES AND INFLUENCE 1961

1 'Of John Davidson', *Collected Poems* (Macmillan, New York, revised edition, 1967).
2 Elkin Mathews and John Lane, London, 1893.
3 Routledge, London, 1936.
4 Leipzig, 1928.
5 Grant Richards, London, 1903.
6 Lawrence and Bullen, London, 1893.

22 CONTEMPORARY SCOTTISH LITERATURE AND THE NATIONAL QUESTION 1965

1 Nelson, London, 1924.
2 Michael Joseph, London, 1940; new edition 1961.
3 Donaldson, Glasgow, 1947.
4 Stevens and Sons, London, 1967.
5 Macdonald, Edinburgh, 1964.
6 Gollancz, London, 1962.
7 Museum Press, London, 1956.
8 Gollancz, London, 1968.

23 THE SCOTTISH RENAISSANCE MOVEMENT AFTER FORTY YEARS 1966

1 Routledge, London, 1936.
2 Macmillan, London, 1946.
3 Penguin Books (Pelican Guide to English Literature), Harmondsworth, 1961.
4 Oliver and Boyd, Edinburgh, 1966.
5 Hutchinson, London, new edition, 1966.
6 Oxford University Press, 1936.
7 Edinburgh University Press, 1961.
8 Stevens and Sons, London, 1967.
9 Michael Joseph, London, 1961.

24 THE UPSURGE OF SCOTTISH NATIONALISM 1967

1 MacLehose, Glasgow, 1937.

25 POETRY AND SCIENCE 1967

1 Ernest Benn, London, 1924.
2 *Sentences and Paragraphs* (Lawrence and Bullen, London, 1893).
3 C. A. Watts, London, 1949.
4 *In Memoriam James Joyce* (Maclellan, Glasgow, 1955).
5 Collier-Macmillan, New York and London, 1953.
6 Cambridge University Press, 1936.
7 Faber and Faber, London, 1929.